The
Crystal
Bible volume 2

The
Crystal
Bible volume 2

Judy Hall

 Walking Stick Press
Cincinnati, Ohio
www.writersdigest.com

Published in the U.S. by Walking Stick Press, an imprint of F+W Media, Inc.
10151 Carver Road, Suite 200, Blue Ash, OH 45242
(800) 289-0963

First published in Great Britain in 2009 by
Godsfield, a division of Octopus Publishing Group Ltd
2–4 Heron Quays, London E14 4JP
www.octopusbooks.co.uk

ISBN 978-1-58297-701-0

A CIP catalog record for this book is available from the Library of Congress.

Printed and bound in China

10 9

NOTE: An asterisk placed after a word indicates that the word or term may be
looked up in the Glossary section (see pages 376–383) for a full explanation.*

*CAUTION: No medical claims are made for the stones in this book and the
information given is not intended to act as a substitute for medical treatment.
If in any doubt about their use, a qualified crystal-healing practitioner
should be consulted. In the context of this book, illness is a dis-ease*, the final
manifestation of spiritual, environmental, psychological, karmic*, emotional or
mental imbalance or distress. Healing means bringing mind, body and spirit back
into balance and facilitating evolution for the soul; it does not imply a cure. In
accordance with crystal-healing consensus, all stones are referred to as crystals
regardless of whether or not they have a crystalline structure.*

CONTENTS

CRYSTAL REFERENCE

CRYSTAL ABUNDANCE

In this companion volume to The Crystal Bible, *you will find more than 200 crystals and combination stones not detailed in the first volume, plus a few crystals into which there has been greater exploration. This additional volume has become necessary because of the abundance of crystals on the market. Most have high vibrations* that bring about spiritual alchemy and multi-dimensional healing. Some are higher resonances* of existing stones—Greenlandite of Aventurine and Spectrolite of Labradorite, for instance—and take the energy of the existing stones to a new level. Other stones have been used for millennia but are finally more accessible—Russia is now sending crystals to the West, as is China, and the Himalayas have also revealed their bounty. Though far from accessible, the incredibly ancient rocks of Greenland revealed by receding ice are also offering up remarkable stones.*

Preseli Bluestone

Not only are new sources of stones opening up, but the internet and online auction sites now make it possible to obtain a stone from anywhere in the world almost instantly. While online descriptions of stones—especially of their size—should be checked carefully before making a purchase, some excellent crystals can be obtained this way and the fun of bidding makes the process more special: success indicates that a stone is truly meant for you.

Tiffany Stone

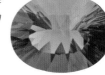

Mystic Topaz

When buying stones, try to remember that biggest is not necessarily best, nor does the most beautiful stone equate to the most potent. It also is not necessary to obtain a faceted stone. Although faceted stones make beautiful jewelry and are a delight to wear, raw rock can be as powerful, depending on what you want to do with the stone. Try to make 'fit for purpose' your criteria when buying—and consider the energy of each particular stone. When your heart feels the energy, you choose wisely.

Stichtite

The Crystal Directory (see pages 34–355) describes how stones work spiritually, karmically*, environmentally, psychologically, mentally, emotionally and physically, so that you can choose exactly the right stone for your needs. Indicating where to position the stone for maximum impact and healing, the Directory helps you to combine and place stones to enhance energy, protect your space, open chakras and subtle-energy meridians*, and journey* safely into the multi- and inter-dimensional worlds that enfold us. All crystals need cleansing and activating before use and at the back of this book (see pages 356–375) you will find an essential Quick Reference section to get you started, including a chakra guide.

Tugtupite

Calcite Fairy Stone

Quantum Quattro

Tangerine Aura Quartz

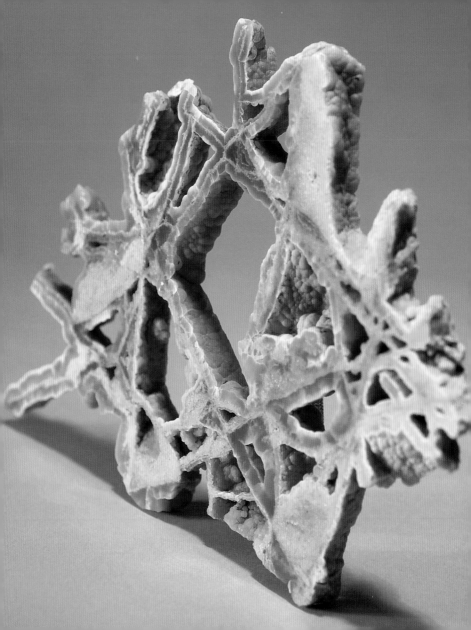

CRYSTAL VIBRATIONS

No one knows how or why humans first came to use crystals, but there is evidence that they have been doing so for thousands of years. Amazing crystals are still making themselves known to us, and all but a few have their origin deep within the earth. The exceptions are the result of 'supernatural' events, such as Fulgarite, born from lightning-struck sand. The resulting crystals seemed like gifts from the gods and how highly they were prized is illustrated by the use of Libyan Gold in the funerary ornaments of Tutankhamun.

Miniature storehouses, born as the earth solidified, crystals record the development of the earth over millions of years. They metamorphosed as the planet itself changed—we might think of them as the earth's DNA or a mineral blueprint of evolution. Whatever form they take, the crystalline structure of these stones absorbs, conserves, focuses and emits energy, especially on the electromagnetic waveband. And because crystals are such efficient energy-enhancers and space-clearers, by gridding* them (see pages 28–31) you can create a safe space to live, love, work and play.

CRYSTAL HISTORY

Flint

You may think that crystals are a New Age fad, but they are actually one of the oldest forms of healing and have always been used for protection. Flint in the form of a pebble or a polished axe has been found in many Neolithic graves and crystals were sacred across the ancient world. Specularite, for example, was mined in Africa from 40,000 BCE for cosmetic and ritual purposes, symbolizing the blood of the earth, and was sprinkled on the bodies of the dead for thousands of years. According to an ancient medical text, in Iraq 5,500 years ago Lapis Lazuli and Jasper were laid around a living person to cure their ills and Bloodstone was used for diseases of the blood, exactly as today. In Egypt in 1900 BCE, Lapis Lazuli, Jasper, Carnelian and Turquoise were placed around the necks of newborn babies to protect them.

Specularite

Crystals are an integral part of mythology. Wearing Lapis Lazuli jewelry, the Sumerian goddess Inanna (a forerunner of Aphrodite and Venus) journeyed into the underworld carrying her Lapis Lazuli rods that measured time and the length of a person's life. It was believed that crystals were the flesh of the gods and that the gods were crystal beings. The Libyan Gold Tecktite, Blood of Isis, Lapis Lazuli and Turquoise in Tutankhamun's funerary jewelry were not just for decoration: they protected and conveyed his soul to the next world. A journey of over

Blood of Isis

500 arid miles (800 kilometers) had been undertaken to obtain Libyan Gold for the scarab in his pectoral, which depicted the daily voyage of the sun and the moon boat through the sky.

In India, astrological remedial gems have been used for thousands of years and, just as in Egypt, mythology tells that a pair of celestial serpents fought and their perspiration fell to earth as gemstones. In China too, crystals belonged to the

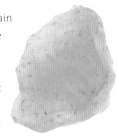

Libyan Gold Tecktite

Tutankhamun's pectoral with the sun scarab in the center, below the moon boat.

realm of the gods and in both China and Japan it was thought that gems rained down from a lapidary sky. Many cultures envisaged a series of crystal domes surrounding the sky around which the planets rotated and stars held their place. Indigenous Australians took the view that fossils and gems came from the Dreamtime, an idyllic period rather like the time of the Garden of Eden. Norwegian Vikings erected a chapel on the Isle of Man floored with Quartz, with a Quartz reliquary box, possibly to intensify the vigor of the holy bones within it. Quartz had been used for thousands of years to amplify energy and construct stone circles. The builders of Stonehenge, in the English county of Wiltshire, laboriously transported Preseli Bluestone 250 miles (400 kilometers) to the center of their sacred healing circle.

Preseli Bluestone

BIBLICAL CRYSTALS

In Ezekiel 28:12–14, the prophet Ezekiel addresses the King of Tyre, saying to him:

> *Thus saith the Lord God; Thou sealest up the sum, full of wisdom, and perfect in beauty.*
>
> *Thou hast been in Eden the garden of God; every precious stone was thy covering, the sardius, topaz, and the diamond, the beryl, the onyx, and the jasper, the sapphire, the emerald, and the carbuncle, and gold: the workmanship of thy tabrets and of thy pipes was prepared in thee in the day that thou wast created.*
>
> *Thou art the anointed cherub that covereth; and I have set thee so; thou wast upon the holy mountain of God; thou hast walked up and down in the midst of the stones of fire.*

This nostalgic picture of a king adorned with crystals walking among stones of fire in the Garden of Eden is in the Old Testament, a book revered by three world faiths. Throughout both the Old Testament and the New Testament there are numerous references to crystals. According to the Revelation of St John the Divine, the New Jerusalem will be built upon a crystal foundation, which in turn rests on an essential piece of priestly apparel—the Breastplate of the High Priest, an item adorned with gems. In Exodus 28: 17–20 the breastplate is described as follows:

> *And thou shalt set in it settings of stones, even four rows of stones: the first row shall be a sardius, a topaz, and a carbuncle: this shall be the first row.*
> *And the second row shall be an emerald, a sapphire, and a diamond.*
> *And the third row a ligure, an agate, and an amethyst.*
> *And the fourth row a beryl, and an onyx, and a jasper: they shall be set in gold in their inclosings.*

The Jewish High Priest wearing the breastplate on his chest.

Translation problems make it impossible to know exactly which stones were used in the breastplate—different versions of the Bible cite different ones. Sapphire, for instance, was unknown in that part of the ancient world, so 'sapphire' refers to Lapis Lazuli, which itself was brought all the way from what is present-day Afghanistan. 'Sardius' is Sardonyx, but 'carbuncle' may be Garnet or Carnelian, 'emerald' may be Green Aventurine and 'diamond' could be Clear Quartz. Contrary to popular opinion, the stones of the breastplate could not have been the source of the birthstones we know today.

Onyx was mounted on the breastplate's shoulders and this stone often has markings that are said to resemble heavenly writing. Josephus, a Roman historian writing some 1,500 years after the Exodus, gives in *Jewish Antiquities* a description of the use of the breastplate as an oracle:

Onyx with markings, simulating the spheres.

> *For as to those stones that the high priest bore on his shoulders, which were sardonyxes (and I think it needless to describe their nature, they being known to everybody), the one of them shined out when God was present at their sacrifices... bright rays darting out thence, and being seen even by those that were most remote; which splendor yet was not before natural to the stone.*

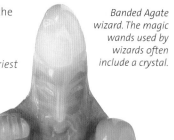

Banded Agate wizard. The magic wands used by wizards often include a crystal.

Although Josephus is not the most reliable witness, it is interesting that he assumes everyone is familiar with the nature of a Sardonyx.

To return to Ezekiel, the prophet saw many wondrous things and gave vivid descriptions of his visionary experiences. Ezekiel 1: 4–28 illustrates how his call to prophesy was filled with crystal imagery:

And I looked, and, behold, a whirlwind came out of the north,
a great cloud, and a fire infolding itself, and a brightness
was about it, and out of the midst thereof as the color
of amber [also translated as 'awesome crystal'], out of the
midst of the fire...
Now as I beheld the living creatures, behold one wheel upon the
earth, by the living creatures, with his four faces.
The appearance of the wheels and their work was like unto the
color of a beryl...
And the likeness of the firmament [dome] upon the heads of the
living creature was as the color of the terrible crystal...
And above the firmament [dome] that was over their heads was
the likeness of a throne, as the appearance of a sapphire stone...
As the appearance of the bow that is in the cloud in
the day of rain, so was the appearance of the
brightness round about. This was the appearance
of the likeness of the glory of the Lord.

This describes the famous 'chariot of fire' that so many people today interpret as a spaceship coming down to land. So, for Ezekiel, there was nothing ungodly about crystals, they were an integral part of his divine world.

An awesome Beryl
flashing fire.

19

CRYSTAL STRUCTURE

The internal structure of any crystalline formation is constant and unchanging. It is this inner structure, rather than the minerals from which a crystal is formed, that is crucial to crystal classification, and each family of crystals has its own specific identity due to chemical impurities, radiation, earth and solar emissions and the exact means of their formation. In some cases, the mineral content differs slightly, creating the various colors. While a number of crystals may be formed out of the same mineral or combination of minerals, each type crystallizes out differently and the shapes affect the way in which energy is focused.

THE EARTH'S CRUST

The earth began as a whirling gas cloud of cosmic debris containing the raw materials for crystals. This contracted into a molten ball that was white-hot. Over millions of years this molten magma cooled into a thin crust—the earth's mantle—that is relatively about as thick as the skin on an apple. Inside the mantle, mineral-laden molten magma continues to boil, cool and bubble and new crystals form. Some, such as Quartz, form from the fiery gases and molten minerals in the magma. Superhot, they are propelled upward by the movement of tectonic plates on the earth's surface. As gases penetrate the crust and meet solid rock, they cool and solidify—a process that may take eons of time or be fast and furious. Large crystals grow if the process has been relatively slow or if the crystal forms in a gas bubble. Faster processes create small crystals. Stopping and starting the growth process creates effects such as phantom or self-healed* crystals. If the process is exceptionally fast, a glass-like amorphous crystal is formed.

Other crystals are formed when minerals melt and re-crystallize under intense pressure and enormous heat. These crystals, known as metamorphic, undergo a chemical change that reorganizes the original lattice. Calcite and other sedimentary crystals form from a secondary process when rocks at the surface weather and mineralized water drips through rock, or travels along a river laying down eroded material as new crystals or the minerals become cemented together. Other crystals form from evaporation—these crystals are laid down in layers and are softer in texture. Crystals are often found attached to or embedded within the bedrock, known as the matrix.

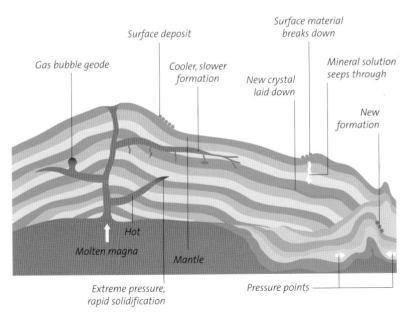

Gas bubble geode

Surface deposit

Cooler, slower formation

Surface material breaks down

New crystal laid down

Mineral solution seeps through

New formation

Hot

Molten magma

Mantle

Extreme pressure, rapid solidification

Pressure points

CRYSTAL PROTECTION

Crystals subtly affect all the levels of your being and the space in which you live and work. Symptoms labeled as illness may, in fact, be signs of dis-ease*, blocked creativity or emotional angst—the final manifestation of spiritual, environmental, psychological, karmic*, emotional or mental imbalance or distress. Healing means bringing your mind, body and spirit back into harmony, and facilitating evolution for the soul. This does not imply a cure, particularly in cases where the soul is evolving through an—outwardly negative—experience, but crystals adjust how you perceive that learning, support optimum well-being and accelerate insight and spiritual growth.

CRYSTALS SPEAK

So how do we know what crystals do? Well, it's simple. They tell us. The ancients thought that stones were alive but only took a breath every one or two hundred years, and many cultures believed that they were incarnations of the divine. Crystal healers agree that these wonderful gifts from Mother Earth are living beings and see them as incredibly old and wise. Treat your crystals like friends. Talk to your stones, hold them, meditate quietly, invite them to assist and ask how they wish to work. You may be surprised by how easy it is to communicate with them and how much more effective energy-work is when the language of crystals takes on a whole new meaning. Talking to crystals is particularly useful with the newer, high-vibration* stones because each one is individual and not every crystal will resonate with everyone. Communicating with them will tell you which one is right for you.

The first thing a crystal communicates is that it is an efficient tool for energy-enhancement, healing and spiritual growth, but each crystal

A crystal will communicate its purpose if you are ready to listen.

Cathedral Quartz

works uniquely according to your individual vibration and needs. Do not limit your crystal by assuming that it only does certain things. All possibilities are open, and the more you attune to and harmonize with crystals, the more they will delight—and surprise.

HIGH-VIBRATION CRYSTALS

Many new crystals have an exceedingly high vibration that brings about multi-dimensional healing and

23

spiritual alchemy—if your vibrations harmonize. These crystals may take some getting used to since they emphasize that you must do your own healing and evolutionary work in this dimension before moving onto a higher vibratory level—which is then expressed on the physical plane. As with most crystals, they act as a mirror of your inner energies, which may come as something of a shock if you have unacknowledged qualities within. Although they assist in embodying your highest being and manifesting your core spiritual identity—love—in matter, crystals are not a short-cut to bliss or ascension*. However, they do facilitate that shift when appropriate and ground it.

Paraiba Tourmaline jewelry

To see if a high-vibration crystal will resonate with you, hold it gently and sit quietly. Your body may vibrate as it attunes to the crystal or you may be instantly transported to another energetic dimension, which means this crystal will work with you. If this does not happen, choose another crystal and try again later when your vibrations have shifted. Most high-vibration stones work slowly to bring about physical change, if indeed they affect the physical body, because they act on the subtle levels of being first. If a high-dimension* stone provokes a healing crisis* or catharsis, remove it and hold a Smoky or Chlorite Quartz between your feet to stabilize your energies.

POWER STONES

Crystals such as Smoky Elestial Quartz, Quantum Quattro or any of the red Quartzes re-empower you if your physical or psychological energy has become depleted or drained. Pink stones assist with emotional empowerment as do many specific stones (see the Crystal Directory on pages 34–355). White or Amethyst Elestial Quartz, Selenite and other high-vibration stones empower at a spiritual level, and these stones are particularly effective in a scepter* formation (see page 272).

To empower yourself with these stones, simply relax and hold the appropriate crystal for 10–15 minutes. Breathe gently, let your eyes go out of focus and be open to an in-flooding of energy as you ask that the stone restores your power. You can also empower yourself by wearing a dedicated crystal (see page 358).

BORROWING VIRTUE

Most stones work exceedingly well if they are small, especially the high-vibration crystals, but occasionally the power surge of a large stone is required to bring about a particular effect. If you need the energy of a huge crystal but cannot afford one, or it has to be portable, 'borrow virtue' by placing a smaller stone on top of the large one and leave the two to attune to each other for 15 minutes or so. The small stone will draw on the energy of the large to do its work, no matter how distant they are from each other. When cleansing the small stone (see page 358), ask that the cleansing also works on the larger one.

Orange River Quartz (scepter)

ENERGY ENHANCEMENT AND SPACE CLEARING

Energy depletion occurs when your environment is affected by geopathic stress* or electromagnetic smog*. Placing crystals around a room or in the environment neutralizes and cleanses negative energies, making the space safe and sacred, energetically balanced and purified. A space can also be 'polluted' by negative emotions emanating from those within it. Hang a large Chlorite Phantom or Smoky Elestial

25

point down in the lavatory cistern to energetically cleanse the whole house. You can also place crystals to draw more love or abundance into your life or to enhance an existing loving relationship or family life.

After environmental factors, the most common cause of personal energy depletion is family, friends and clients. Needy people 'hook' into the subtle bodies* or physical organs to gain the nourishment they crave—they are psychic vampires*—and thoughts may be sent to control what you do. If your energy is high, your chakras aligned and your auric protection strong, it is much more difficult for negative energies, psychic vampirization or controlling thoughts to affect you. The simplest way to raise your vibration is to wear an appropriate crystal—remember to cleanse and activate it before use and to purify it regularly (see page 358). The best way to establish which crystal to wear is to dowse for it (see page 360) or simply choose one to which you feel strongly attracted.

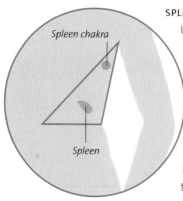

The visualized pyramid draws energy from a crystal such as Greenlandite, enclosing and protecting the spleen.

SPLEEN PROTECTION

Using a combination of crystals and the power of your mind helps to cut off energy vampirization*. If you feel tired in someone's company or when they phone, or have an ache beneath your left armpit, tape a spleen-protection stone such as Greenlandite or Gaspeite about a hand's breadth under your left armpit. Visualize a large, three-dimensional pyramid going down to your waist at your back and front to protect your spleen (make sure the pyramid has a floor). To re-empower yourself, replace the stone with Quantum Quattro or another

Within the image: Spleen chakra, Spleen

26

power stone. A similar stone-and-pyramid set-up can protect your liver from other people's anger and your solar plexus from those desperate for emotional nourishment. Place the stone a hand's breadth under the left armpit for emotional nourishment, and a hand's breadth under the right for the liver and anger.

Quantum Quattro

SAFE SPACE

Crystals can hold the space while you leave your body and travel the dimensions or go deep within yourself, and they make your living or working environment a much nicer place. Holding the space in any kind of gathering dramatically alters and enhances the dynamics and is essential if you are to work safely spiritually. However, you need to be grounded in your body to create and hold safe space. If ungrounded, you are open to subtle invasion. Fortunately gridding* with crystals both grounds and guards your physical body and facilitates your movement into multi-or inner-dimensions*. Large Smoky Elestials are the perfect stones for creating safe space, but large raw Labradorite works equally well. To protect your space from environmental pollution, large Amazonite or Black Tourmaline are favorites, but Greenlandite or Poppy Jasper work well too, as do Elestials. A basic triangle of Bronzite with a reversed triangle of Black Tourmaline over the top prevents ill-wishing or other negative energy from bouncing back and forth (see page 31).

Poppy Jasper

Gridding three stones in a triangle or six in a Star of David cleanses, protects and energizes your space, and other layouts are also possible (see pages 29–31). Sick building syndrome, for instance, needs the powerful energy generated by a zig-zag pattern. It is worth experimenting with the energetic effect of various stones and shapes, then add a high-vibration or grounding crystal and feel the difference.

27

GRIDDING

Gridding is the art of placing stones to create an energetic net to protect and energize space. The easiest way to grid a room or other space is to place a crystal in each corner since this creates an energy grid across the whole room. However, you can grid a room with whichever pattern feels right at the time (see options on pages 29–31).

Dowsing establishes the exact placement for crystals when gridding—join the crystals with a wand or long-point crystal, such as a Lemurian, to set the grid. Wands are the traditional tools of shamans, healers and metaphysicians. The magic wands of myth and legend are believed to have been used by crystal healers in the ancient civilizations of Atlantis and Lemuria. Wands have the ability to focus energy tightly through their tip, and the healing ability of wands is vastly expanded when dedicated with intent (see page 358). When using a wand, it is important to consciously allow universal healing energy to flow in through your crown chakra and down your arm to the hand holding the wand, and then into the wand where it is amplified and passed on (using your own energy for this purpose is inefficient as this makes you weak and depleted and in need of healing). Remember to cleanse and activate crystals before use, setting out your intention clearly (see page 358).

When gridding, the lines of force may have to pass through walls and solid objects (see opposite). Use either the power of your mind or a crystal wand to connect the points: take it up to the point on the wall, watch it pass through the wall and then walk around to the other side to recommence the line. See also the one-way portal on page 208.

Lemurian (natural wand)

28

TRIANGULATION

You will need:

- 3 cleansed and activated crystals
- Crystal wand

Triangulation gridding works well to neutralize negative energy and bring in positive energy.

Place one crystal centrally along a wall and two others on the wall opposite at

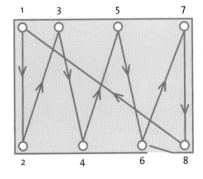

an equal angle if possible. If working on a whole house, the lines of force pass through walls, so connect the points with a wand to strengthen the grid (see opposite).

ZIG-ZAG

You will need:

- 8 cleansed and activated crystals
- Crystal wand

The zig-zag layout is particularly useful for dealing with sick building syndrome and environmental pollution. Place appropriate crystals as shown on the diagram, remembering to return from the last stone laid to the first. Cleanse the stones regularly.

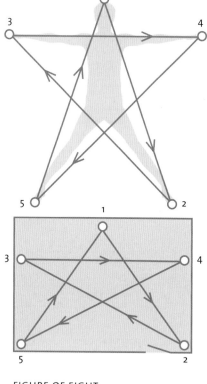

FIVE-POINTED STAR

You will need:

- 5 cleansed and activated stones
- Crystal wand

This is a useful protection layout or caller-in of love and healing and it enhances your energy. Follow the direction of the arrows on the diagram when placing crystals and remember to return to the start crystal to complete the circuit. Like the Star of David, this layout can be used to grid around a body and also for a room or other space.

FIGURE OF EIGHT

You will need:

- 5 cleansed and activated high-vibration stones
- 5 cleansed and activated grounding stones

This layout draws spiritual energy down into the body and melds it with earth energy drawn up from the feet to create perfect balance. It also opens a cosmic anchor*

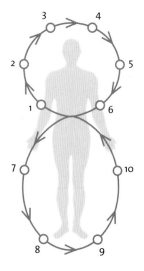

30

*to ground you between the core of the earth and the galactic center,
creating core-energy solidity that equips you to ride out energetic
changes and channel high-vibration energy down to earth. Place high-
vibration stones, such as Amphibole, Cacoxenite, Blue Moonstone, above
the waist to the crown of the head, and grounding stones, such as Poppy
Jasper, Agate, Septarian, below the waist, down to the feet. Remember to
complete the circuit back to the first stone placed.*

STAR OF DAVID

You will need:

- 6 cleansed and activated crystals
- Crystal wand

*The Star of David is a traditional
protection layout but also creates an
ideal manifestation space when laid
with large Grossular Garnet,
Ammolite or other abundance stones.
Lay the first triangle and join up the
points, then lay another triangle the
other way up, over the top. Join up the
points. (If using Bronzite and Black
Tourmaline to neutralize ill-wishing*,
lay the Bronzite triangle first and
cleanse the star daily.)*

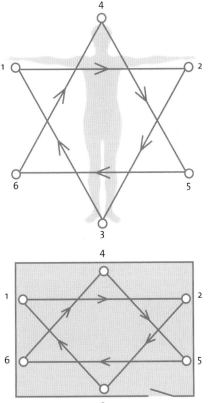

31

THE GREENLAND STONES

Tugtupite

Exciting new stones on the market today come from mysterious Greenland, source of the most ancient rocks on earth. The world's largest island, Greenland is a land of contrasts: hot thermal springs and ice-cold glaciers; towering mountains and deep fjords. Home to the fascinating aurora borealis (the northern lights) and the midnight sun, this is a place of spectacular nature and extremes, from deafening silence to a winter of perpetual darkness. This remote country was inhabited over 5,000 years ago by Inuit people from Canada, and the Vikings under Erik the Red reached Greenland in fragile boats over 1,000 years ago. Dangerous exploration continues in Greenland to this day. One intrepid miner describes edging up a treacherous path on a cliff high above a fjord to reach stones that he has to carry gingerly down the mountain in a backpack. The path is so narrow he cannot get his high-tech mining gear up and has to pick the stones out of the beds by hand. Another miner has to helicopter his stones out as there is no road. Not surprisingly, the supply of stones such as Tugtupite, Ussingite and Nuummite is limited, although some of these stones are found in other countries, too. Greenland gems such as Greenlandite, Hackmanite and Fiskenaesset Ruby are exquisite, many having high vibrations that quietly facilitate spiritual evolution, returning us to oneness and a gentle energy that teaches us to respect and honor the earth and everything in and upon it. Out of the ancient past comes hope for humanity's future.

Nuummite

Most of the Greenland stones are fluorescent, which means that under energetic activation, such as from the sun or ultra-violet rays, they emit electromagnetic radiation that we perceive as colored light—a truly magical experience. Fluorescence is the result of a shift to a higher energetic state within the stone, so it is not surprising that these stones are particularly effective energy healers. Other Greenland stones are tenebrescent, changing color in heat or daylight. To shamans, such stones have an aura around them, which may be why they were sacred to ancient people.

Ussingite

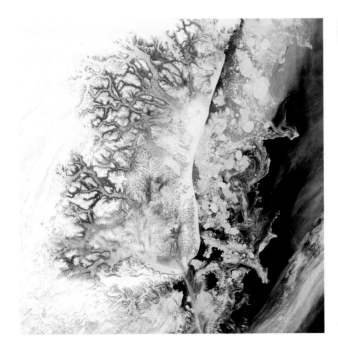

Kakortokite

From space Greenland, with its sparkling icecap, looks just like a gigantic crystal.

CRYSTAL DIRECTORY

It is important to identify crystals accurately and the stones are, where possible, shown both raw and polished or faceted. Rather than picturing exquisitely beautiful crystals, we have shown what you will find in a shop. Identification of stones is complicated because some old stones have new names or the same stone might have different names. Cathedral Quartz, for instance, is now known as Lightbrary and Atlantis Stone, a name also applied to at least three other crystals. Some new Quartzes are particularly difficult to tell apart. Although their appearance varies only slightly, their energy is hugely different. 'Shift Crystals' from Brazil look and feel like Himalayan Growth Interference (also named Nirvana Quartz and Ice Quartz) and Glacial Etched Quartz (also known as Ice Quartz) is similar, while the term 'Celestial Quartz' is applied to two distinctly different stones.

This Directory helps you to navigate your way to exactly the right stone (the contents are listed in Crystal Reference at the front of the book, pages 6–9). If you can't find specific combination stones, use two crystals together and ask their energy to synergize.

ACTINOLITE

White
(raw)

Green
(raw)

COLOR	Green and black, or white
APPEARANCE	Translucent to transparent, vitreous, bladed crystals, often included in Quartz or compact opaque mass
RARITY	Easily obtained
SOURCE	United States, Brazil, Russia, China, New Zealand, Canada, Taiwan

ATTRIBUTES Useful if you encounter blockages or resistance on your spiritual path, Actinolite dissolves that which is unwanted or inappropriate. An effective stone for psychic shielding, it expands the biomagnetic sheath* and seals its edges.

Spiritually, Actinolite connects to higher awareness, bringing body, mind, psyche and spirit into balance. Psychologically, it offers a new orientation and enhances self-esteem. It is an aid to visualization and imagery, expanding and enhancing spontaneous creativity.

36

By bringing all physical functions into harmony and stimulating growth, Actinolite assists the body in adjusting to changes or recovery from trauma.

HEALING Beneficial for stress; said to assist in the healing of asbestos-related tumors and support the immune system, liver and kidneys.

POSITION Hold, grid (see pages 28–31) or place as appropriate.

SPECIFIC COLORS AND FORMS

Black Actinolite cleanses and protects the base chakra. Gently removing all that is outworn and outgrown in the psyche, it opens the way for new energies to manifest. Black Actinolite provides an efficient shield against any negative thoughts, including your own.

Actinolite Quartz is helpful when you have lost your way and are looking for a new direction. Indicating the path for constructive evolution, highlighting right timing and showing the value in 'mistakes', it is beneficial for detoxing and metabolism.

Witches Finger from Zambia, which may have white Actinolite, Tremolite, Rutile or Mica included* in Quartz, is a useful stone for shamanic or earth healing*. In those who are attuned to it, a Witches Finger is an efficient healing tool during chronic or severe illness as it stimulates the flow of *qi** and accelerates the healing process. It cuts away all that is outworn and then soothes and heals the site. This formation can also be used for auric shielding* or to grid* the environment during periods of chaotic upheaval. Its properties vary according to the inclusion.

*Witches Finger
(natural formation)*

ADAMITE

*Natural crystals
on matrix*

COLOR	Yellow
APPEARANCE	Vitreous, transparent crystal or druse
RARITY	Rare
SOURCE	Mexico, Greece, United States

ATTRIBUTES A strongly creative stone, Adamite has little direct spiritual effect other than enhancing metaphysical gifts* and communication with those in other dimensions. But, if you are ruled by emotion, it creates emotional equilibrium and will help you to find a calm, centered space around which emotions can rage without affecting your inner serenity.

Mentally, this stone brings heart and mind together as it links the solar plexus, heart and throat chakras with the universal mind, providing clarity and inner strength when dealing with emotional issues and strengthening your spiritual will.

38

Emotionally, Adamite assists in clearly communicating your needs, especially when you need to change an emotional interaction to allow more room for expressing feelings. This is the perfect stone to attract more joy into your life.

Psychologically, Adamite is useful if you have to focus on specific tasks or face difficult choices. It helps in consulting your inner self and in directing you to where answers lie. The answer might not be at all what you were expecting—this stone suggests surprising and innovative solutions, but they work if you trust the process.

Being a creative stone, Adamite helps to move forward confidently into an unknown future and activates entrepreneurial skills. It induces the ability to identify new avenues for growth in both your business and personal life and is the perfect stone to program (see page 358) to attract a new job or prosperity.

HEALING Supports the heart, lungs and throat, cellular memory*, the endocrine system and glands; is beneficial for seasonal affective disorder (SAD), PMS and chronic fatigue.

POSITION Hold, grid (see pages 28–31) or place as appropriate.

AEGIRINE

Green-red
(raw)

Black
(natural
wand)

COLOR	Green-red or black
APPEARANCE	Transparent to opaque, long crystal, sometimes striated or small crystals on a matrix
RARITY	Easily obtained
SOURCE	Greenland, United States, Africa

ATTRIBUTES Focusing energy for personal or environmental healing, Aegirine is a powerful energy generator. Spiritually, this stone empowers the quest for your true self and teaches how to be true to that self. Aegirine assists in facing your karma* confidently and with integrity. A protective stone that is extremely helpful in psychic attack* and mental influence, Aegrine dissolves thought forms* and helps to

40

repair the biomagnetic sheath* after the removal of attachments* or negative energy.

Psychologically, this stone facilitates integrity and enhances self-esteem. Promoting sincerity in all that you do, it imparts the ability to do what is needed from the heart.

Mentally, Aegirine turns negative thoughts positive. This stone helps you to see the bigger picture and encourages you to follow your own truth without conforming to group pressure or the ideas or ideals of others. It shows how to focus your goals wisely, setting your intent without emotional investment in the outcome.

Emotionally, Aegirine heals relationship problems and transmutes grief after separation. It removes energy blockages from the emotional body and enhances positive vibrations.

Physically, by boosting the body's self-healing systems, Aegirine enhances the healing power of other crystals.

HEALING Supports cellular memory*, the immune, metabolic and nervous systems, and the liver, gallbladder, spleen, muscles and bones. It overcomes muscle pain, facilitating the removal of toxins.

POSITION Hold, grid (see pages 28–31) or place as appropriate. To stimulate the immune system, place over the thymus. To dissolve thought forms, place on the throat, third eye or soma chakra.

AGATE: BOTSWANA AND GRAY-BANDED AGATE

Botswana
(tumbled)

Gray-banded
(tumbled)

COLOR	Gray, gray and pink (Botswana is pinker)
APPEARANCE	Closely banded opaque stone
RARITY	Easily obtained
SOURCE	Botswana, United States, Morocco, Czech Republic, Brazil, South Africa

ATTRIBUTES Banded Agates stimulate the crown chakra, bringing celestial and earth energy into the subtle bodies* and harmonizing them with the physical body. A powerful holistic healer, Banded Agates remove dualities and conflict, maintaining well-being. This crystal is extremely effective for multi-dimensional healing and soul-work, the bands across its surface taking you traveling into another reality, different streams of consciousness or other lives.

A useful environmental healer when gridded* around a house, Banded Agate prevents out-of-body visitations from another soul and turns back unwelcome spirits. Traditionally, Banded Agate has been used to overcome physical, emotional and mental poisoning or toxicity and is a useful receptacle for negative energy.

Placed on the third eye, Banded Agate quickly cuts mental cords to a guru, a partner from a past life or a parent who manipulates an earlier childhood connection to retain control in the present, replenishing the energy lost in such situations. It is particularly useful where someone is being 'prayed for', whether by a priest or cult-leader, to bring that person 'back to the fold'—or under control once again—since this stone returns the compulsive energy back to its source and leaves the person free to live life as he or she wishes.

Psychologically, Banded Agate teaches that sexuality is a natural function and that sensuality is the appreciation by the senses of the fullness of life. It releases emotional repression and encourages artistic expression. Useful for people who are easily hurt, this stone teaches users to look for solutions rather than dwell on problems and shuts off obsessive thoughts and destructive mental patterns. Giving the broader picture, it encourages you to explore unknown territory and creativity while at the same time paying appropriate attention to detail.

Emotionally, this stone can be programmed (see page 358) to protect you and your family and to encourage supportive love, which is objective and non-smothering.

Botswana Agate also assists anyone working with fire or smoke, and aids smokers who want to quit. It is said to repel spiders.

HEALING Enhances cellular memory* and multi-dimensional healing; benefits depression, detoxification, fertility, the brain, oxygen-assimilation, the chest, skin and the circulatory and nervous systems. It is useful for reprogramming cellular memory after mortification of the flesh, emotions or spirit in a previous or present life.

POSITION Hold, grid (see pages 28–31) or place as appropriate. Place on the third eye to release guru connections. May cause giddiness; if so, remove.

AGATE: **CRACKLED FIRE AGATE**

Tumbled

COLOR	Orange
APPEARANCE	Crazed and banded translucent stone
RARITY	Fairly easily obtained from crystal shops
SOURCE	United States, Czech Republic, India, Iceland, Morocco, Brazil

ATTRIBUTES A powerful energy attuned to the vermilion flame* of spiritual will and an effective 'ass-kicker' stone, Crackled Fire Agate emanates life force and *joie de vivre*. Fiercely protective, it provides an impenetrable shield against ill-wishing*, gently returning it to source to know the harm it is doing and then dissipating it.

Physically an enlivener, Fire Agate stimulates vitality and creativity on all levels. Enhancing libido, it fires up the base chakra and eliminates cravings and destructive desires, treating addictions.

HEALING Restores vitality and overcomes fatigue, prevents burn-out and hot flushes; improves night vision; resonates with the triple-burner meridian* and the reproductive and digestive systems.

POSITION Wear for long periods.

AGATE: SNAKESKIN AGATE

*Natural
formation*

COLOR	White and brownish gray
APPEARANCE	Snakeskin-like crystal
RARITY	Rare
SOURCE	United States, India, Morocco, Czech Republic, Brazil, Africa

ATTRIBUTES Attuned to the south on the medicine wheel (see pages 368–375), Snakeskin Agate is a stone of invisibility and a natural shape-shifter. Helping to blend in and travel without being seen in both the physical and spiritual upper and lower worlds*, it is a useful accompaniment for soul retrieval*.

Spiritually, Snakeskin Agate strengthens the base and sacral chakras, rooting the soul into the body and the earth, and facilitating full acceptance of incarnation.

Psychologically, Snakeskin Agate, being an exceptionally cheerful stone, assists in eliminating worry and depression from everyday life and connects you instead to the joy of living. It reminds you that, just as a snake sheds its skin, you can slough off your past and be reborn.

45

When placed on the lower chakras, this stone activates the rise of kundalini* and instigates regeneration. It lends you the cunning of a serpent when handling devious people or difficult situations.

Physically, under the homoeopathic principle of 'like cures like', this stone has long been used to smooth wrinkles and heal skin diseases.

HEALING Has traditionally been used for psoriasis, hearing disorders and the stomach.

POSITION Hold, grid (see pages 28–31) or place as appropriate. Bathe skin with the gem essence (see page 361). Hold to connect to snake medicine or place in the south of the medicine wheel.

AGATE: **TREE AGATE**

Tumbled

Raw

COLOR	White and green
APPEARANCE	Spotted and veined opaque stone
RARITY	Easily obtained
SOURCE	United States, India, Morocco, Czech Republic, Brazil, Africa

ATTRIBUTES A useful earth and environmental healer, Tree Agate
is an effective support for plants and trees of all kinds. Gridded*
around a growing area, it improves germination and fertility. Making
a powerful connection to the nurturing energy of nature and nature
spirits, Tree Agate enhances your rapport with living things, facilitating

47

communication with trees or plants. Keep one in your pocket to enhance your connection with nature in the raw and keep you safe in the wilderness.

Psychologically, Tree Agate instills a feeling of safety in the most challenging of situations. Imparting strength and perseverance, it helps in facing difficult circumstances with equanimity and in identifying the gift or karmic* lesson behind them. This stone encourages a positive sense of self and unshakeable self-esteem.

Emotionally, Tree Agate affords protection against negativity in yourself or others. Physically, by restoring and reviving vitality and imparting strength, Tree Agate supports the immune system.

HEALING This crystal is beneficial for the immune system and helps to fight infections.

POSITION Hold, grid (see pages 28–31) or place as appropriate. If your immune system is weak and susceptible to infection, tape Tree Agate over your thymus and leave in place overnight.

AGRELLITE

Raw

COLOR	White
APPEARANCE	Pearly, striated opaque stone
RARITY	Rare
SOURCE	Canada

ATTRIBUTES Useful for psychological healing and for overcoming writer's block, Agrellite highlights your attempts to control others, supporting independence and self-respect in both parties.

Psychologically, by surfacing matters repressed deep within the psyche that prevent soul growth, this stone defeats an inner saboteur and accesses your untapped potential. It detects blockages within physical or subtle bodies*, which may require additional healing crystals, by a distinctive energetic response.

HEALING Enhances healing, receptivity to radionics*; assists the immune system, bruises, swellings, infections, chemotherapy and over-alkalinity.

POSITION Hold, grid (see pages 28–31) or place as appropriate.

ALEXANDRITE

Shaped

Crystal in matrix

COLOR	Green-red
APPEARANCE	Gritty and opaque, transparent when faceted, shines red according to light source
RARITY	Rare
SOURCE	Russia, United States, Brazil, China, Ireland, Switzerland, Australia, Czech Republic, France, Norway

ATTRIBUTES A symbol of royal power and an efficient guardian stone, Alexandrite supports longevity, being a useful purifier and renewer, and is said to bring about a joyful inner transformation. Karmically*, this stone links to the esoteric knowledge once stored in the library at Alexandria. Worn over the heart, Alexandrite is said to bring luck in love and to impart grace and elegance to the wearer. With its ability to show two colors at once, Alexandrite allows you to see both sides of the

50

picture and links the heart and the mind so they come from a dispassionate, illumined perspective that encompasses and integrates the rational and the intuitive viewpoints.

Faceted

Psychologically, Alexandrite, a regenerative stone, rebuilds self-respect and self-worth. Through realignment and centering you around your self, it reinforces your sense of who you really are. This stone strengthens willpower and dreaming, and assists in accurately assessing emotions—both your own and those of others.

Mentally, this stone inspires the imagination and attunes to your inner voice. A comforter that facilitates emotional maturity and encourages joyfulness in everyday life, Alexandrite teaches how to expend less effort. Physically, this stone harmonizes male and female energies and encourages tissue regeneration.

Raw

HEALING Balances the nervous and glandular systems; soothes inflammation, tension in neck muscles and the side effects of leukaemia. It supports the pineal and pituitary glands, spleen, pancreas, liver, male reproductive organs and neurological tissue.

POSITION Hold, grid (see pages 28–31) or place as appropriate.

AMBLYGONITE

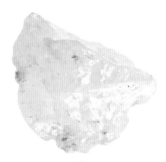

Raw

COLOR	Yellow
APPEARANCE	Lustrous, opaque, light color
RARITY	Easily obtained
SOURCE	United States, Brazil, France, Germany, Sweden, Myanmar, Canada

ATTRIBUTES Amblygonite is an extremely creative stone for the arts, promoting and enhancing music, poetry and creativity of all kinds. Meditating with it or keeping it close by expands your talents.

A stone of psychological and emotional balance, Amblygonite assists in nurturing yourself and reconciling dualities, integrating the polarities of being. Activating the solar plexus and higher crown chakras, this stone unites the emotions and the mind, and aligns all the chakra systems so that energy flows more freely between the subtle bodies*. Amblygonite encourages empathy, service and thoughtfulness toward those around you without falling into the trap of martyrdom or victimhood.

Spiritually, by strengthening your sense of self-worth, Amblygonite awakens your *knowing* that you are a divine soul who is immortal and passes on to other planes of existence after earth-life is over.

Emotionally, this is a useful stone for gently releasing emotional hooks from the solar plexus, especially where these belong to past partners or parents who still try to retain control. Amblygonite also assists in ending relationships without angry consequences.

In physical healing, Amblygonite activates the electrical systems of the body and, taped over the thymus, protects against computer emanations in those who are sensitive.

Environmentally, this stone is an efficient grid* for areas of discordance or public disorder, bringing peace and tranquillity, especially where young people are involved.

HEALING Helpful for stress, attention-deficit hyperactivity disorder (ADHD) and hyperactivity; reported to heal genetic disorders, headaches, bone disorders, irritable bowel syndrome (IBS), stomach and digestion problems.

POSITION Hold, grid (see pages 28–31) or place as appropriate.

AMMOLITE

*Sliced and
polished*

COLOR	Multi-colored
APPEARANCE	Opalized ammonite shell, intensely colored flash
RARITY	Rare
SOURCE	Canada, Morocco

ATTRIBUTES Activating metaphysical powers and inter-dimensional exploration, Ammolite is particularly effective when placed on the soma chakra and third eye. Representing coming full circle and knowing a place for the first time, it has the soul's path encoded within it and is a useful support for rebirthing. Spiritually, this stone takes you deep into your center and into completion. Activating personal empowerment and the spiritual will, Ammolite converts negative energy into a gently flowing positive spiral. A powerful karmic* cleanser, placed on the third eye this stone releases mental obsessions and past-life soul imperatives*.

Psychologically, Ammolite stimulates survival instincts and the knowledge that you will get there if you persevere. Physically, Ammolite is excellent for anything that needs structure and clarity, relieving birth trauma that interferes with the craniosacral flow, and is helpful in all craniosacral work. Environmentally, this is an effective earth-healing* stone.

Feng Shui masters call Ammolite the Seven Color Prosperity Stone. They believe Ammolite stimulates the flow of *qi**, life-force, through the body. According to them, this stone is exceedingly fortunate and they suggest keeping one in your home to bring wealth, health, vitality and happiness; and in business premises to promote beneficial business dealings. When worn, the stone is said to impart charisma and sensuous beauty to the wearer.

HEALING Helpful for overall well-being and longevity, cell metabolism, depression, labor pain, osteomyelitis, ostitis and tinnitus; awakening kundalini* energy and cellular memory*; stabilizing the pulse and overcoming degenerative disorders. It supports the cranium and inner ear, lungs and limbs.

POSITION Hold, grid (see pages 28–31) or place as appropriate.

FENG SHUI COLORS Red represents growth and energy; orange stands for creativity and increased libido; green represents wisdom, intellect and entrepreneurship; yellow is associated with wealth; blue represents peace and health.

ANNABERGITE

Tumbled

COLOR	Apple green
APPEARANCE	Opaque stone
RARITY	Easily obtained
SOURCE	Canada, United States, Germany, Sardinia, Italy, Spain, Greece

ATTRIBUTES Spiritually, Annabergite teaches that everything is perfect exactly as it is, showing you the harmony of your highest self and opening up all possibilities. Placed on the third eye, this mystical stone enhances visualization and intuition, and assists contact with wise beings of the universe.

Psychologically, placed on the soma chakra, this stone enables knowing who you truly are and reflecting this out to the world. This crystal is elusive, appearing when the time is right and bringing with it the knowledge you need, and so it is a useful indicator of the right timing for psychological change.

Annabergite aligns the biomagnetic sheath* and chakras, cleansing the earth chakra and strengthening the biomagnetic energies. In the physical meridians*, it enhances the flow of energy and harmonizes them with the earth's meridian grid, facilitating multi-dimensional cellular healing.

Physically, Annabergite opens healing potential and prepares the body to receive radiotherapy and to fight infections, and it enhances receptivity when undergoing radionic* or any form of energy medicine. It can stimulate ambidextrousness and support the learning of languages or shorthand, and reading and understanding symbols or dream imagery.

HEALING Supports cellular memory* and overcomes dehydration, tumors, cellular disorders and infections.

POSITION Hold, grid (see pages 28–31) or place as appropriate.

ASTROPHYLLITE

Tumbled

COLOR	Yellow-gray
APPEARANCE	Metallic or pearly blades
RARITY	Rare
SOURCE	United States

ATTRIBUTES Spiritually, Astrophyllite highlights your unlimited potential, heightens your perception and makes you sensitive to unspoken needs. Activating the ability to 'dream true' to see your soul path, it promotes out-of-body experiences, acting as guide and protector in other realms.

Psychologically, by enabling you to attain an objective view of yourself, it eliminates without guilt anything that is outworn, reminding you that as one door closes another opens. Promoting intimacy and increasing sensitivity of touch, it is helpful for massage or acupressure.

HEALING Beneficial for epilepsy, the reproductive, hormonal and nervous systems, PMS, menopausal disturbances, cellular regeneration, the large intestine, spinal alignment and fatty deposits.

POSITION Hold, grid (see pages 28–31) or place as appropriate.

ATLANTASITE

Tumbled

COLOR	Green and lilac
APPEARANCE	Opaque combination of two clearly defined colors
RARITY	Becoming more easily available
SOURCE	Australia, South Africa, Canada

ATTRIBUTES A combination of green Serpentine and purple Stichtite, Atlantasite accesses past lives in Atlantis, reconnecting to your ancient wisdom and encouraging you to complete projects set in motion at that time.

By stimulating spiritual evolution, this stone assists those who misused their spiritual powers in ancient civilizations and helps in recognizing the right use of power and the true nature of spiritual empowerment. Atlantasite clears and aligns all the chakras.

Psychologically, Atlantasite lowers stress levels and encourages thinking before speaking. Useful for gently encouraging children to modify inappropriate behavior, this stone is also helpful for breaking away from the results of poor choices or old wounds, healing outworn patterns and instilling a more positive approach. It is an effective harmonizer of disputes.

Environmentally, Atlantasite is a useful earth healer*, bringing peace into the environment and, when buried in the earth, undertakes earth clearing and energy restructuring in places where there has been death and destruction.

HEALING Beneficial for cellular memory*, stress, blood disorders, hypoglycaemia and diabetes.

POSITION Hold, grid (see pages 28–31) or place as appropriate.

(*See also* Stichtite, pages 331–332.)

ADDITIONAL FORM
Picrolite was highly prized in prehistoric times. A form of green Serpentine, this is a protective stone that clears and balances the chakra systems and promotes stamina. A useful earth healer, it can be gridded* to draw rain to areas of drought. Emotionally, Picrolite supports a rocky relationship by encouraging recognition of the positive qualities in a partner. Physically it assists the heart, adrenals and endocrine system, encouraging the assimilation of protein. Gemmy Picrolite has a somewhat lighter vibration.

Picrolite (raw)

AVALONITE

ALSO KNOWN AS DRUSY BLUE CHALCEDONY

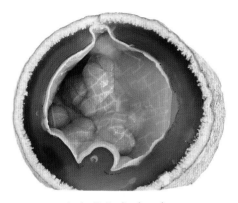

Avalonite in sliced geode

COLOR	Blue
APPEARANCE	Tiny crystals, almost velvety, often within a geode
RARITY	Rare
SOURCE	United States, Austria, Czech Republic, Slovakia, Iceland, England, Mexico, New Zealand, Turkey, Russia, Brazil, Morocco

ATTRIBUTES Avalonite enhances visualization and journeying*, opening psychic awareness and telepathy between soul partners. This stone takes you into the mythical realms where fairy tales and legend offer deep wisdom, acting as a translator and facilitator for creatively

61

reworking the myths in your life. Communicating with fairies, elves and devas*, Avalonite links into ancient magic and helps you to access and gain insight into knowledge held in the collective unconscious. To contact your inner wise woman or priestess incarnations, gaze into the depths of Avalonite and allow it to gently transport you inward.

Psychologically, this stone harmonizes the emotional, mental and spiritual knowledge at the center of your being. Enhancing mental practicality and stimulating innate wisdom especially when faced with new situations, this stone is perfect for those who fear failure or are unable to love, as it opens the heart and allows you to discover the perfection of your true self and recognize that you are never alone. It is an effective healer for disillusionment, bringing about a profound trust in the universe.

As an environmental protector, Avalonite absorbs negative energy and transmutes it to prevent the onward transmission, but it requires regular cleansing and recharging (see page 358).

HEALING Beneficial for sensitivity to weather or pressure changes.

POSITION Hold, grid (see pages 28–31) or place as appropriate.

BARITE

Greenish (natural bladed formation)

White (raw)

COLOR	White, orange, greenish
APPEARANCE	Vitreous clear crystal, bladed or fibrous mass
RARITY	Easily obtained
SOURCE	United States, Britain, Germany

ATTRIBUTES This stone facilitates communicating intuitive vision. A traditional journeying* stone, Barite stimulates both dreaming and dream recall. If anonymity and stealth are required for ritual working, Barite confers this and guides you safely back.

Spiritually, this is a useful stone for cleansing and rebalancing the entire chakra system. Psychologically, Barite enhances autonomy. If you have conformed to others' ideals instead of your own, or have been at the beck and call of others, Barite sets you free. Conversely, it supports loyalty to an appropriate person or ideal. This stone overcomes shyness and assists with interpersonal communication and mental focus. It teaches you where your boundaries lie. A strongly motivating stone, Barite benefits people whose energies are scattered or exhausted.

Mentally, Barite is supportive for the memory and encourages efficient functioning of the brain, heightening your ability to organize and express thoughts.

Emotionally, Barite is beneficial for platonic friendships and encourages intimacy and insight into relationships of all kinds. A powerful transformer, it may bring about a catharsis in which old emotional patterns, obsessions and fears are released (a process best undertaken with a qualified therapist), and other crystals may be required to restore equilibrium. The emotional catharsis may release long-repressed emotions and restructure the emotional body to restore calm.

HEALING Assists vitality, over-sensitivity to cold or temperature changes, memory, chronic fatigue, detoxification, the brain, vision, addiction and sore throat. It balances brain chemistry and calms the stomach and nervous system.

POSITION Hold, grid (see pages 28–31) or place as appropriate.

BERYLLONITE

Raw

COLOR	White to pale yellow
APPEARANCE	Delicate translucent crystal
RARITY	Rare
SOURCE	Brazil, United States, Afghanistan

ATTRIBUTES Spiritually opening metaphysical gifts* and containing crystallized light with an exceedingly high vibration*, Beryllonite connects to the original blueprint* to create quintessential well-being. Dis-ease* at all levels falls away, centering you in your self, showing you that whatever you are experiencing is the perfect basis for evolution and indicating the qualities your soul is developing through any situation, no matter how dire.

HEALING Works best beyond the physical level of being, calling in the perfect blueprint and realigning cellular structures to a time before dis-ease existed.

POSITION Hold, or place with care.

BIXBITE

Faceted   *Raw*

COLOR	Bright red
APPEARANCE	Translucent or transparent crystal
RARITY	Extremely rare
SOURCE	United States (may be lab-grown with somewhat lesser properties)

ATTRIBUTES A creative and powerful stone, promoting courage, passion and willpower without egotism, Bixbite encourages respect for others. This stone stimulates the base chakras and links to the heart, grounding you in compassionate love and releasing karmic* conflict and ancient wounds. Its fiery color derives from manganese, required for cell reproduction and fatty acids for the formation of new blood cells.

HEALING Promotes self-healing and cell repair; supportive during convalescence, increasing stamina and vitality; assists the reproductive organs, liver and blood, metabolic and enzyme processes, teeth and bones.

POSITION Hold, grid (see pages 28–31) or place as appropriate. Place over the base and sacral chakras to increase fertility and creativity.

BLOOD OF ISIS

Faceted

COLOR	Red
APPEARANCE	Transparent crystal with 'smoke' effect
RARITY	Rare and expensive
SOURCE	Red Sea, Egypt

ATTRIBUTES Blood of Isis is gem-quality Carnelian, which was popular for protective amulets and offerings to the gods not only in Egypt but also in Europe, Myanmar and Japan. It was almost certainly one of the stones used in the Breastplate of the High Priest (see pages 17–18) and attunes to Isis energy, the divine feminine principle.

The goddess Isis was both a powerful priestess, with power over life and death, and the archetypal devoted wife and mother. Each year in her honor, a great mystery was enacted in the temples: that of birth, death and regeneration. Meditating or sleeping with this stone under your pillow invokes a profound connection to the universal feminine and the goddess-within, and also helps remove the veils of Isis to reach spiritual clarity and true sight.

The medieval lapidary of King Alphonso the Learned of Spain, translated from a much earlier Arab text preserving very ancient knowledge, calls this the 'stone of sleep' and also attributes to it the quality of emitting light. Said to impart a deep stupor, it was apparently used to dull pain, especially during surgery.

Spiritually, the stone assists in re-membering the lost and forgotten parts of your self, especially the opposite gender to the body you now inhabit. It facilitates making an inner marriage, uniting your masculine and feminine qualities, and is helpful for men who have lost touch with the creative, empowered feminine part of their psyche.

Psychologically, Blood of Isis is an excellent stone to foster forgiveness. The ancient Egyptians wore Carnelian to calm anger, jealousy, envy and other negative symptoms. The goddess Isis forgave her sister for stealing her husband, and her brother-in-law for killing him. She knew the depths of grief and the stone also assists with grief work, ameliorating loss and bringing acceptance of the cycles of life.

Physically, this stone is helpful at menopause for a woman who mourns the loss of her fertility and for 'empty nest syndrome', attuning her to a new purpose—becoming a truly wise woman.

HEALING Traditionally used for healing blood and the organs of fertility: said to help with PMS, infertility and menopausal symptoms.

POSITION Wear or position as appropriate.

BLUE ARAGONITE

Tumbled

COLOR	Blue
APPEARANCE	Opaque stone (may be color-infused)
RARITY	Easily available
SOURCE	United States, Namibia, Britain, Spain, Morocco

ATTRIBUTES The delicate blue of Blue Aragonite derives from copper, a powerful energy conduit that heightens and grounds spiritual communication. Copper has long been sacred to the goddess of love, Venus, and this gentle stone purifies and aligns all the subtle bodies* with the physical and balances yin-yang energies, leading to optimum well-being.

Uniting the third eye, throat and heart chakras, Blue Aragonite assists in expressing spiritual vision. Psychologically, this stone instills a sense of resolute optimism and assists in finding the source of problems you encounter, turning them into opportunities for evolution. Blue Aragonite is useful for inner-child* work and for manifesting your soul's plan for the present life.

Emotionally, this stone uplifts and calms the spirit and facilitates the expression of deep emotions. To attract more love into your life, and especially if you yearn for your spiritual twinflame*, program Blue Aragonite to call this into your life now (see page 358).

Physically, Blue Aragonite assists with any form of breath- or voice-work, strengthening the lungs and throat. It assists in being comfortable within your physical body.

Environmentally, it is a powerful earth-healer* and soul-healer. Gridded* around a house, Blue Aragonite keeps the environment stable and harmonious and transmutes pollution and negativity of any kind.

HEALING Beneficial for stress, cellular memory*, Reynauds disease and releasing spasm. It supports the respiratory tract.

POSITION Hold, grid (see pages 28–31) or place as appropriate.

BLUE MOONSTONE

Shaped and polished

COLOR	Blue on white (color enhanced)
APPEARANCE	Scintillating patches in a clear crystal
RARITY	Easily obtained but expensive
SOURCE	Russia

ATTRIBUTES A refined, high-vibrational* stone, color-infused Blue Moonstone is an activation stone *par excellence*, having a powerful effect on unawakened potential and creating a gateway to exceedingly high levels of consciousness and multi-dimensions. This stone creates a subtle geometric merkaba*-shaped energetic pathway in the physical brain, linking the alta-major (past-life) chakras with the hypothalamus, hippocampus, pineal and pituitary glands, and the third eye and soma chakras. This opens a higher-dimensional* space within the brain, anchored to the thymus and higher heart chakra so that it manifests within the physical world. Blue Moonstone attunes the metabolism to assimilate the minerals and nutrients that the activated lightbody* requires to function on the earth plane.

71

Spiritually, Blue Moonstone enables you to have a foot in both worlds—physical and spiritual—being 'here' and 'there' at the same time with no duality or conflict and complete clarity of awareness. It also activates a cosmic anchor*. On the soma chakra, it brings ideas into manifestation by first creating an energy structure.

HEALING Placing Blue Moonstone on the neck where the spinal column meets the skull has the same effect as a craniosacral treatment, releasing muscle tension and bringing subtle energies, blood vessels and nerves passing through this area into more perfect function.

POSITION Wear or place as appropriate.

ADDITIONAL FORM

Rainbow Moonstone carries the vibration of cosmic light and offers spiritual healing for the whole of humanity. Taking you on inter- and multi-dimensional journeys*, it reminds you that you are part of an ongoing, ever-unfolding cycle, and links into your overall soul as well as your current life plan*. Helping you to see the unseen, intuitively read symbols and synchronicities, and opening you to spiritual gifts, Rainbow Moonstone may leave sensitive people feeling psychically or emotionally overwhelmed, although it provides insight in appropriate circumstances. This stone is powerfully attuned to the cycles and phases of the moon and may need removing at full moon. Rainbow Moonstone is beneficial for the internal organs, eyes, arteries and veins.

Rainbow Moonstone (polished)

BORNITE

Tumbled

COLOR	Gold with colored flashes
APPEARANCE	Opaque, metallic, tarnishes to iridescent
RARITY	Easily obtained
SOURCE	United States, Canada, Morocco, Germany, Poland, England, Chile, Australia, Kazakhstan, Czech Republic, France, Norway

ATTRIBUTES Opening psychic abilities and enhancing inner knowing, Bornite teaches trust in the intuitive process. Spiritually, by assisting with visualization and creating your own reality, Bornite fosters concern about all beings on the planet, advocating social justice and equality for all.

Psychologically an effective protector against, and transmuter of, negative thoughts and beliefs, Bornite teaches how to negotiate obstacles with ease and encourages finding happiness in the present moment. This stone assists in dealing with traumatic situations and identifying the lessons behind them. Integrating mind, body, emotions and soul, Bornite filters out what is no longer relevant and assists in moving on.

Mentally, Bornite identifies the source of detrimental thoughts so that they are eliminated. An effective tool during any kind of rebirthing work, this stone can be programmed (see page 358) to send or receive healing from a distance—in which case it should be carried or worn over the thymus.

HEALING Assists with regeneration, cellular memory*, cellular structures, metabolic imbalances, over-acidity, assimilation of potassium and swelling. It dissolves calcified deposits and calms spasm.

POSITION Hold, grid (see pages 28–31) or place as appropriate; wear set in silver.

COMBINATION STONE

Bornite on Silver reinforces the silver cord* that connects the subtle bodies to the physical, ensuring safe return during journeying*. Silver is a stabilizing metal that strengthens the qualities of the stone to which it is attached and focuses its energy appropriately. Silver is a feminine, moon-attuned metal and, heightening perception and intuition, this combination acts as a reflective mirror for mystic visions, scrying or inspiration. It assists with accessing and reframing the source of third-eye blockages, especially where these have been deliberately induced in the past. Emotionally, Bornite on Silver enhances mothering oneself and the nurturing process, and heightens platonic or romantic love. Physically, this combination facilitates the reprogramming of cellular memory, supports the cellular structures in the body, the assimilation of potassium and metabolic imbalances. It assists in dissolving calcified deposits and swelling.

Bornite on Silver (raw)

BRAZILIANITE

Raw

COLOR	Yellow-green
APPEARANCE	Transparent, slightly ribbed
RARITY	Rare
SOURCE	Brazil

ATTRIBUTES Brazilianite has a zingy, high-energy vibration* that empowers the spiritual will and assists manifestation. Said to connect to Atlantis, this highly creative stone spiritually opens metaphysical gifts* and shows how to achieve apparently supernatural feats that are within expanded human capabilities. If you misused such energies in Atlantis, it cleanses the past and re-empowers your soul integrity.

Psychologically, if you have difficulty in establishing boundaries for yourself and others, Brazilianite assists in knowing where you end and others begin, teaching how to say no and preventing psychic intrusion into your space. It overcomes a victim or martyr mentality, especially if this has a past-life root, teaching instead how to be a proud survivor. A stone of right action, Brazilianite assists in setting limits and is particularly helpful in laying down rules for teenagers testing parental

75

boundaries. Brazilianite also assists if others push your boundaries inappropriately—and shows how to expand your boundaries if these are too tight because of fear or previous abuse. It helps in taking responsibility for yourself, standing on an edge and moving forward confidently knowing that you follow the rightness of your soul path.

Emotionally, it assists in becoming aware of your vulnerabilities, especially if these have long been denied. If emotions such as resentment have been holding you back, this stone transmutes them and assists in forgiving yourself. Giving emotional strength, Brazilianite teaches how to find your core strength rather than growing a carapace to cover vulnerability but leaving a black hole in your emotional center.

Physically, Brazilianite assists energy flow and circulation within the body, clearing meridians* and removing excess heat.

HEALING Said to release pollutants such as heavy metals, supporting the kidneys and other excretory organs.

POSITION Hold, grid (see pages 28–31) or place as appropriate.

BRONZITE

Tumbled

COLOR	Brown and black
APPEARANCE	Mottled stone
RARITY	Easily obtained
SOURCE	Germany, Finland, India, Sri Lanka, United States

ATTRIBUTES Bronzite facilitates simply 'being', entering a dynamic state of non-action and non-doing. Spiritually, this is the perfect stone if you have difficulty in stilling yourself, since it brings total serenity. Marketed as effective against curses and sold as a magical protector, Bronzite turns back negative thoughts and ill-wishing*. However, it returns ill-wishing, curses or spells back to the source considerably magnified, perpetuating the problem as it 'bounces' backward and forward, becoming stronger each time, and makes the ill-wisher feel extremely ill while the 'recipient' remains protected but aware of the energetic disturbance. It is more effective to use Bronzite in combination with Black Tourmaline, as this absorbs the ill-wishing, immediately stopping the interaction and taking attention away from the source.

Psychologically, this 'stone of courtesy' strengthens non-judgmental discernment, pinpoints your most important choices and promotes decisive action. This protective, grounding* crystal is helpful when you feel powerless in discordant situations or are in the grip of events beyond your control. Holding Bronzite increases self-assertion, restores composure and assists in keeping a cool head. With its assistance, you can take an objective perspective and see the bigger picture. It is helpful for overcoming stress and reversing wilfulness, teaching how to go with the flow of divine will. If you have become stuck in any negative pattern, Bronzite releases it.

Physically, Bronzite is useful for supporting and balancing masculine yang energy within the body or the psyche.

HEALING Helpful for chronic exhaustion, the assimilation of iron, cramp and nerves, and for removing pain and over-alkalinity.

POSITION Hold, grid (see pages 28–31) or place as appropriate. Use in a Star of David formation with Black Tourmaline to turn back ill-wishing.

BUSTAMITE

*Shaped and
polished*

COLOR	Pinky-red
APPEARANCE	Vitreous, opaque and patterned
RARITY	Easily obtained but expensive
SOURCE	South Africa, Sweden, Russia, Peru, Argentina, Austria, Bulgaria, Germany, Honduras, Italy, Japan, New Zealand, Norway, Britain, Brazil

ATTRIBUTES Bustamite carries a powerful energy that brings about deep connection to the earth and facilitates earth healing*, repairing and realigning the meridians of the earth's etheric body*. Spiritually, it is excellent for gridding* a safe space in which to carry out ritual work, initiation or meditation. Stimulating conscious dreaming and intuition, Bustamite enhances channeling* and accesses the angelic realms. It is said to lose its luster in the presence of danger.

Mentally, this stone helps you to retain composure and creates inner congruency, helping to stand back from disharmonious experiences while remaining physically present, or facilitating your physical absence from detrimental situations. This stone turns ideals and ideas into positive action.

Emotionally, Bustamite removes old pain, harmonizing the emotional energy system and healing cellular memory*. Physically, this stone realigns the energy meridians of the physical and subtle bodies*. When Bustamite assists with healing, you follow your life path with great vitality.

HEALING Beneficial for cellular memory, stress-related illness, calcium deficiencies, circulation, headaches and fluid retention, Bustamite supports the legs and feet, heart, skin, nails, hair, motor nerves, muscle strength, spleen, lungs, prostate gland, sexual organs, endocrine and digestive systems, and balances the pancreas.

POSITION Hold, grid (see pages 28–31) or place as appropriate.

COMBINATION STONE

Bustamite with Sugilite unites heaven and earth. It increases spiritual and psychic awareness while enhancing groundedness, and it opens intuition, improving your ability to listen to the voice of your self. Using this stone, sensitive people are helped to adapt to being in the earth environment while keeping their spiritual connection open to nourish the core of their being. Psychologically, this is a useful stone for anyone who feels they do not fit in. Program it (see page 358) to draw like-minded souls together and to channel more love into the earth. Physically, Bustamite with Sugilite is excellent for relieving migraine and headaches.

Bustamite with Sugilite (tumbled)

CACOXENITE

Shaped

COLOR	Yellowish-orange
APPEARANCE	Radiated, feathery inclusion
RARITY	Rare
SOURCE	England, Sweden, France, Germany, Holland, United States

ATTRIBUTES Known as a stone of ascension*, Cacoxenite heightens spiritual awareness. Spiritually, this stone is used in meditation or past-life regression. It takes you to core soul memories that require healing or integration before present-day spiritual evolution can occur. Included* within Amethyst, Cacoxenite activates the third eye and crown chakras, increasing receptivity to receive new ideas. This crystal heightens the effect of full or new moon rituals.

Psychologically, it is helpful for overcoming fear and clearing stress. Harmonizing the personal will with the Higher Self* and accentuating the positive in all that you do, Cacoxenite assists in releasing inhibitions and restrictions. If apparently insurmountable problems confront you, Cacoxenite creates a peaceful space to withdraw into, encouraging you to see events in a positive light.

Environmentally, Cacoxenite assists with planetary re-alignment to stimulate the vibratory evolution of the earth and can be gridded* for earth healing*.

HEALING This stone is a holistic healer that promotes awareness of the psychosomatic causes of dis-ease* and the holistic nature of healing. It supports cellular memory*, and the heart, lungs, adrenals and thyroid; assists respiratory ailments, colds and flu. It balances hormonal and cellular disorders.

POSITION Hold, grid (see pages 28–31) or place as appropriate.

(*See also* Super Seven, pages 333–334.)

CALCITE FAIRY STONE

Natural formation

COLOR	Grayish-beige
APPEARANCE	Smooth, rounded and flattened discs
RARITY	Rare
SOURCE	Canada

ATTRIBUTES Looking rather like little aliens, insects or ancient earth goddesses, these Calcite Fairy figures are pseudomorphs created when calcite settled into glacial clay. If a Calcite Fairy Stone adopts you, it acts as a 'little helper', taking care of details and providing a safe and nurturing space in which to work both spiritually and practically.

Spiritually, Calcite Fairy Stones have a strong link to the nurturing energies of the Earth Mother and to female power, and remind us that raising vibrations*, or ascending, does not mean losing touch with the necessities of the earth. This stone teaches care and concern for the planet and all those upon it at a pragmatic rather than an idealistic level. It believes in getting things done in the most practical way possible. It assists in channeling*, but there is nothing airy-fairy about the information it offers—it is basic, grounded and to the point. A useful stone for opening a shamanic anchor* for lower-world* journeys* or the earth portion of a cosmic anchor*, it attaches you to the earth's core so that you can ride out and ground earth-energy changes, but it requires a higher-vibration* stone, such as Stellar Beam Calcite, to reach the galactic center*.

Psychologically, Calcite Fairy Stone assists in dismantling defensive walls you have built around old hurts that lock you into old pain. In dissolving a 'flight-or-fight' reflex or conditioned reaction, it teaches how to respond positively to each new situation.

Each stone has a unique energy according to its shape; meditate with it to learn how it wants to work with you and the specific gifts it offers.

HEALING Excellent for arthritic pain and dissolving calcifications.

POSITION Hold or position as appropriate.

COBALTO-CALCITE

*Natural crystals
on matrix*

COLOR	Vivid pink
APPEARANCE	Small, transparent to opaque crystals
RARITY	Easily obtained
SOURCE	Germany, United States, Britain, Belgium, Czech Republic, Slovakia, Peru, Iceland, Brazil, Romania

ATTRIBUTES Cobalto-calcite symbolizes unconditional love and
forgiveness and is attuned to the pink flame* of pure, compassionate
love. A stone of self-discovery, it connects heart with mind. If you are
uncertain where you need to go spiritually, gentle Cobalto-calcite helps
you to find your innate talents and life purpose.

Psychologically, this beautiful crystal helps to transfer ideas into
action without forcing the pace. It harmonizes the intellect and the
emotions, bringing the two into balance. This compassionate stone
is effective for emotional healing and overcoming emotional blocks,

85

loneliness, grief or a broken heart. It calms intense feelings, assisting in loving yourself and others, and promotes a sense of feeling good about your life. Encouraging emotional maturation, it sends out a profoundly nurturing energy that helps you to mother yourself. It is extremely supportive for those who have chosen to carry pain for other people or the planet, and for those who have given up hope. It also shows whether taking on other people's pain is appropriate, gently cutting the ties if it is not and promoting forgiveness on both sides.

For distance healing, program Cobalto-calcite (see page 358) to send pink light to support someone in becoming all that they might be, then place the stone on a photograph of that person, or program it to heal dis-ease* wherever it may be.

HEALING Works best at the emotional level of being, erasing scars and bringing more love into the physical body.

POSITION Hold, grid (see pages 28–31) or place as appropriate.

(*See also* Erythrite, page 127.)

CALCITE: **HEMATOID CALCITE**

*Natural
formation*

COLOR	Reddish yellow
APPEARANCE	Large squares or planes of opaque crystal
RARITY	Fairly easily obtained
SOURCE	United States, Britain, Belgium, Czech Republic, Slovakia, Peru, Iceland, Romania

ATTRIBUTES Combining the stabilizing power of Hematite with the purifying energies of Calcite, Hematoid Calcite is an excellent stone for grounding* and assimilating influxes of energy—hold it or place over the base chakra for five or ten minutes or until the energy stabilizes. Carry this powerfully protective stone when you are in a strong energy field, particularly if the energies clash, as it quickly cleanses and harmonizes the environment.

Psychologically, this stone is helpful for anyone who has become locked into a predator pattern, stopping at nothing to get what they want and ignoring the needs and feelings of others; or for someone who is the apparent victim of such a person, but who is, in reality, punishing themselves for their own perceived guilt and inadequacy. Hematoid Calcite enables you to step forward to mutual cooperation.

Mentally, Hematoid Calcite is a supportive stone for the memory, so if you have 'senior moments' or lose things or cannot remember birthdays or names, keep this stone with you. It ameliorates mental confusion, restoring lucidity and structuring thought.

Physically, Hematoid Calcite instills vitality and supports self-healing, encouraging the body to mobilize its natural defences.

Environmentally, Hematoid Calcite is helpful for gridding* a workplace, particularly if this is a site of ego conflict or manipulation. Hematite stabilizes the emotional field and Calcite pours soothing energy into the environment, restoring peace and harmony.

HEALING Beneficial for the memory, blood cleansing, oxygenation and stress.

POSITION Hold, grid (see pages 28–31) or place as appropriate.

Honey Phantom Calcite (natural cluster)

(*See also* Hematite with Rutile, pages 152–153.)

ADDITIONAL STONE

Honey Phantom Calcite (Mariposa Calcite) gives a protective coating of purifying light to the biomagnetic sheath* and imparts physical endurance to the body. It is an effective healer for any form of abuse. A grounding stone that breaks old patterns and teaches right use of power, it assists in manifesting abundance on earth through your own efforts.

CALCITE: **ICICLE CALCITE**

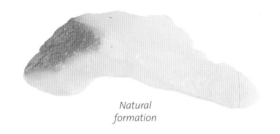

*Natural
formation*

COLOR	Whitish yellow and orange
APPEARANCE	Long, finger-like, opaque bi-color crystal
RARITY	May need searching for
SOURCE	United States, Britain, Belgium, Czech Republic, Slovakia, Peru, Iceland, Romania

ATTRIBUTES Icicle Calcite is a spiritual and pragmatic guidance crystal that fires creativity at all levels. Spiritually, it is a powerful amplifier of energy with strongly purifying and cleansing properties that quickly remove stagnant energies wherever they are located. The white portion of Icicle Calcite acts like a wand to pull multi-dimensional dis-ease*, disharmony, negativity or blockages from the physical or etheric body* and, once the crystal has been cleansed, the site can then be repaired and re-energized with the orange portion, bringing the body back into balance on all levels.

Psychologically, Calcite connects the mind and the emotions and increases the ability to see things in a new way. Icicle Calcite helps you to understand and clear the root causes of psychosomatic dis-ease or ancestral-line* DNA imbalances. It takes you back into past situations, reframes* them and transmits healing backward and forward down the ancestral line so that the problem does not arise in the present.

Emotionally, Icicle Calcite gently releases fear and alleviates emotional stress, replacing it with serenity. It insists that you step forward into the future to live out your purpose with courage, conviction and the certainty that you are following the path of your soul. Whenever you feel in need of support, hold Icicle Calcite and request assistance.

HEALING Works etherically or physically to remove blockages and re-energize cells.

POSITION Use as a wand.

CALCITE: **STELLAR BEAM CALCITE**

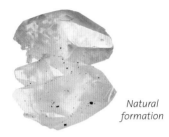

Natural formation

COLOR	Amber, yellow or whitish-yellow
APPEARANCE	Clear, blade-like double-terminated crystal
RARITY	Available from mineral suppliers and crystal shops
SOURCE	Tennessee (United States)

ATTRIBUTES Named for its multi- and inter-dimensional properties and for its perceived ability to link to spaceships and extra-terrestrials, the double terminations of Stellar Beam Calcite channel a dual beam of powerful energy that lifts to an exceedingly high vibration* and, on the soma or stellar gateway chakras, facilitates travel across vast distances in time and space. It is excellent in the center of the medicine wheel.

Spiritually, on the third eye or crown chakra, this stone opens the higher crown and soul star chakras and facilitates attunement to divine energy, higher guidance and elevated levels of consciousness. Taking you directly into the heart of All That Is*, it lights the way back and assists in remembering what happens in outer or inner dimensions*, accelerating spiritual growth. Stellar Beam Calcite takes you to the galactic center* to anchor the upper end of a cosmic anchor*, but

91

requires a lower-vibration stone, such as Calcite Fairy Stone, to anchor into the earth's core.

Psychologically, it assists in breaking old patterns, including spiritual beliefs or pathways that no longer serve your purpose, and moving forward on your soul path. It takes you to the 'planning meeting' in the between-life state* to ascertain your soul purpose and the life you were born to live and brings forward wisdom and skills from the far past. It attunes to your soul group* and the higher purpose of the group.

Emotionally, Stellar Beam Calcite helps you to immerse yourself in mutual love, desire and tenderness. An amplifier and purifier of energy, this stone cleanses anything negative picked up during spiritual journeying* or healing work.

HEALING Works beyond the physical level of being to heal the soul, aligning and integrating energies into subtle bodies* and healing the etheric blueprint*.

POSITION Hold or place as appropriate. Grid (see pages 28–31) to encourage extra-terrestrial contact or to create sacred space.

ADDITIONAL STONE

Starburst Dogstooth Calcite disperses blockages, connects you to the infinity of All That Is and takes you traveling through past, present or future lives on earth or with the stars to map your overall soul purpose. It can be used to stabilize brain patterns in epilepsy, ameliorate vertigo or tinnitus and restore the etheric body following drug abuse or the side effects of prescription drugs.

Starburst Dogstooth Calcite (natural formation)

92

CALLIGRAPHY STONE

Sliced and polished

COLOR	Lavender, white and yellow
APPEARANCE	Banded stone that suggests glyphs and letters
RARITY	Rare form of Fluorite
SOURCE	China

ATTRIBUTES A form of Fluorite that assists in reading sacred symbolism, revealing multi-layered meanings, both inner and higher, and attuning to the wisdom of past and future. This stone connects the third eye, soma, throat and past-life chakras, facilitating the expression of other-dimension concepts in language understandable in functional reality.

Psychologically, Calligraphy Stone assists with breaking the patterns of the past, opening your mind to higher spiritual realities. Environmentally, by drawing off negative energies, Calligraphy Stone defends against electromagnetic radiation.

HEALING As this stone is delicate, it is better to use Fluorite for healing.

POSITION Grid (see pages 28–31) or place with care.

CASSITERITE

Turquoise (crystals
on matrix)

Gray
(raw)

COLOR	Vivid turquoise blue, yellow, gray
APPEARANCE	Small prismatic or pyramidal crystals
RARITY	Easily available
SOURCE	Brazil, Cornwall, United States, China

ATTRIBUTES A form of tin, Cassiterite was traditionally linked to astrology and astronomy and assists in understanding the major cycles of life. Affording useful protection at every level, spiritually Cassiterite reminds you of your inherent perfection and divinity. With the help of Cassiterite, you can manifest your dreams and hopes for the future.

Psychologically, this stone assists in objectively perceiving how and why things were as they were, opening the way for compassion and forgiveness for all concerned and releasing cellular memories* so that

94

deep soul healing can take place. A stone of tough love, Cassiterite encourages doing exactly what is necessary and no more for yourself and others, cutting through a tendency to sacrifice or martyr yourself and mitigating a savior complex.

Mentally, Cassiterite imparts mathematical precision, giving a razor-sharp mind and the insight needed to see into the source of a problem and reframe* it.

A powerful emotional healer, Cassiterite is a useful stone for anyone who was severely disapproved of in childhood or for other situations such as rejection, abandonment, prejudice or alienation. Making an excellent container for negative energy, it gently dissolves the resulting pain and is particularly useful where this underlies eating disorders or compulsive behavior. The stone supports transitions of all kinds.

HEALING Beneficial for eating disorders, obesity, malnutrition, cellular memory, the nervous and hormonal systems and secretions.

POSITION Hold, grid (see pages 28–31) or place as appropriate.

Gray (crystals on matrix)

95

CAVANSITE

Tumbled

*Natural crystals
on matrix*

COLOR	Vivid turquoise blue
APPEARANCE	Translucent to transparent, vitreous, crystalline or pearly radial spheres, rosettes or fans on a matrix
RARITY	Easily obtained
SOURCE	India, United States, Brazil, New Zealand

ATTRIBUTES A stone of purification and regeneration, Cavansite facilitates conscious astral journeying* and past-life exploration. Karmically*, with the assistance of this stone, trauma can be reframed at source so that it does not manifest in the present day (use under the guidance of an experienced past-life therapist). Placed on the third eye, Cavansite stimulates channeling* and metaphysical awareness, and combines this with pragmatic everyday learning and logical thought.

Psychologically, this life-affirming stone brings optimism and inspiration into your world. A self-reflective stone that assists in going deep within, it redresses destructive behavior or ingrained thought patterns, enabling you to be comfortable in your physicality and encouraging self-respect. Mentally, Cavansite helps you to think before you act and, combining logic and intuition, shows the way to work through problems and assists in communicating all you have seen.

Physically, this stone facilitates endorphin release and the conductivity of electrical impulses around the body, enhancing the feel-good factor and bringing about cellular healing. A protective stone, Cavansite shields a healer or past-life therapist during a session. Environmentally, Cavansite sensitizes you to the need to look after the environment and instills an appreciation of the beauty all around. It is excellent for gridding* to safeguard your home or car.

HEALING Supports cellular memory* and healing of the eyes, teeth, sore throat, kidneys, bladder, blood and tinnitus; said to assist the endocrine system, recurrent disease, calcium deficiency, bone loss, joint flexibility, migraine and fragmented DNA; stabilizes the pulse.

POSITION Hold, grid (see pages 28–31) or place as appropriate.

CELESTOBARITE

Raw

COLOR	Orange, gray and white bands
APPEARANCE	Banded, opaque stone
RARITY	Easily obtained
SOURCE	England, Poland, Denmark, Australia, United States

ATTRIBUTES Celestobarite cuts through blockages and takes you to the edge and beyond. Spiritually, it encompasses past, present and future and explores the multi-dimensional layers of being. With strong shielding energy, this is an excellent journeying* stone that holds you suspended between the earth and soul star chakras and takes you safely into the shamanic worlds in which reside soul aspects and entities*. Celestobarite is perfect for creating a shamanic anchor* for both lower- and upper-world* journeys and it activates a cosmic anchor*, stabilizing your energy to the core of the planet and the center of the galaxy, for which it needs bands top and bottom.

Celestobarite is a shamanic oracle that shows you both sides of an issue, elucidating what is not clear but leaving you to decide what to believe or put into practice.

Belonging to the south on the medicine wheel (see pages 368–375), this stone has an affinity with Coyote, a joker energy that presents the darker side in a joyful way and reminds you that nothing stays the same. It teaches how to laugh at yourself and the absurdities of the human condition. If you feel as though an answer or insight is just out of your grasp, holding Celestobarite will bring the answer to the surface and you will see how it has been staring you in the face all along.

HEALING Brings about multi-dimensional healing beyond the physical level of being, but can also help you to feel more integrated in the physical body.

POSITION Hold, grid (see pages 28–31) or place as appropriate.

CHALCOPYRITE

Tumbled

COLOR	Brassy yellow when polished
APPEARANCE	Opaque crystal that tarnishes to multi-colored
RARITY	Easily obtained
SOURCE	France, Chile, Namibia, Zambia, Peru, Germany, Spain, United States

ATTRIBUTES A powerful energy conduit, Chalcopyrite puts you through 'the fires of truth', tempering your soul, and assists in the assimilation of spiritual knowledge. Spiritually, this stone is an aid to achieving the state of 'no mind' required for deep meditation and contemplation of the perfection of the universe. Linking to ancient civilizations, it assists in ascertaining the cause of present life difficulties or diseases.

Psychologically, Chalcopyrite shows that prosperity is a state of mind and helps to attract abundance into your life. Mentally, Chalcopyrite assists accurate perception and logical thought while listening to your inner voice.

Physically, this stone stabilizes cell energy as higher frequencies are integrated and is effective for heightening the effect of acupuncture or acupressure as it dissolves energy blockages and enhances the movement of *qi** around the body. Grid* around the couch, bed or chair for maximum assimilation of energies. It is also supportive during Tai Chi. Environmentally, this stone is reported to locate lost objects; the stone itself disappears and reappears through different realities.

HEALING Beneficial for cellular memory*, energy blockages, hair growth, thread veins, brain disorders, excretory organs, tumors, infectious diseases, RNA/DNA, arthritis, bronchitis, inflammation, fever.

POSITION Hold, grid (see pages 28–31) or place as appropriate.

CHRYSOTILE

ALSO KNOWN AS CHRYSOTITE

Tumbled

COLOR	Yellow and green
APPEARANCE	Concentric dark and light banded stone
RARITY	Medium
SOURCE	United States, Canada, India, Russia, Australia, Arabia

ATTRIBUTES If you angle Chrysotile into the light, it is possible to see ancient writing inscribed within it that links to the knowledge of the ages and it is possible that this was one of the stones in the Breastplate of the High Priest (see pages 17–18). A shamanic stone, Chrysotile is useful when working the crystal medicine wheel (see pages 368–375) as, deep within it, your power animal waits to make itself known so that you can embody it, journey* and learn from its wisdom.

Spiritually, this powerful stone assists in clearing away the debris of the past to reveal and integrate your core self. Psychologically a stone of

102

integrity and self-honesty, Chrysotile shows where you seek to control others, assisting in letting that go while steering your destiny. This stone can be used to bring you what you desire, but you need to be sure of the full implications of that desire before using it.

Physically, when placed over the thymus, Chrysotile works on the etheric blueprint* to heal cellular memory* and correct imbalances and blockages that could manifest as physical disease unless redressed.

HEALING Beneficial for chronic fatigue, inflammation, multiple sclerosis, irritating coughs and emphysema. It supports the parathyroid, throat, brainstem, central meridian channel, veins and arteries.

POSITION Hold, grid (see pages 28–31) or place as appropriate.

CLEVELANDITE

Natural formation

COLOR	White
APPEARANCE	Opalescent, transparent to translucent blades
RARITY	Rare
SOURCE	Pakistan

ATTRIBUTES This is a useful stone to carry during a profound life change because it helps in moving forward into the future with equanimity. Encouraging planning shrewdly and wisely where necessary and trusting where appropriate, Clevelandite provides safe passage for your journey*.

Spiritually a stone of initiation and transformation, Clevelandite links to the three phases of the goddess and womanhood—maiden, mother and crone—facilitating the transition through each stage and bringing about rebirth. It is the perfect stone for croning ceremonies—a welcome into the sisterhood of mature wise women.

Psychologically, Clevelandite assists in turning difficult circumstances into positive, life-affirming situations. It helps you to focus on exactly what kind of change you need to bring about and shows the gifts and tools at your disposal to assist in manifesting it.

Useful for emotional healing, when placed on the solar plexus this stone releases deeply held emotional fears of abandonment, rejection and betrayal, or the consequences of such experiences, and facilitates self-nurturing.

HEALING Lends support during puberty and menopause. Supports the cell membranes and joints, and overcomes cardiovascular disorders and stroke-damage, colitis and allergies.

POSITION Hold, grid (see pages 28–31) or place as appropriate.

CONICHALCITE

*Natural crystals
on matrix*

COLOR	Bright green when raw, metallic when polished
APPEARANCE	Vitreous mass or translucent crystal
RARITY	Easily obtained
SOURCE	United States, Mexico, Chile, Poland, Zaire

ATTRIBUTES A powerful energy conduit, Conichalcite provides a shield against energetic disturbances. Stimulating intuition, it centers the mind for meditation, removing concerns about the everyday world and opening the way for limitless possibilities to manifest themselves.

Psychologically, Conichalcite promotes an inner strength flexible enough to accommodate change. Mentally assisting communication, this stone brings heart and mind together to create personal empowerment and facilitates the ability to talk with plants.

HEALING Beneficial for detoxification, mucus, the kidneys and bladder, psoriasis and herpes.

POSITION Hold, grid (see pages 28–31) or place as appropriate.

COVELLITE

Tumbled

COLOR	Dark blue
APPEARANCE	Lustrous, metallic opaque stone, sometimes tarnished
RARITY	Easily obtained
SOURCE	Italy, United States, Germany, Sardinia, Wales, Alaska

ATTRIBUTES Attuned to the Higher Self*, Covellite transforms dreams into concrete realities and stimulates your metaphysical abilities*. Spiritually, this reflective stone opens a doorway to the past and to the wisdom acquired in other lives. It is a useful adjunct to the rebirthing process or to any trip into the lower world*.

Psychologically, Covellite is a helpful stone if you are feeling vulnerable and too easily stimulated by others. Supporting your intention and assisting in integrating your shadow qualities* and facing your karma*, this stone overcomes discontent, instilling satisfaction with life. Strengthening creativity, it assists in coming to terms with sexuality, improving libido if required. Covellite harmonizes body, mind and soul and facilitates the process of loving yourself unconditionally while eliminating vanity and arrogance.

Mentally, this stone releases anything holding you back, particularly ingrained beliefs from other lives. It facilitates rational analytic thought and the decision-making process and enhances communication. Emotionally, Covellite overcomes despondency and anxiety, replacing negative emotions with loving serenity.

Physically, Covellite protects the body against radiation and facilitates energy flow through cells, detoxifying and removing stagnant energy. If physical dis-ease* has a karmic cause, Covellite helps you to explore and reframe* contributory factors, but this is best done with the assistance of a qualified therapist.

HEALING Beneficial for detoxification, radiation-induced disease, birth, digestion, tumors, the ears, eyes, nose, mouth, sinuses, and throat and fungal infections.

POSITION Hold, grid (see pages 28–31) or place as appropriate.

CREEDITE

*White (crystals
on matrix)*

COLOR	White, orange
APPEARANCE	Transparent to opaque, or needle-like crystals set on a matrix
RARITY	Easily obtained
SOURCE	United States, Mexico

ATTRIBUTES Creedite facilitates out-of-body experiences*, guiding the soul to its destination and promoting total recall of the experience. Spiritually, it attunes to a high vibration* and clarifies channeled* messages and impressions received from the higher planes, bringing these into physical embodiment. This stone assists in reading the universal wisdom embodied in ancient texts and enhances communication and understanding of wisdom at any level including the Akashic Record*.

Emotionally, Creedite assists in understanding the reasons and gifts behind experiences, including those from past lives. A stone that encourages dispassionate observation, Creedite releases you from an ingrained need to be a drama queen—or a martyr—enabling you to stand in the peaceful center of your emotions rather than being overwhelmed by them.

This stone is effective for cleansing, realigning and recharging all the chakra systems of the energetic bodies.

HEALING Beneficial for fractures, torn muscles and ligaments, for stabilizing the pulse and assimilating vitamins A, B and E.

POSITION Hold, grid (see pages 28–31) or place as appropriate.

SPECIFIC COLOR

Orange Creedite speeds up the ability to move between multi-dimensional levels of consciousness, attuning the physical body to the changing vibration and imparting urgency to spiritual evolution. This cluster formation radiates energy out to the surrounding environment and absorbs detrimental energies. It is especially useful for cleansing and recharging a room or workspace and can be gridded* and left in place. This stone will purify other crystals but will need cleansing afterward.

*Orange Creedite
(natural formation)*

CROCOITE

*Natural
formation*

Crystals on matrix

COLOR	Red
APPEARANCE	Small, needle-like crystals or long striated wand
RARITY	Rare
SOURCE	Tasmania, Russia, California (United States)

ATTRIBUTES A highly energized, vital and fertile stone, Crocoite provides impetus for a breakthrough at any level.

Psychologically supporting everything you feel passionate about, and assisting the flow of kundalini* energy in tantric love-making, this stone energizes the creative process and brings about a profound spiritual shift by igniting the fire in your belly and aligning it with the fire of awakened spirit.

HEALING Imbues the body with energy, stimulating the immune system and the reproductive organs. It is said to pinpoint the best time for conception.

POSITION Hold over the lower chakras or grid around the bed (see pages 28–31).

DALMATIAN STONE

Tumbled

COLOR	White with black and brown spots
APPEARANCE	Spotted stone
RARITY	Easily obtained
SOURCE	Mexico

ATTRIBUTES Opening the base, sacral and earth chakras, Dalmatian Stone imparts a sense of physicality to the soul and reminds that you are a spiritual being on a human journey. Grounding* and entering your body, it assists in coming to terms joyfully with being in incarnation. A protective influence, Dalmatian Stone is said to sound a warning when danger is near, assisting in maintaining composure under all circumstances.

Psychologically, attuning to the innocent child within and fortifying the spirit, this stone stimulates your sense of fun and is a useful pick-me-up for depression or energy depletion. As it contains Tourmaline, Dalmatian Stone quickly transmutes negative energy and outworn patterns. If you are prone to over-intellectualization or excess

112

thinking, Dalmatian Stone helps you to get out of your head and into your body.

Mentally, this playful stone helps to avoid excess analysis and moves you forward in life, but at the same time it suggests that reflecting on possible actions and planning with care may be appropriate in certain circumstances.

Emotionally, this stone encourages fidelity and harmonizes emotions. It assists in overcoming potential revenge scenarios that would be most hurtful to yourself. Physically, Dalmatian Stone is said to be beneficial for animals and athletes. Children benefit on all levels from this lively stone and it is particularly useful at night to assist safe sleep and prevent night terrors.

HEALING Beneficial for cartilage, nerves and reflexes and sprains; balances yin-yang and mood elevation, and guards against nightmares.

POSITION Hold, grid (see pages 28–31) or place as appropriate.

DANBURITE: **GOLDEN DANBURITE**

Tumbled

COLOR	Yellow or golden yellow
APPEARANCE	Translucent or transparent, striated crystal
RARITY	Becoming widely available
SOURCE	Madagascar, Myanmar, Afghanistan

ATTRIBUTES Attuned to the golden flame* of the illumined mind, Golden Danburite works on the highest frequency of the heart and higher heart energy, linking to the universal mind and angelic realms.

Spiritually instilling serenity and eternal wisdom, in meditation this stone goes to a pure state of consciousness and accesses profound guidance, taking you to hear the music of the spheres. By the bedside, it accompanies the dying on the journey beyond death, enabling conscious spiritual transition.

Karmically*, Golden Danburite facilitates deep change and acts as a soul cleanser, releasing miasms*, emotions and mental soul imperatives* that have been carried forward. This stone dispels mental hooks located in the subtle bodies*. It accesses the soul plan* for your current lifetime and points the soul in a new direction. Mentally, this stone enhances brain function and information-processing.

HEALING A powerful healing stone that works best psychosomatically. Helps allergies and chronic conditions; has a strong detoxifying action, treats the liver and gall bladder; assists muscular and motor function.

POSITION Place as appropriate—over the heart, or under a pillow for lucid dreams.

ADDITIONAL FORMS

Aqua Aura Danburite is enhanced with gold to provide a high-vibration* link to All That Is*. Connecting the spiritual and physical hearts and activating compassion and forgiveness for the past, this stone opens its arms and welcomes soul fragments* home.

Aqua Aura Danburite (treated natural point)

Drusy Danburite is coated in fine Quartz points, amplifying heart energy to a finer vibration and drawing in archangels and higher powers, promoting an inflow of Buddha energy and universal love. This stone fosters harmony, making it easier to accept and give help and to show thankfulness and appreciation. Increasing compassion, Drusy Danburite instills the ability to laugh at life even in the most difficult circumstances. This combination is a wonderful gift for the terminally ill or the deeply troubled soul.

Psychologically, Drusy Danburite promotes ease, changing recalcitrant attitudes and instilling patience and peace of mind—it is perfect for those who find it difficult to have patience and trust in 'right timing'. Drusy Danburite has a strong emotional detoxifying and purifying action. Combine with Smoky Quartz for maximum effect.

Drusy Danburite (coated natural formation)

DATOLITE

*Yellow (natural
formation)*

COLOR	Yellow or green
APPEARANCE	Transparent to opaque, vitreous crystal or mass
RARITY	Rare
SOURCE	Mexico, United States, South Africa, Tanzania, Scotland, Russia, Germany, Norway, Canada

ATTRIBUTES Datolite has a strong connection to the Akashic Record*
and, placed on the third eye or past-life chakras, provides a download of
karmic* and historic information that may take time to process and
integrate but ultimately shows the overall soul plan* for all your lives. A
useful stone for karmic and ancestral-line* healing, Datolite facilitates
the retrieval of information encoded in the subtle DNA, connecting to
ancestral patterns and events so that you understand why your family
is as it is, and facilitating healing of the past if appropriate.

Spiritually, Datolite also activates personal soul and far memory and opens the soul star chakra. Psychologically, this stone assists in recognizing the transience of all things, ensuring that you know that 'this too will pass' and, therefore, it is a useful stone during violent upheaval or tumultuous change as it provides enormous comfort and a place of inner peace to hold on to, dissolving fear and releasing grief.

Mentally, Datolite is a problem-solving stone that enhances study skills. It improves clarity of thought and deepens concentration, leading to an ability to remember fine detail where appropriate and teaching how to discard the remainder. This stone facilitates mature thought and the flow of ideas. Emotionally, this stone brings you closer to those you love and removes obstacles that arise from a past inability to enjoy intimacy.

HEALING Improves concentration and cellular memory*; is beneficial for diabetes, hypoglycaemia and the nervous system, adapting it to the new vibrations.

POSITION Hold, grid (see pages 28–31) or place as appropriate.

DENDRITIC CHALCEDONY

Tumbled

COLOR	Black and white
APPEARANCE	Fern-markings in opaque stone
RARITY	Easily obtained as a tumbled stone
SOURCE	Worldwide

ATTRIBUTES Dendritic Chalcedony encourages living in the present moment and offers support when facing unpleasant matters.

Psychologically a joyful stone facilitating a friendly approach to other people, it promotes tolerant interaction without judgment and assists with processing memories.

HEALING Beneficial for chronic illness, problems associated with smoking, the immune system, assimilation of copper, inflammation of the female sexual organs, thrush and the liver.

POSITION Hold, grid (see pages 28–31) or place as appropriate.

118

DIOPSIDE

Green (natural formation)

COLOR	Green, black, white
APPEARANCE	Long crystals often on a matrix or cluster
RARITY	Easily obtained
SOURCE	United States, Sweden, Canada, Germany, India, Russia, China

ATTRIBUTES A stone of service, Green Diopside increases compassion, opening your heart to the suffering of others and encouraging you to be of service to the planet through a profound sense of connection with the earth. Spiritually, by teaching humility and assisting in honoring what you really feel, this stone supports in following your intuition and enhances your ability to *sense*.

A useful healer for psychological conditions, this stone teaches the value of trust and forgiveness and assists in reconciling with anyone or anything that has hurt you in the past, gently pushing you toward

119

making the initial move. If you have always felt that you lacked something, but were not necessarily sure what it was, Diopside gently assists you to let go the need and be aware of your gifts.

Mentally, Diopside is helpful for creative pursuits or academic study as it stimulates intellectual faculties and the art of analysis. It has long been used to support the study of mathematics.

Emotionally, Diopside is beneficial for those who cannot show their grief as it promotes letting go. If you feel overburdened or overwhelmed by the problems of life, it teaches how to live life with appreciation and *joie de vivre*.

Physically, Green Diopside enhances recovery from surgery, trauma or severe illness.

Black Diopside is attuned to the root and earth chakras and to the telluric currents* of the earth, bringing these back into balance and harmony.

HEALING Green Diopside supports cellular memory*, physical weakness, acid-alkaline balance, the lungs, circulation, hormonal balance and blood pressure; it is beneficial for inflammation, muscular aches and spasm, stress, the kidneys and the heart. Black Diopside is useful for earth healing* or for support during terminal or chronic conditions.

POSITION Hold, grid (see pages 28–31) or place as appropriate.

DUMORTIERITE

Raw

Tumbled

COLOR	Blue or blue-gray
APPEARANCE	Dense, dusty, mottled opaque stone with iridescent flashes, blue inclusion, or crystalline
RARITY	Easily obtained
SOURCE	United States, Brazil, Namibia, Sri Lanka, Madagascar, Canada, France, Poland

ATTRIBUTES Dumortierite makes you more receptive when in contact with angelic or spirit guides. Spiritually, it shows your archetypal eternal self, reconnecting to innate wisdom. Placed behind the ear, it opens clairaudience*; placed further back on the past-life chakra or on the soma chakra it activates past-life memories. Taking you to the beginning of your soul journey* to examine contracts and agreements made over eons of time, it assists in renegotiating these if they are no longer applicable. On the soma chakra, this stone breaks ties that no longer serve and facilitates the rescinding of vows. Identifying and releasing past-life causes of dis-ease*, difficult circumstances or

121

relationships in the present life, Dumortierite highlights the patterns that underlie addictions and compulsions so that cellular memory* is reprogrammed. It breaks a karmic* cycle of co-dependency, helping carers realize that they cannot 'do it for an addict' or anyone else or control addictive behavior.

Psychologically, Dumortierite assists in standing up confidently for yourself and adapting to functional reality, offering patience or courage, and activating your instinct for self-preservation by instilling unshakeable self-confidence. Calming over-excitability, promoting detachment and opening positive self-love and *joie de vivre*, this stone helps you remain young at heart with a constructive attitude to life. Useful for people who deal with crisis and trauma on a daily basis, it creates calm and focuses relief efforts. If you are chaotic and disorganized, it helps you take control of your life and overcomes stage-fright, shyness, stress, phobias, insomnia, panic, fear, depression or stubbornness.

Mentally, Dumortierite promotes clarity and self-discipline and enhances organizational abilities, focus and linguistic capabilities for communication with other cultures; it facilitates efficient filing.

Emotionally, this stone stabilizes a rocky relationship and attracts a soulmate—although there may be difficult lessons to learn in the process. Dumortierite assists in seeing the worth in each human being and reasons for the interaction. It highlights why you chose to learn through difficulties and challenges, and assists in thanking the other person for their role in your karmic learning process.

HEALING Works best at the psychosomatic level, but is beneficial for cellular memory, hypersensitivity, wasting disorders, sunburn, epilepsy, headaches, nausea, vomiting, cramp, colic, diarrhea and palpitations.

POSITION Hold, grid (see pages 28–31) or place as appropriate.

EILAT STONE

Tumbled   Raw

COLOR	Green, blue and turquoise
APPEARANCE	Mottled, opaque stone
RARITY	Easily obtained
SOURCE	Israel, Jordan

ATTRIBUTES Spiritually joining the higher heart, heart and throat chakras, Eilat Stone instills a sense of wonder at the beauty of the earth. This stone balances yin and yang and brings about a lightness of being.

Mentally, since it combines Malachite, Turquoise, Chrysocolla, Azurite and other minerals and is known as the sage stone, Eilat Stone offers wisdom and creative solutions to problem-solving.

Emotionally, Eilat Stone harmonizes and yet stimulates feelings, ensuring your emotional life is calm but not flat, and encourages telepathy between soul partners. This stone is particularly helpful for

123

emotional healing where there has been incest, rape, physical violence, misogyny or sexual repression. Releasing fear and depression, it brings in creativity and emotional self-expression and encourages you to own your power.

An excellent healer on the physical level, Eilat Stone is an effective cleanser for the thymus. Flushing out hurt and loss, it removes toxins and blockages created from soul-shattering events in current or previous lives, facilitating speaking about and release from past hurts. Bringing about acceptance and inner reconciliation, it integrates soul fragments* and wipes the Akashic Record* clean, reprogramming soul and cellular memory* and reintegrating the self.

HEALING Beneficial for cellular memory, bone and tissue regeneration, the sinuses, re-ordering cellular growth rate, fever, pain, tumors, the liver, the thyroid and menstrual cramps.

POSITION Hold, grid (see pages 28–31) or place as appropriate. Wear over the thymus.

NOTE The Malachite component of this stone may occasionally cause palpitations. If so, remove and calm with Smoky Quartz, Rhodochrosite or Tugtupite.

EPIDOTE

Tumbled

COLOR	Green
APPEARANCE	Vitreous mass or translucent crystals often in Quartz
RARITY	Easily obtained
SOURCE	United States, Bulgaria, Austria, France, Russia, Norway, South Africa, Pakistan, Mozambique, Mexico

ATTRIBUTES Epidote increases spiritual attunement and removes ingrained resistance to spiritual awakening. Not everyone responds well to this stone, however, as it can have the opposite effect—increasing negativity and bringing to the surface feelings and thought patterns that require considerable effort to transform.

Psychologically, Epidote enhances perception. Offering you the courage to enjoy life to the full and the ability to manifest dreams, it strengthens your sense of identity and personal power. This is the perfect stone for those who fall easily into victimhood or martyrdom, dispelling self-criticism and helping you to look objectively at your strengths and weaknesses and at those of other people. Teaching how to set realistic goals, it moves you away from unattainable expectations and the inevitable disappointments that rise when you plan from your emotions.

Clearing negative emotional states such as stress, self-pity and anxiety, Epidote purifies the emotional body, releasing grief and old emotional trauma. It keeps you centered no matter the situation you find yourself in. Its detoxification effect may create a powerful release of negative energy from the subtle bodies* and physical body, sometimes experienced as a once-and-for-all catharsis, or abreaction (best undertaken with a qualified crystal therapist), which clears the emotional blueprint* and cellular memory*.

Physically useful in convalescence, Epidote supports the body's healing processes and ensures that you look after yourself in the best way possible. It may well surface the underlying core causes of obesity and so facilitate weight loss, but you may need the assistance of a qualified therapist or healer to work through the issues.

HEALING Helpful for emotional trauma, stamina, the nervous and immune systems, cellular memory and dehydration. It supports the brain, thyroid, liver, gallbladder and adrenal glands. As a gem essence (see page 361) it is said to soften the skin.

POSITION Hold, grid (see pages 28–31) or place as appropriate.

(*See also* Dream Quartz, pages 248–249.)

ERYTHRITE

ALSO KNOWN AS COBALT BLOOM

Crystals on matrix

COLOR	Purple, violet, magenta, fuchsia pink
APPEARANCE	Dense crystalline or radiating coating
RARITY	Fairly easily obtained
SOURCE	Mexico, Morocco, Australia, Poland, Spain

ATTRIBUTES Erythrite strengthens core energy at any level, whether it be of the spine, the body, the lightbody* or the planet.

Psychologically, it offers the confidence, surety and personal empowerment that arise out of an unshakeable assurance of inner strength. Erythrite also strengthens the physical heart and bonds of true love, uniting people with loving compassion.

HEALING Helpful in supporting bone marrow, blood cells and core cellular structures and in overcoming skin disorders.

POSITION Hold or grid (see pages 28–31).

EUDIALYTE

Shaped formation

COLOR	Red, green and black
APPEARANCE	Mottled, opaque to transparent stone
RARITY	Becoming more easily obtainable
SOURCE	Greenland, Russia, Canada, Madagascar, United States

ATTRIBUTES Imbued with strong life-force connected to kundalini*
energy, Eudialyte opens the heart chakra, links it to the base and earth
chakras and aligns chakra flow to connect spirit and mind with the
emotional body, bringing about profound reorientation. Karmically*,
by showing how to rectify unfortunate choices and open to truth,
Eudialyte teaches that you can grow spiritually through joy and

fulfilment rather than suffering, embracing the fullness of all that life on earth has to offer. If you need a situation or relationship to end, Eudialyte assists in doing so with grace and peace rather than conflict.

Spiritually, if you feel angry at God, Eudialyte assists in exploring why, facilitating journeying* to past lives if necessary. A stone of purification and at-onement, it heals the split and reconciles you to the divinity in yourself and aligns you to your true purpose.

Psychologically a stone of personal empowerment, Eudialyte chases away depression and dissatisfaction, releasing negative emotions such as jealousy, anger, guilt, resentment and animosity. Promoting self-forgiveness and healthy self-love, it expedites profound change, instills confidence and assists in learning from apparent mistakes. This stone teaches that you cannot be well—or happy—if your creativity is blocked or unexpressed. It assists in finding an outlet, treasuring your gifts.

Emotionally, drawing together soul-companions, it reveals the reason for the reunion. If you meet a 'soulmate' who does not want to know, or you are strongly attracted to someone but question whether a sexual relationship is right or whether there is some other purpose to the meeting, meditating or sleeping with Eudialyte reveals the answer—which may come about in an unexpected way.

HEALING Beneficial for multi-dimensional cellular healing, energy depletion, harmonizing brainwaves, stabilizing the nervous system and the optic nerve, Alzheimer's, Parkinson's Disease, MS, lupus and encouraging the body to heal itself.

POSITION Hold, grid (see pages 28–31) or place as appropriate.

FISKENAESSET RUBY-IN-MATRIX

Polished

COLOR	Deep red, silver-black
APPEARANCE	Translucent stone
RARITY	Very rare
SOURCE	Greenland

ATTRIBUTES A high-energy stone, Fiskenaesset Ruby is one of the oldest forms of this gem on the planet. Spiritually, by assisting communication with the spirit world and inducing trance, Fiskenaesset Ruby facilitates entering a deep, altered state of consciousness with ease. It forms a powerful shield against psychic attack* and vampirism of heart energy and has traditionally been regarded as a major protector for family and possessions. Ruby is said to give warning by darkening when danger or illness threatens. Activating the alta-major (past-life) chakra, it is extremely helpful in core soul healing and past-life work as it accesses soul memory and spiritual learning, and brings about multi-dimensional cellular healing. The stone helps to overcome spiritual depletion where too much energy has been given to others to assist their evolution to the detriment of your inner self.

Psychologically, this stone promotes individuality while at the same time retaining interconnectedness with the rest of humanity. It encourages passion for life, improves motivation and assists in setting realistic goals, teaching you how to plan for the future without emotional involvement or unhelpful projections*. Facilitating dynamic leadership, courage and selflessness, this stone encourages you to 'follow your bliss'. Ruby promotes positive dreams and clear visualization. One of the stones of abundance, it assists in retaining wealth and passion.

Emotionally, Fiskenaesset Ruby teaches emotional independence and autonomy, bringing about the realization that you alone are responsible for creating and maintaining your well-being and happiness, and are not dependent on any external source, including a partner or loved one. However, passionate Ruby also deepens true love and rekindles libido.

At a physical level, Fiskenaesset Ruby strengthens the flow of life-force, stimulating the immune system and the circulation. Overcoming exhaustion and lethargy, it imparts vigor to life and is beneficial for recovery from extended stress or chronic illness.

HEALING Beneficial for physical vitality, blood and lymph, the circulatory system, fertility, sexual potency, hyperactivity, detoxification, over-acidity, insomnia and restricted blood flow, fevers and infectious disease. It supports the heart, adrenals, kidneys, reproductive organs and spleen.

POSITION Wear, hold, grid (see pages 28–31) or place as appropriate.

FLINT

Black-white (natural formation)

COLOR	Black, white, blue, gray, brown, yellow, orange
APPEARANCE	Dense and glassy, often coated white
RARITY	Readily available
SOURCE	Worldwide

ATTRIBUTES Sacred since time began, Flint is a powerful stabilizer and cleanser and draws the help of the gods to an enterprise. Originally black, it weathers to different colors. Used for eons to accompany the dead to the next world, Flint calls guides and power allies. Protective, it turns back curses and ill-wishing* and is said to prevent nightmares.

Spiritually, Flint hones the spirit and cuts away all that is outworn and outgrown, slicing through psychological blockages and problems and ties etherically* linking people. At the chakras, it dissolves cords and heals the site. Flint shards perform etheric surgery and cauterize past-life wounds, clearing the etheric blueprint*, physical or etheric bodies. With its stabilizing action, Flint brings structural integrity to mental and physical bodies. Creating a shamanic anchor* for journeys* to re-member your soul, Flint creates the inner-core solidity to ride out earth changes. An effective conductor for electromagnetic energy, Flint enhances energy flow and is a powerful earth healer.

Symbolizing the deep masculine and Green Man earth mysteries, this nurturing stone also provides a strong link to the Earth Mother, taking you into her womb to reconnect to wise femininity and priestess power. Perfect for rites of passage that mark the transitions of womanhood, it assists men in connecting to their feminine qualities.

*Gray-white
(natural
formation)*

HEALING Disperses pain and dis-ease*; supports the reproductive system, cellular memory*, tissue restructuring and skin elasticity; overcomes depression and obsessive disorders, warts, moles and wrinkles, stones and growths. It is excellent for jaw or back pain.

*Black
(tumbled)*

POSITION Grid (see pages 28–31), hold or wear. Place orange or dark Flint on the earth chakra and white or blue Flint or Selenite on the soul star to activate the cosmic anchor*. Combine with Selenite or Natrolite to ground* vibrational downloads* and create a stable matrix within the earth during profound change, or to reverse polluted earth-energy flows. Combine with Nuumite for entity removal*.

*Orange
(natural
formation)*

SPECIFIC COLORS
Black or Brown Flint assists in understanding the deeper causes of depression and accepting the shadow* side of your nature, finding the gift within.

Orange Flint gives inner strength during difficult times, lifting obsessive tendencies.

Blue Flint lifts you above the mundane into higher spiritual understanding of dis-ease. Mentally supportive when you are struggling with causes of problems and blockages, Blue Flint clears these, facilitating concentrated, focused thought.

*Blue
(natural
formation)*

FRONDELLITE

Raw

COLOR	Pinkish-bronze
APPEARANCE	Ribbed and opalescent
RARITY	Rare
SOURCE	United States

ATTRIBUTES A form of Fuchsite mica, Frondellite is a powerful cleanser for psychic infections especially those lodged in the third eye, removing negative energy, implants* and power struggles that cross the psychic airways from a different time and space and dissolving thoughts and ill-wishing* from the present day. However, the effect can be nauseous as a psychic detox takes place that may need other stones to move it out of the physical body. Frondellite is best used with Strengite to transmute the process.

Psychologically, Frondellite is helpful for those with an obsessive fear of dirt and bacteria, taking you back to uncover the cause and reframe the experience. In the process you may experience emotional catharsis and replay very dark feelings and this is best done under the guidance of a past-life therapist.

Mentally, Frondellite organizes disorganized thought and brings order out of chaos enabling you to see the pattern or solution instantly. In this respect, it is useful in game or role playing.

Emotionally, Frondellite assists in releasing negative emotions and too strong a hold on the past, freeing you up for change and transformation.

Physically, Frondellite can be beneficial in stimulating T-cell production and balancing the immune system.

HEALING Works best beyond the physical level of being, but can be used as a wrist rest to prevent carpal tunnel syndrome or RSI.

POSITION Hold, grid (see pages 28–31) or place as appropriate.

COMBINATION STONE

Frondellite with Strengite has a more gentle purification and transmutation energy, lifting you above the cause of dis-ease* or phobia to observe and detach without fully entering the experience. It cleanses the third eye and strengthens it so that the psychic infection cannot re-enter.

Frondellite with Strengite (raw)

FULGARITE

*Sandy-beige
(natural formation)*

*Gray (natural
formation)*

COLOR	Sandy-beige, gray, yellowish
APPEARANCE	Tiny grains cemented into a tube
RARITY	Easily obtained
SOURCE	United States, Sahara, Gobi Desert

ATTRIBUTES Fulgarite is formed when lightning hits sand—an event that tightly focuses an enormous amount of energy into a tiny space. Despite its delicacy, Fulgarite has traditionally been a powerful shamanic soul tool, as this stone holds high-frequency energy from the strike. When a shaman takes a journey* to retrieve lost child or soul parts*, those parts are placed into Fulgarite for safe travel during the return. Fulgarite is then placed over the heart chakras and the lost child or soul part is gently blown home, the lightning strike opening the way. The stone also transports soul parts left at a traumatic past-life death, trauma, disappointment or other event that tethers the soul into another life. This stone assists a journey into the between-life state* to ascertain why a soul did not fully incarnate in the present. Purifying soul fragments passed through the pipe, Fulgarite brings the soul home for reintegration.

Traditionally used spiritually to blow prayers to the universe, Fulgarite is a powerful tool for manifesting dreams. Set your intention, speak it out loud and blow through the Fulgarite to set it free to manifest in the best way possible for your highest good. Accelerating the spiritual growth of humanity, the center of the tube is a conduit for divine energy to pass into the physical. It creates an energy vortex from the chakras into the subtle bodies* that purifies, realigns and re-energizes as it moves through the frequencies, taking body and soul to a higher level and opening the way for new patterns to imprint. A perfect shamanic anchor*, Fulgarite opens the earth section of a cosmic anchor*, attaching you deep into the earth's core.

Psychologically, Fulgarite facilitates letting go of anything blocking progress, opening the way for new behaviors that serve your higher being and present state of evolution.

Mentally, by bringing thought into form, Fulgarite teaches how to hold only the highest and most positive of intents.

Physically, Fulgarite can be gridded* around the body to draw off negative energy or blockages and to replenish energy lost to psychic vampirization* or chronic dis-ease*.

HEALING Blasts through restrictions and constrictions that block energy or blood flow, and raises energy levels and libido, but its most profound work is at the soul level.

POSITION Hold or place as appropriate. Handle Fulgarite gently and do not apply pressure.

GAIA STONE

Shaped

COLOR	Deep green
APPEARANCE	Transparent, obsidian-like clear crystal
RARITY	Easily obtained
SOURCE	Artificially manufactured from volcanic ash from Mount St Helens, United States

ATTRIBUTES Gaia Stone is also known as the Goddess Stone as it brings about a profound connection to the divine feminine within women and men. Spiritually, having been born out of fire, the stone shows the value in the spiritual purification and transmutation that occurs through psychological catharsis and alchemical processes within the body or the earth.

This stone opens and unites the earth and heart chakras and harmonizes the entire chakra flow. Having a powerful link to the Earth Mother, environmentally Gaia Stone attunes to devas* and the *anima terra*, the soul of the earth, and takes you journeying* to the place outside our solar system where that soul originated. This stone is comforting for those who do not feel that the earth is their real home, activating the earth section of a cosmic anchor* and stabilizing your inner-core energy field or acting as a shamanic anchor* for lower-world* journeys.

By creating close harmony with the earth and the environment, Gaia Stone assists in healing the etheric energy grid of the planet, especially when gridded around areas of disharmony or pollution. Promoting compassion and empathy, it teaches that everything on and in the earth is a unity, and is a useful stone for exploring the west on the crystal medicine wheel (see pages 368–375).

Emotionally, Gaia Stone draws painful wounds out of the emotional body and neutralizes past trauma, replacing negativity with unconditional love for yourself and for others.

Physically, Gaia Stone attunes you to the energy flows of the earth and to the divine feminine as manifested through the Earth Mother. A stone of prosperity and abundance, Gaia Stone stimulates healing ability of all kinds.

HEALING Particularly useful for self-healing and overcoming emotional wounds and past trauma. Placed on the third eye, it alleviates psychosomatic dis-ease* and migraine and can bring beneficial healing and cooling to eye conditions.

POSITION Hold, grid (see pages 28–31) or place as appropriate. Wear constantly for self-healing.

GASPEITE

Polished ball

COLOR	Dark and light apple green
APPEARANCE	Opaque, mottled and veined
RARITY	Rare but increasingly available especially as jewelry
SOURCE	Canada, Australia

ATTRIBUTES Gaspeite is one of the stones lending strength during the evolution of the earth and to all those upon it. Spiritually, it fortifies the soul and grounds spiritual energy into the body assuring that, if you need help, you only have to ask. Meditate with Gaspeite while sitting on the ground, setting out any difficulties and trusting that the answer will come in the most appropriate way. Hold it whenever you need safe passage as it facilitates moving through dark or dangerous places without being noticed. If you have a lower-world* journey* to make

140

during shamanic or soul-retrieval* work, Gaspeite wraps you in a cloak of invisibility and invincibility.

Wear protective Gaspeite over the spleen chakra (under your left armpit) if you are vampirized by an energy pirate or undermined by a needy person, and wear it under your right armpit for protection against another person's anger—especially if you have cut off their energy supply by closing your spleen chakra and they retaliate with anger or resentment.

Emotionally, Gaspeite is helpful when you feel resentful or bitter about life or that someone has had the gall to do something hurtful or destructive. Dissolving anger, hurt, distress or pain in the heart and opening the higher heart chakra, this stone cleanses the liver chakra area beneath your right armpit of your anger and any spite that may be sent your way by someone else, bringing in calm emotions. This stone bridges the emotional and physical levels of being and ameliorates the psychosomatic effects of the mind on the body when emotions and thoughts that no longer serve have physicalized into stone-like concretions or blockages that need to be dissolved.

HEALING Supports the liver and gallbladder and is beneficial for gallstones, duct blockages, cirrhosis and intestinal problems, sedating or stimulating the tract as required; soothes nausea and travel sickness.

POSITION Hold, grid (see pages 28–31) or place as appropriate. Place under the armpit for energy protection. Keep Gaspeite in your pocket while traveling.

Shaped

GOETHITE

*Ribbed crystals
on matrix*

COLOR	Brown
APPEARANCE	Deeply ribbed opaque stone or 'stars'
RARITY	Easily obtained
SOURCE	United States, Germany, England, France, Canada

ATTRIBUTES Meditating with Goethite feels like being suspended in a still, silent point of non-action and non-doing. With Goethite, you simple *are*. It opens a cosmic anchor*, attaching you safely between the core of the earth and the galactic center*.

Spiritually, this stone resonates to the number 44, the number of metamorphosis. It facilitates clairaudience* and metaphysical abilities*. It is useful for any form of divination, revealing soul intention for the future in situations where knowing this is helpful for your journey.

Goethite purifies the emotional body. Releasing hooks and past-life feelings and beliefs about yourself that no longer serve your purpose, it fills your heart with compassion for what you have been through, showing the gift in the experience.

Physically, this stone supplies the energy necessary for enjoying the human experience and enhances the flow of oxygen around the body. A useful communication tool, it combines inspiration with the pragmatic ability to get things done and assists the physical body in recovery following any kind of trauma.

Environmentally, being strongly attuned to the healing power of nature, this stone enhances dowsing abilities, aligning to the note of the earth. Taking you to meet devas* and the *anima terra*, soul of the earth, it sensitizes you to subtle energies and the currents within the earth and the human body, and facilitates the fine-tuning of the energy meridians* of the planet. Goethite clears the earth and the base chakras, aligning the whole chakra system to connect the earth and higher mind.

HEALING Supports weight training. Assists epilepsy, anaemia, menorrhagia and the ears, nose, throat, alimentary canal, veins, oesophagus and bone marrow.

POSITION Hold or position as appropriate. Grid (see pages 28–31) for extraterrestrial contact.

SPECIFIC FORM
Iridescent Rainbow Goethite cuts through depression, gloom and despondency, instilling light and hope into your life. It is particularly useful for enhancing metaphysical gifts.

NOTE Goethite forms the stars in Star Hollandite Quartz (see pages 304–305).

Iridescent Rainbow Goethite (raw)

GREENLANDITE

Green (polished)   *Bluish-green (raw slice)*

COLOR	Grayish or bluish-green when raw (deep blue-green when polished), violet
APPEARANCE	Dense, opaque stone with metallic glow
RARITY	Rare
SOURCE	Greenland

ATTRIBUTES Greenlandite is a higher resonance* of Aventurine. Forming part of the cape of the Bishop of Greenland, this stunning gemstone is 3.8 billion years old. With ancient energies encoded into its striations, it teaches how to care for the earth and live in harmony with nature.

Spiritually, Greenlandite activates and protects the heart chakra, guarding against psychic vampirism* of heart energy. An excellent protector for the spleen chakra against energy pirates, it works on extremely subtle levels to free you from karmic enmeshment* with souls in and out of incarnation. A positive stone, Greenlandite diffuses negative situations and turns them around.

Psychologically, Greenlandite reinforces leadership qualities and decisiveness. This stone assists stammers and severe neurosis, bringing an understanding of what lies behind the conditions. Promoting compassion, empathy and the act of trying again, Greenlandite takes you back into the past to find sources of dis-ease*.

This stone brings together the intellectual and emotional bodies. A mental stabilizer, Greenlandite balances your state of mind, stimulates perception and enhances creativity. Linking to the wisdom of the universal mind, the stone assists in accepting alternatives and possibilities, especially those presented by other people.

Emotionally, Greenlandite calms anger and irritation. Assisting emotional recovery and the ability to live within one's heart, it is the perfect stone for strengthening mature love.

Physically, Greenlandite promotes a feeling of well-being. It balances male-female energy and encourages regeneration of the heart.

Environmentally, having a strong connection to the devic kingdom*, Greenlandite grids* against geopathic stress* and facilitates earth healing* and the realignment of the earth's grid. Wearing Greenlandite absorbs electromagnetic smog* and protects against environmental pollution. Worn or taped to a mobile phone, this stone protects the sensitive person.

HEALING Supports the eyes, thymus gland, connective tissue, nervous system, adrenals, lungs, sinuses, heart, muscular and urogenital systems, blood pressure, metabolism, cholesterol and arteriosclerosis; helps skin eruptions and allergies; relieves migraine headaches and soothes eyes; is anti-inflammatory. As an elixir, assists skin problems.

POSITION Hold or place as appropriate. For spleen-chakra protection place below the left armpit or wear at the base of the sternum.

HACKMANITE

Tumbled

COLOR	Blue, lilac, pink
APPEARANCE	Dense opaque or crystalline stone
RARITY	Rare (heated amended stones are available)
SOURCE	Greenland, Canada, Russia, Australia, Afghanistan, Myanmar, Pakistan

ATTRIBUTES A higher resonance* of Sodalite, Hackmanite has an extremely fine vibration while remaining connected to the earth. Activating a cosmic anchor* and protecting the biomagnetic sheath*, it opens an in-body expansion into the infinity of being and integrates the lightbody*. It efficiently cuts ties at the subtle chakra levels.

Spiritually, this refined stone unites intuition with logic, accessing the higher mind and connecting it to the physical plane to create the illumined mind. It facilitates deep meditative states and attunes to spiritual gifts that bring joy, freedom and healing.

Psychologically, Hackmanite assists in understanding the situation in which you find yourself, aligning to the soul's purpose in taking on such an experience. It is a useful stone for accepting your shadow

146

energies* and finding the treasure within them. It transforms a defensive or over-sensitive personality, illuming and releasing core fears, phobias, guilt and control mechanisms that hold the soul back from full expression. It enhances self-esteem, self-acceptance and self-trust. With a powerful desire for truth and idealism, Hackmanite urges you to remain true to your self and stand up for your beliefs.

Mentally and karmically*, Hackmanite sets you free from intellectual bondage and rigid mindsets, especially from religious ideals imprinted in the past, opening your mind to infinite new possibilities. Allowing a rational and yet intuitive perception, it assists in verbalizing feelings, creating space to put your new insights into practice.

Environmentally, Hackmanite clears electromagnetic pollution. It is helpful when gridded* against sick building syndrome, electromagnetic smog* or multiple chemical allergies.

HEALING Supports metabolism and the lymphatic system, immune system, throat, vocal cords and larynx. Beneficial for calcium deficiencies, radiation damage, insomnia, hoarseness, digestive disorders, fevers, blood pressure, torn ligaments and absorption of fluid.

POSITION Hold, grid (see pages 28–31) or place as appropriate.

COMBINATION STONE
Hackmanite with Violet Ussingite works extremely well to earth exceptionally high spiritual vibrations* and to ground the expanded awareness of an ascended soul into the physical realm.

NOTE If the combination stone is not available, use individual Ussingite above Hackmanite, preferably mounted in silver.

Hackmanite with Violet Ussingite (raw)

147

HALITE

*White
(natural
formation)*

COLOR	White, pink, blue
APPEARANCE	Fragile, crusty transparent small or large cubic crystals
RARITY	Easily obtained
SOURCE	United States, France, Germany, North Africa

ATTRIBUTES Efficient for purification, Halite stimulates spiritual discernment and multi-dimensional evolution. Spiritually, by drawing out any impurities lodged in your soul or etheric bodies* and creating inner balance, Halite assists in harnessing your will to the guidance of your Higher Self* and creates a more objective perspective. This protective stone guards against negative energies, entity* attachment or psychic attack*, especially when under the influence of drink or drugs or in spaced-out spiritual states. It is particularly useful if you become the object of someone else's unreasonable lust or needy feelings.

Psychologically, Halite dissolves old patterns, negative thoughts and ingrained feelings, such as anger, and helps you to transcend problems. Ameliorating anxiety and bringing contentment, Halite transmutes feelings of abandonment or rejection, promoting emotional well-being and increasing goodwill.

Physically, this stone stimulates the meridians* of the body and enhances acupuncture or acupressure, grounding* the healing properties of other crystals.

HEALING Supports detoxification, metabolism and cellular memory*; beneficial for water retention, intestinal problems, bi-polar disorder, respiratory disorders and the skin.

Pink (raw)

POSITION Place in your immediate environment or a pouch. As it quickly absorbs negative energy and damp, cleanse frequently in brown rice and keep in a dry place, but place in the bath or under shower for purification (it dissolves, cleansing the energies).

SPECIFIC COLORS
Pink Halite is effective for detaching entities and spirit possession and for preventing reattachment or fresh spirit attachment*. This color encourages spiritual development, raising personal vibrations, stimulating metaphysical abilities* and removing negativity. Emotionally, it facilitates well-being and a sense of being loved. Psychologically, it dispels a sense of oppression and acts as a diuretic.

Blue Halite is an efficient opener for metaphysical gates. It heightens intuition and encourages mystical awareness. It reprograms a distorted vision of reality and cleanses mental attachments or undue influence from the third eye and the subtle bodies*. Physically, this stone is beneficial for iodine absorption, and the thyroid, thymus and thalamus.

Blue (natural formation)

149

HANKSITE

Gray (natural formation)

COLOR	Green, gray, white, brown, yellow
APPEARANCE	Translucent crystal, greasy or powdery with clay inclusions
RARITY	Rare but increasingly available
SOURCE	California

ATTRIBUTES Containing borax and Halite, Hanksite formed through evaporation and is found in deep mud, symbolizing wisdom awaiting release from the dross of the past. This stone is deeply purifying and assists breathing in toxic places. Accessed through past-life and soma chakras, Hanksite retrieves true feminine power and intuition. It combines particularly well with Lemurian Seed crystals.

Spiritually, by promoting multi-dimensional evolution, Hanksite contains powerful knowledge to accelerate expanded consciousness locked away since the ancient times of Lemuria and Atlantis. Facilitating reconnection to these civilizations and to personal power and wisdom held then, it cautions that this power must be used for the good of all, not for selfish gain. A stone of forgiveness, the Halite component heals mistakes and misuses of power and reminds you not to repeat such experiences. Hanksite makes an effective psychic protector, especially against spirit attachment*. Purifying and cathartic on all levels, it clears chakras and cleanses other stones. Facilitating a rapid detox of detritus from many lifetimes, it cleanses ancient anger, jealousy and resentment or manipulation and transmutes their effect in the physical body, stabilizing mood swings. Drawing out impurities and creating inner balance, it assists in attuning to the guidance of your spiritual rather than your emotional self. Recreating a playful, innocent inner child* state, Hanksite can also surface childlike fear and feel cold and repulsive.

Mentally, Hanksite creates a more objective perspective, clearing thought and behavior patterns that no longer serve a purpose.

Environmentally, it has been described as 'a time bomb of what things eventually return to'—a mirror of the world before humankind began and a state our planet could return to if humankind continues to violate it. This crystal will support the planet in regenerating when the ozone layer and air are depleted. It assists in applying ancient wisdom to modern problems.

HEALING Useful for water retention and detoxification, metabolism and cellular memory*, intestinal problems and the skin. Helpful for colds and breathing difficulties caused by an excess of mucus or inflammation.

POSITION Place at the feet. Grid (see pages 28–31) into a Star of David with Smoky Elestial at the center to draw off toxicity, or use as a stabilizer for a Lemurian crystal. If headache and nausea occur, push the energy out into a Smoky Quartz placed on the earth chakra.

NOTE Dissolves when wet. Keep dry and cleanse in uncooked brown rice.

HEMATITE WITH RUTILE

*Natural
formation*

COLOR	Silver and gold
APPEARANCE	Beautiful silver and gold opaque stone
RARITY	Rare
SOURCE	Africa, Australia

ATTRIBUTES Hematite with Rutile combines the grounding* and energizing functions of Hematite with the cleansing properties of Rutile into a high-vibration* stone that activates the past life and soma chakras and deep soul connections.

Spiritually, placed on the soma and soul star chakras, this stone attunes to the true self and assists in embodying it into the physical realm so that it functions beyond duality or division. The combination purifies and reintegrates dismembered parts of your soul, wherever they may be and from whatever timeframe. It brings about profound multi-dimensional healing, cleansing chakras up to the highest levels, anchoring the lightbody* and bringing about an unshakeable connection with the highest vibrations in the universe.

This combination is particularly useful for deep karmic* and soul cleansing. It corrects the etheric blueprint* and repairs the cellular memory*, re-energizing and realigning the physical body.

Psychologically, Hematite with Rutile offers insight into the psychosomatic causes of dis-ease* and then assists in rebalancing the emotional and other subtle bodies*. This powerfully protective and regenerative stone helps with reconciliation and the bringing together of opposites, assisting both impersonal and personal relationships. Whatever needs balancing in your life will be brought into equilibrium by this stone.

HEALING Works best beyond the physical level of being, acting on the subtle bodies to bring about multi-dimensional healing.

POSITION Hold, grid (see pages 28–31) or place as appropriate.

(*See also* Rutile, pages 318–319.)

Natural formation

HEMIMORPHITE

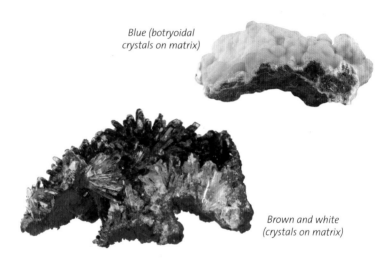

Blue (botryoidal crystals on matrix)

Brown and white (crystals on matrix)

COLOR	Blue, brown, white
APPEARANCE	Tiny transparent needle-like striated or pyramidal crystals on a matrix, or botryoidal crust
RARITY	Easily obtained
SOURCE	England, Mexico, United States, Zambia

ATTRIBUTES Hemimorphite is an extremely protective stone, particularly against malicious thoughts and manipulation. In ancient times, it was reputedly used to counteract poison. Spiritually, this stone facilitates raising vibrations* of the physical and subtle bodies* and communicating with the highest spiritual levels and multi-dimensions.

This stone is not an easy ride, as it promotes self-development in the quickest way possible. Insisting on personal accountability, it links to your Higher Self*, encouraging you to take responsibility for your happiness or dis-ease*, and teaches that you create your reality through your thoughts and attitudes. It highlights external influences that do not accord with your soul plan* and assists release from these.

Psychologically, this stone shows how to develop inner strength and manifest your highest potential while maintaining awareness of being part of humanity. Instilling a sense of social responsibility, it is useful for remaining energized and committed throughout projects, seeing them through to the end.

Emotionally, Hemimorphite gently relieves angst. If you invariably pitch your expectations and goals too high to achieve, it helps in setting and attaining realistic goals without being emotionally attached to the result. This optimistic stone assists in looking back on, and reframing*, irritating and ingrained traits, and helps being totally open and honest in emotional communication. Physically, Hemimorphite supports you in regaining full health on all levels.

HEALING Supports weight loss, pain relief, blood disorders, the heart, cellular memory* and cellular structures; helps genital herpes, warts, ulcerative conditions, hormonal imbalances, burns and restless legs.

POSITION Hold, grid (see pages 28–31) or place as appropriate. Tumbled Hemimorphite is best for personal wear or healing placements.

Blue (tumbled)

155

HERDERITE

Brown (raw)

COLOR	Golden, gray, brown, green, purplish-lavender
APPEARANCE	Opaque or translucent stone with natural facets and terminations
RARITY	Rare
SOURCE	Brazil, South Africa, United States, Germany, Russia

ATTRIBUTES A high-vibration* stone, Herderite aligns the subtle chakras, raising consciousness to the highest possible levels and awakening the illumined mind. Stones from different locations vary in color and are specific in their action, affecting people according to their personal energetic blueprint* and readiness to move to a new stage of evolution.

Spiritually, when Herderite opens the third eye, it involves full body awareness of the multi-dimensional self and a deep connection to the earth. Holding this stone, your body feels perfectly supported by the earth so that you walk lightly but purposefully upon it.

Herderite promotes the evolution of the physical brain to manifest heightened awareness and the energies of the higher mind on the earth. Physically, it re-patterns the etheric blueprint so that brain injuries or blockages are brought back to the optimum pattern. It is helpful for improving concentration and memory. Attuning to Herderite facilitates restructuring at every level.

HEALING Working mostly beyond the physical level of being to effect multi-dimensional healing, Herderite assists headaches, migraines and brain-damage and supports brain function, the pancreas and spleen.

POSITION Hold, grid (see pages 28–31) or place as appropriate. Place over the third eye to clear migraine arising from the blocking of metaphysical gifts*.

SPECIFIC COLOR
Golden Herderite links to the divine within and assists in recognizing that you are god. This stone takes you into a blissful space that appears 'far out', yet is actually an inner dimension, embodying your divine being more fully. It particularly resonates with the soul star and stellar gateway chakras.

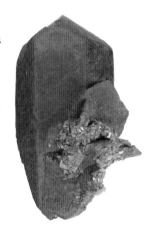

*Golden Herderite
(natural formation)*

HEULANDITE

Peach (natural formation)

COLOR	Peach, white, green
APPEARANCE	Crystalline to vitreous opaque pearly crystals on a matrix
RARITY	Easily obtained
SOURCE	India, Iceland

ATTRIBUTES Heulandite is an extremely beneficial stone if you want to evolve. Karmically*, it assists in reconnecting to ancient knowledge and skills from the ancient civilizations of Lemuria and Atlantis and from other past lives. Facilitating the traversing of inter-and inner-dimensional* spaces, it accesses and provides insights into the Akashic Record* and takes you back into the karmic past to release negative emotions and to recover from loss of any kind. It then shows how such knowledge can be applied to your present life.

Psychologically, Heulandite facilitates the change of ingrained habits or behaviors, especially those held at a cellular level, replacing them with openness to new ways and exciting possibilities.

Emotionally, this is a useful stone for releasing jealousy and other negative emotions and for alleviating patronizing attitudes of superiority and condescension or feelings that you are better than someone else. Green Heulandite, in particular, avoids judgmental or condemning attitudes. It assists in recognizing the equality of value of each soul and promotes forgiveness in whichever direction it is required.

Physically, each color of the stone works on different physical and subtle levels: white on the brain and nervous system; pink on the endocrine system; and green on the heart, ameliorating the effect of painful emotions on the body and replacing them with the joy of living.

Dedicate Heulandite and leave it in your environment to quietly bring about the changes sought, although it needs cleansing regularly.

HEALING Beneficial for cellular memory* and mobility; supports weight reduction, growth, the lower limbs, blood flow, the kidneys and liver.

POSITION Hold, grid (see pages 28–31) or place as appropriate.

HUEBNERITE

ALSO KNOWN AS HUBNERITE

Natural formation

COLOR	Reddish-black
APPEARANCE	Striated or bladed, opaque, slightly metallic
RARITY	Rare
SOURCE	United States, Mexico, Peru

ATTRIBUTES Huebnerite is a useful detoxifier, cleansing gall, bile and bitterness from the physical and emotional levels of being and re-energizing the emotions. Opening the earth and base chakras and activating a cosmic anchor*, it sends negative energy to earth for transmutation and assists in assimilating high-vibration energy downloads*, which can be passed to the earth for healing. It may need other stones to complete the process. Physically, this stone invigorates and recharges.

HEALING Supports the liver, spine and pancreas.

POSITION Hold, grid (see pages 28–31) or place as appropriate.

JASPER: **LEOPARDSKIN ORBICULAR JASPER**

Orange bi-colored (tumbled)

COLOR	Green or orange bi-colored
APPEARANCE	Opaque leopard-like markings
RARITY	Easily obtained
SOURCE	South America

ATTRIBUTES A bridge to the deepest mysteries of duality, Leopardskin Jasper assists in redressing the balance between light and dark, teaching how to recognize dark as a complement to light rather than its opposite. Associated with the west on the medicine wheel (see pages 368–375) and strongly protective, this is a shamanic shape-shifter's stone, helpful during journeying* and putting you in touch with Jaguar, Cougar, Leopard and Panther allies. Shutting off your outer vision and focusing perception, Leopardskin Jasper assists in listening to your inner voice. Paradoxically, by reflecting the outside world, Leopardskin Jasper clears ingrained assumptions and teaches you to see what *is*, assessing your situation with clarity.

161

Spiritually assisting in fulfilling karmic* agreements or soul contracts made before incarnating, Leopardskin Jasper highlights where those contracts are no longer appropriate and assists in rescinding or renegotiating the terms and intent, breaking ties where necessary.

Psychologically, this stone reduces insecurities, heals the emotional body and strengthens a sense of self. The perfect tool for balance between passivity and activity, spirituality and emotion, Leopardskin Jasper delineates your life path. It provides protection while you are meeting challenges and fulfilling goals. If you leave part of yourself in the future when planning ahead, this stone gently returns you to now.

Emotionally, this stone overcomes guilt, fear and emotional stress, bringing in calm tranquillity.

Physically, Leopardskin Jasper activates twelve-strand DNA healing*, fortifies your body's natural resistance and assists in maintaining optimum health and well-being.

Environmentally, Leopardskin Jasper engenders respect for the innate wisdom and healing methods of native peoples and encourages a connection between humankind and the animal world, bringing about environmental harmony.

Orange bi-colored (tumbled)

HEALING Helpful for cellular memory*, DNA, tissue regeneration, digestive processes, excretion, abdominal pain, skin diseases, kidney or gallstones and for overcoming body odor and insomnia.

POSITION Hold, grid (see pages 28–31) or place as appropriate.

JASPER: **OCEAN ORBICULAR JASPER**

ALSO KNOWN AS THE ATLANTIS STONE

Polished natural formation

COLOR	Multi-colored
APPEARANCE	Whorls, contour lines and bands of opaque stone, interspersed with druse
RARITY	Rare but easily obtained
SOURCE	Madagascar

ATTRIBUTES A stone of renewal and strength connected to Atlantis and holding mystic knowledge within it, Ocean Jasper takes you back to reclaim wisdom when you meditate with it. Assisting in reframing* and transmuting the misuse of spiritual power at any time, this stone teaches wise use of power and will. Helpful for healers and counselors,

Ocean Jasper helps you in loving yourself and others, and in being more empathetic to emotional and mental needs while remaining objective and detached. If Drusy Quartz is within the stone, it focuses and intensifies the healing intention.

Spiritually, the swirling patterns symbolize the interconnectedness of all things—a reminder that nature is cyclical, rhythmical and fluid. Ocean Jasper assists in coping with change and in giving service to humanity. Its circular markings resonate with circular breathing, which it facilitates, and with anything that runs in cycles or circulates.

Psychologically, the Green Jasper component heals and releases dis-ease* and obsession, balancing parts of life that have become all-important to the detriment of others.

Tumbled

Emotionally, with its gentle nurturing energy, Ocean Jasper brings to the surface long-hidden and unresolved emotional issues and helps in facing the future positively, accepting responsibility for yourself. This stone instills patience.

Physically detoxifying, Ocean Jasper is a useful lymphatic drainage stimulator, eliminating toxins that cause body odor.

HEALING An all-round healer. Alleviates stress and supports the immune system, lymph, circulation, debilitated internal organs, the female reproductive system, PMS, digestion, the upper torso and digestive tract; beneficial for tumors, gum infections, eczema, cysts, colds, hallucinations, insomnia, inflammation, skin disorders and bloating.

POSITION Hold, grid (see pages 28–31) or place as appropriate.

JASPER: **POPPY JASPER**

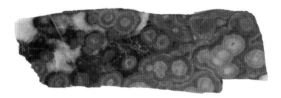

Natural slice

COLOR	Red
APPEARANCE	Mottled opaque stone with flower-like markings
RARITY	Easily obtained
SOURCE	California, United States, China, South Africa

ATTRIBUTES Joyful and potent, Poppy Jasper is named for its orbicular 'flowers'. A powerhouse that is gently stimulating or fiery as required, it is a strongly physical stone that resonates with the base chakra to bring you vitality and passion, grounding* energy into the body and stimulating libido. Conversely, it calms an over-stimulated base chakra and disperses sexual frustration, soothing an over-active libido. Useful when fresh motivation is needed, this stone acts like an adrenaline kick. Following the whorls of Poppy Jasper facilitates shamanic lower-world* journeys* and improves dream recall, providing protection at all times. By rectifying unjust situations, it reminds humanity to help each other. Poppy Jasper balances yin and yang, and aligns the physical, emotional and mental bodies with the etheric realm. Clearing electromagnetic and environmental pollution, it assists when dowsing.

165

Psychologically, Poppy Jasper imparts determination. Bringing the courage to get to grips with problems assertively, it encourages self-honesty. Supporting during necessary conflict, it brings problems to light before they become too big and provides insights into difficult situations. Sustaining and supporting during times of stress, this stone brings tranquillity and wholeness, calming the emotions when held.

Mentally, Poppy Jasper assists quick thinking, promotes organizational abilities and the ability to see projects through. It stimulates the imagination and transforms ideas into action.

Physically, Poppy Jasper extends sexual pleasure. Supportive during prolonged illness or hospitalization and re-energizing the body, this is a stone of health, strengthening and detoxifying the circulatory system and the blood and liver. Poppy Jasper activates the base chakra and assists birth and rebirthing. It cleans and stabilizes the biomagnetic sheath* and strengthens boundaries, including cell walls. Helpful for allergies to animals, it assists in attuning to what they need for healing, providing on-going energetic support. This stone is excellent for repelling stalkers and ex-partners who won't let go.

Tumbled

HEALING Supports the circulatory, digestive and sexual organs and ameliorates allergies. It is said to dissolve blockages in the liver or bile ducts and balance the mineral content of the body.

POSITION Place on the base chakra or as appropriate, preferably in contact with the skin. Use for long periods of time. Place under the pillow to stimulate dream recall or grid around the bed (see page 28) to enhance sexual pleasure or repel stalkers ensuring safe sleep.

JASPER: **RAINFOREST JASPER**

Raw

COLOR	Green and white
APPEARANCE	Mossy opaque stone
RARITY	Easily obtained
SOURCE	South America

ATTRIBUTES Connecting to nature and to the earth, Rainforest Jasper unites the earth, base and spleen chakras to create emotional stability.

Spiritually, if you have gone astray at a soul level, this stone takes you back to your roots to re-anchor yourself and reassess your situation objectively. Re-activating herbal-healing knowledge from the far past, this natural healer draws attention to the action of plants and passes

167

on such knowledge, especially through the female line. This stone accesses ancestral matriarchs to reconnect to the family myths and wisdom by which they lived.

Psychologically, with its ability to pause the mind and encourage you to accept yourself as you are without needing to change, this stone of being facilitates moving effortlessly back into balance. It encourages deep self-respect for yourself and others.

Mentally, Rainforest Jasper offers objectivity, clarity, imagination and practical creativity. Emotionally, it encourages stability and pragmatism.

Physically and environmentally, this stone balances humidity, creating conditions neither too damp nor overly dry. It is especially useful for improving cellular memory*.

HEALING Beneficial for cellular memory, flu, colds, susceptibility to damp, viral infections and fluid imbalances.

POSITION Hold, grid (see pages 28–31) or place as appropriate.

KAKORTOKITE

ALSO KNOWN AS LOPAR'S BLOOD

Polished

COLOR	White, red and black
APPEARANCE	Flecked, opaque stone
RARITY	Rare
SOURCE	Greenland, Alaska

ATTRIBUTES Kakortokite is a high-energy stone imbued with life-force and vitality, although it does not reach the highest of vibrations*. Spiritually, this stone teaches how to 'breathe and be', experiencing at one and the same time a physical connection with the earth and a spiritual connection with the infinity of being. It shows that what is in front of your eyes is the perfect manifestation of where and what you need to be right now.

Kakortokite is formed geothermally from red Eudialyte and black Arfvedsonite in white Syenite: a powerful fusion of energy and color. This Plutonian stone unites earth, base, heart, crown and soul star chakras, opening the way for an in-pouring of light and activating a cosmic anchor*, securing it in the earth's core. Connecting to the galactic center*, this stone acts as a conduit for the cosmic life-force to refertilize the earth and enables riding out energetic changes to come. It also assists lower- and upper-world* journeys*.

Karmically*, it draws together soul companions and members of a soul group* and throws light on the reason for the reunion, which may be complex and to do with ancient soul purpose. This stone is useful for checking out whether soul contracts and soul imperatives* are still valid. If letting go is required, Kakortokite helps in cutting ties and forgiving yourself and the other party.

Psychologically, Kakortokite strengthens confidence in your abilities—and enhances the trust of others. The sheer effort of mining this stone indicates a quality of indomitable will and determination to overcome all obstacles. The sureness of foot needed to convey it down the cliffs helps in adapting to any circumstances and negotiating your way skilfully through adversity.

Emotionally, Kakortokite ameliorates jealousy, animosity, anger and resentment and assists in forgiveness. A stone of cheerfulness, it overcomes depression and seasonal affective disorder (SAD) as its bright vibrations lift the spirits and chase away winter gloom. Physically, Kakortokite re-energizes and re-oxygenates the body and the blood.

HEALING Useful for energy depletion, SAD, multi-dimensional cellular healing; said to strengthen the optic nerve; supports the liver, blood and nervous system.

POSITION Wear or position as appropriate.

(*See also* Eudialyte, pages 128–129.)

KYANITE: **CRYSTALLINE KYANITE**

Polished

COLOR	Blue
APPEARANCE	Lightly striated clear blue crystal
RARITY	Easily obtained
SOURCE	United States, Brazil, Switzerland, Austria, Italy, India

ATTRIBUTES A higher resonance* of opaque Kyanite, self-purifying clear blue Crystalline Kyanite has an extremely light and fast vibration that quickly activates the higher chakras and the illumined mind. Useful for passing rapidly into deep meditation and opening metaphysical gifts, it induces multi-dimensional connections and heals the etheric blueprint*.

Spiritually, Crystalline Kyanite connects to your soul path and true vocation. It must be used with integrity of purpose or misuse will rebound on the wearer. Showing where you abused trust in the past, it unlocks a third eye or metaphysical gates that were closed as a result of psychic spying or the like.

At the emotional level, this stone smoothes the way for lasting relationships. Program a pair (see page 358) to enhance telepathic and intuitive communication and to bring harmony and unconditional love to a partnership.

HEALING Helps ovarian or ovulation pain, the larynx and hoarseness.

POSITION Hold, grid (see pages 28–31) or place as appropriate.

ADDITIONAL FORM
Black Kyanite is an effective earth and psychological healing tool that assists in moving into the between-life state* to access and manifest the current soul plan* and releases soul imperatives* that no longer serve a purpose. This stone shows the karma* currently being created by present choices and assists in foreseeing the outcome of a soul plan. An efficient stone for psychological and auric cleansing, the striations rapidly move negativity out of the subtle bodies*, aligning the chakras. This stone draws dis-ease* and stagnant energy from the physical body, replenishing it with positive life-force. Physically, this stone keeps cells connected to the overall perfect divine blueprint to maintain optimum health. A potent tool for those who have difficulty fully incarnating into earth life, it assists mental cleansing, the uro-genital and reproductive systems, muscles, adrenals, throat and parathyroid. Black Kyanite supports environmental healing, connecting with those who are assisting the evolution of the planet and pulling pollution out of the earth and transmuting it.

*Black Kyanite
(natural formation)*

172

LAZULITE

Raw

COLOR	Indigo-purple
APPEARANCE	Grainy, dense mass with tiny pyramidal crystals
RARITY	Easily obtained
SOURCE	Brazil, Austria, Switzerland, United States, Canada

ATTRIBUTES Drawing in pure universal energy and stimulating intuition, promoting balance and cosmic alignment, Lazulite induces profound states of bliss. Spiritually, placed on the third eye, it creates a serene self grounded in a sense of being part of the divine. Giving insight into underlying causes of psychological and life problems, it provides intuitive solutions. Pinpointing reasons behind addiction, it detaches from desire for more or obsessive control. Psychologically, Lazulite boosts confidence and self-esteem.

HEALING Helps sun-sensitivity, the immune system, cellular memory*, fractures, the lymphatic system, thyroid, pituitary and liver, and migraine.

POSITION Hold, grid (see pages 28–31) or place as appropriate. (*See also* Blue Quartz with Lazulite, page 231.)

LEMURIAN JADE

Midnight (polished)   *Shadow (polished)*

COLOR	Gray-blue-green (Shadow) and black (Midnight)
APPEARANCE	Dense, mottled stone with golden flecks
RARITY	Rare
SOURCE	Peru (one mine only)

ATTRIBUTES This powerful stone stands between the thresholds of two worlds. If you work at the interface between body and higher consciousness, or one person and another, Lemurian Jade facilitates keeping the boundary strong while understanding intuitively what is occurring on the other side. Hold this stone during shamanic work to deepen the connection with the Earth Mother, power allies and nature in the raw. It creates a shamanic anchor* and activates a cosmic anchor*, stabilizing your core energy field to assimilate vibrational shifts and ground earth-energy changes.

Spiritually, Lemurian Jade helps in walking lightly on the earth and restores the balance between nature, planet and humankind. Use it to attune to telluric currents*, practice earth healing* or become one with rocks or stones. A stone of initiation, Lemurian Jade accompanies the dying to their new abode and assists in any transition in life, especially those that occur on the spiritual level. Containing Jade, Quartz, Iron Pyrite and other minerals, this stone is highly protective. With its ability to pass through darkness confidently, teaching the value and gifts found in dark places wherever they may be, Lemurian Jade is a stalwart companion in testing times before the light returns. It draws on to your path anyone from the past with whom there is unfinished business or who is on your soul plan* for the present lifetime. The darker the color, the more this stone facilitates your journey through the mysteries, inner and outer.

Psychologically, Lemurian Jade assists anyone who has had a difficult life in the past, whenever that may be, and heals abuse of any kind. Stabilizing emotions, it opens the heart and instills a sense of gratitude for what *is* rather than what is lacking. Wear it constantly if you suffer from 'poor-me' syndrome—it turns attention to what you can give to others rather than how hard done by you are. When this shift occurs, the stone draws joyful abundance toward you. Attuned to the divine feminine principle, Lemurian Jade assists that energy to manifest in both men and women, bringing about an inner integration and moving beyond a gender-specific perspective on life.

HEALING Provides support during the recovery process or a chronic disease that affects the immune system, which it strengthens. It revitalizes the immune system and the heart.

POSITION Hold or position as appropriate. Place on the earth chakra.

NOTE Lemurian Jade has a similar energy to Healers Gold from Arizona.

LEOPARDSKIN SERPENTINE

Polished

COLOR	Green, gray and black
APPEARANCE	Leopardskin-like opaque stone
RARITY	Rare
SOURCE	Britain, Norway, Russia, Zimbabwe, Italy, United States, Switzerland, Canada

ATTRIBUTES Tactile Leopardskin Serpentine responds to holding and mental connection rather than placement on the body. With its powerful grounding* energy, this shamanic stone keeps you earthed while undertaking lower-world* journeys* and facilitates trance and deep meditation, opening a direct channel to spiritual guidance.

Belonging to the west on the medicine wheel (see pages 368–375), this shamanic stone accesses Leopard energy and facilitates traveling with the Leopard or Jaguar as a power or healing animal, or shape-shifting when necessary. Karmically*, Leopardskin Serpentine assists in reclaiming power, especially where this has been given away, stolen or misused in previous lives or in other dimensions.

Psychologically, Leopardskin Serpentine offers insights into why you are living the life you are, highlighting soul choices and the qualities being brought out, and assists in making any adjustments that may be necessary to align with your soul plan* for the present lifetime.

Environmentally, Leopardskin Serpentine instills a deep love of the earth and wild places. It helps in finding solace in nature and defending the wilderness that oxygenates the planet.

HEALING Detoxifies and balances the thyroid, parathyroid and pancreas.

POSITION Hold, grid (see pages 28–31) or place as appropriate.

LEPIDOCROCITE

*Natural formation
in Quartz*

COLOR	Red
APPEARANCE	Crusty opaque crystals or reddish inclusions
RARITY	Easily obtained
SOURCE	Spain, India

ATTRIBUTES Deepening your intuition and linking this to your practical mind, Lepidocrocite acts as a bridge between matter and consciousness, enhancing the application of spiritual insights to functional reality.

178

Aligning and stimulating all the chakras, Lepidocrocite cleanses the biomagnetic sheath*.

Spiritually, this stone enables the teaching of truth without dogma and the art of observing without making judgments. It strengthens the ability to empower others without entering into power struggles yourself. Giving the strength to make an enduring commitment to your life journey wherever it takes you, it facilitates the work you must do in accordance with your soul plan*. Lepidocrocite assists in recognizing your strengths at whatever level these occur. This stone stimulates the mind and grounds your self into the functional reality of the mundane world.

Mentally, Lepidocrocite dissolves confusion and overcomes negative thoughts, aloofness and disparity, replacing these with unconditional love, whether for yourself, the environment or humanity.

Physically, this stone is useful for calming hyperactivity, bi-polar or attention-deficit hyperactivity disorder (ADHD) and other frenetic-energy imbalances.

HEALING Enhances the healing energy of other stones. It is said to act as an appetite suppressant and be beneficial for the liver, iris, reproductive organs; dissolves tumors and encourages cellular regeneration.

POSITION Hold, grid (see pages 28–31) or place as appropriate.

(*See also* Super Seven, pages 333–334.)

Lepidocrocite
in Quartz point

LIBYAN GOLD TEKTITE

ALSO KNOWN AS LIBYAN GLASS, LIBYAN DESERT TECKTITE

Natural formation

COLOR	Pale yellow, gold, light green, white
APPEARANCE	Smooth or slightly bubbly translucent 'glass'
RARITY	Increasingly available (but may be artificially manufactured)
SOURCE	Libya

ATTRIBUTES Believed to have been formed when a meteorite hit the inhospitable Western Desert and catapulted molten rock and sand into the stratosphere creating a glass-like substance, Libyan Gold is effective for those who do not feel fully connected to the earth or who feel abandoned by their home planet. Valued by the ancient Egyptians for ritual jewelry to bring the Sun God to earth, Libyan Gold formed part of the protective heart scarab that guided Tutankhamun on his after-life journey to the stars (see pages 14–15).

Spiritually, this stone carries powerful sun energy and abundant life-force, acting as a protective amulet for any journey—physical or metaphysical—going beyond the boundaries of what is known and across frontiers of consciousness. It assists in traveling to ancient Egypt to reconnect to wisdom held there—and to identify misuses of power and knowledge. However, the Egyptians guarded their boundaries carefully and uninvited guests were held back by magical incantations. If you find it difficult to travel the road to past, present or future, ask the stone to dissolve the restrictions placed in another life.

Environmentally, Libyan Gold is a useful connector between higher cosmic forces and the planet, grounding* and transmuting this energy into land and body, and opening spiritual vision. It assists in balancing earth changes. Arising from such a phenomenal force, Libyan Gold assists in creating a new life, manifesting your will on earth. It cuts away all that is outworn and outgrown and is useful for etheric surgery, freeing you from the past and reconnecting to your spiritual roots. This stone works intensely, so be sure you are prepared before use.

Natural formation

HEALING Restoring depleted life-force energy; little physical application other than resonating with the kidneys, bladder and gall bladder, and potentially averting traveler's diarrhea.

POSITION Place or wear as appropriate. For journeying*, place over the past-life or soma chakra. For accessing information or inducing visions, place over the third eye.

LIMONITE

Raw

COLOR	Yellow
APPEARANCE	Glassy dense mass, metallic or dull, may be occluded or rusty
RARITY	Easily obtained
SOURCE	Brazil, France, Germany, Luxembourg, Italy, Russia, Cuba, Zaire, India, Namibia, United States

ATTRIBUTES Resonating with the earth, base and sacral chakras, Limonite is iron oxide, a grounding* and protective mineral that stabilizes, imparts endurance and stimulates inner strength, particularly when faced with extreme conditions.

182

Spiritually, Limonite guards against mental influence or ill-wishing* and prevents psychic overwhelming. It affords the physical body protection during metaphysical activities and enhances telepathy.

Psychologically, Limonite is useful for removing yourself from the mire, whatever form that may take. It facilitates standing your ground without needing to fight back and favorably assists legal situations. With the support of other stones, it brings about inner-child* healing.

Mentally, this stone is a powerful intellectual facilitator, sharpening the mind and increasing efficiency of thought and ameliorating confusion. Physically, Limonite is traditionally used as a treatment for dehydration and was said to restore youthful properties.

HEALING Useful for purification, jaundice, fevers, the liver and digestion and overcoming dehydration; supports the muscoskeletal system and the assimilation of iron and calcium.

POSITION Hold, grid (see pages 28–31) or place as appropriate. Limonite is easiest to use in one of its occluded forms.

(*See also* Red and Yellow Phantom Quartz, pages 277–278.)

MARCASITE

Raw on matrix

COLOR	Whitish-yellow
APPEARANCE	Metallic masses or small crystals
RARITY	Easily available
SOURCE	United States, Mexico, Germany, France

ATTRIBUTES Providing a psychic shield and grounding you into the everyday world, Marcasite stimulates metaphysical abilities* such as clairvoyance* and spirit-awareness. Spiritually, Marcasite assists and protects those who undertake house clearing* or entity removal* and supports those who seek to incorporate their spirituality into the functional reality of the everyday world.

184

Psychologically, this stone increases objectivity, encouraging you to take a more detached perspective when seeking insight into yourself or others. It helps in confidently making adjustments necessary for growth and in stepping into your own power without seeking power over others. This is the stone to use if you want your light to shine. Increasing willpower, it promotes going boldly where you have not ventured before. Karmically*, it assists anyone with a longstanding sense of spiritual lack to find true abundance.

Mentally, Marcasite is useful for scattered or confused thinking or impaired memory as it overcomes mental exhaustion, improves concentration and brings clarity to your mind.

Emotionally, Marcasite dispels hysteria and ingrained patterns of martyrdom or victim mentality, alleviating emotional burn-out and inducing emotional prosperity.

Physically, Marcasite resonates with yang energy. It balances the energies of the physical body leading to optimum well-being and high energy levels.

HEALING Helpful for cleansing blood, and for warts, moles, freckles and the spleen.

POSITION Hold, grid (see pages 28–31) or place as appropriate. Wear to overcome depleted energy.

MENALITE

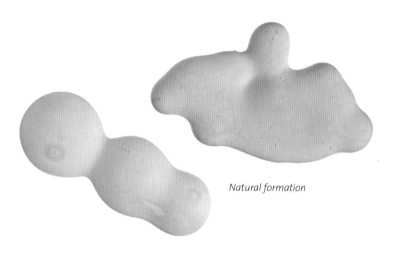

Natural formation

COLOR	White
APPEARANCE	Opaque, chalky stone
RARITY	Rare
SOURCE	United States, Africa, Australia

ATTRIBUTES Enhancing divination and forecasting, Menalite reconnects to the wise feminine and the power of the priestess. An excellent stone for conducting the rites of passage that mark out the transitions through womanhood, Menalite reminds you of the endlessly recurring cycles of life and is particularly useful for rebirth and rejuvenation of any kind.

Spiritually, this stone assists in coming to terms with death, removing fear and assuring that you will survive in another reality. Menalite is a natural accompaniment for meditations to re-member your soul.

This shamanic stone has been used since time began to journey* to other realms and carry out metaphysical rituals. Many of the stones simulate power animals or the ancient fertility goddess, and this nurturing stone provides a link to the Earth Mother, taking you back into her womb for healing and reconnection to the root of being. Similar in energy to Flint or Novaculite, it opens the earth section of a cosmic anchor*, attaching you deep into the core of the earth and solidifying your core-energy field, and is a useful shamanic anchor* for lower-world* journeys. This stone connects to the power allies its shape mimics. Hold one to call on your power animal before ritual working or exploring the crystal medicine wheel (see pages 368–375).

Physically, Menalite is beneficial for transitions, particularly those that affect hormonal balance, such as puberty or childbirth. Keep a Menalite under your pillow during menopause and hold during a hot flush or night sweat.

HEALING Beneficial for fertility, menopause, menstruation, lactation and night sweats.

POSITION Hold, grid (see pages 28–31) or place as appropriate.

MERLINITE

ALSO KNOWN AS PSILOMELANE

Shaped

Polished

COLOR	Black and white
APPEARANCE	Tendril-like, two-color opaque or translucent stone, may have opalescent sheen
RARITY	Easily obtained
SOURCE	New Mexico

ATTRIBUTES Merlinite brings magic and luck into your life. This dendritic* stone holds the wisdom of shamans, alchemists and magician-priests, accessing multi-dimensions, and is a useful companion during between-the-worlds journeying*. Merlinite supports shamanic practices or magical ritual, offering glimpses of the past or future where this is appropriate and bringing about a successful conclusion to spiritual endeavors. A combination of Quartz and Psilomelane, which may be opalized and show flashes of incandescent fire, this stone is attuned to the elements of earth, air, fire and water. It is perfect for the center of the crystal medicine wheel (see pages 368–375) to symbolize unity of the elements and the worlds.

Spiritually, a stone of equilibrium, Merlinite's dual coloring brings harmony, balancing complementaries such as yin and yang, conscious and unconscious, intellect and intuition, and masculine and feminine energies. It is the perfect stone for bringing together the divine feminine and masculine—goddess and god—blending spiritual and earthly vibrations and grounding* them into the body or environment.

Psychologically a powerful energy cleanser, Merlinite reprograms ingrained patterns of behavior in the mental and emotional etheric blueprints*, bringing about profound change. It assists in coming to terms with negative experiences, turning them into positive learning.

Highly effective for karmic* healing, Merlinite reaches into the past to read the Akashic Record* and assists in reframing* beliefs and vows that are creating blockages today.

Physically, Merlinite promotes the circulation of energy and oxygen around the body. An energy-saving stone that slows processes down or stimulates as appropriate, its dendritic tendrils resonate with nerve fibers, increasing energy flow along the spine and through the brain, and it can be of assistance in harmonizing the nervous system to an influx of higher vibrations*.

HEALING Supports the respiratory, nervous and circulatory systems, intestines and heart.

POSITION Place, grid (see pages 28–31) or wear as appropriate.

189

MOLYBDENITE

*Molybdenite in Quartz
(natural crystals on matrix)*

COLOR	Silver
APPEARANCE	Metallic, dense crystal, feels greasy to the touch
RARITY	Rare
SOURCE	United States, England, Canada, Sweden, Russia, Australia

ATTRIBUTES Molybdenite is known as the dreamer's stone. If you need an insightful or healing dream, place appropriately programmed (see page 358) Molybdenite under your pillow.

Spiritually, this stone integrates the everyday self with your Higher Self*. This powerful stone assists healers in their work. It is said to facilitate intergalactic contact. Psychologically, Molybdenite is a useful tool for meeting your shadow* and accessing the gifts it offers. This stone encourages you to perfect your character without judgment, forgiving your former imperfections.

Operating exceptionally efficiently at a mental level, Molybdenite sharpens the mind. Physically, keeping the stone in your energy field ensures continual recharging and rebalancing as it has a strong electrical charge, repairing and re-energizing the subtle energy bodies*.

Molybdenite can be used to harmonize mercury fillings to a more beneficial vibration and to encourage elimination of mercury toxicity from the body.

HEALING Beneficial for jaw pain, the teeth, circulation, oxygenation and the immune system.

POSITION Hold, grid (see pages 28–31) or place as appropriate.

COMBINATION STONE
Molybdenite in Quartz brings light into darkness and assists in knowing you are not alone. Tapping into subconscious knowledge, it opens spiritual insight and links to multi- and inter-dimensional space. This protective combination is beneficial for group working and for harmonizing the vibrations and energy bodies of two or more people. Molybdenite in Quartz effectively removes mental blockages, relinquishing outgrown baggage and sealing the biomagnetic sheath* after removal. It is extremely useful for gaining insight from dreams.

MYSTIC TOPAZ

Faceted

COLOR	Rainbow hue, predominantly purple, blue, green
APPEARANCE	Glittering, transparent faceted crystal
RARITY	Rare, usually found as jewelry
SOURCE	Artificially coated Topaz

ATTRIBUTES The coating of vaporized Titanium oxide (Rutile) lifts the energy of Topaz to an extremely high vibration* that enables multi-dimensional access. Mystic Topaz sheds light on the spiritual path, highlights goals and taps into inner resources.

Spiritually, this crystal brings about the trust in the universe that enables 'being' rather than 'doing'. Cutting through doubt and uncertainty and manifesting your soul plan* for the current incarnation, it supports affirmations, manifestation and visualization, teaching how to set intention from the heart without emotional involvement or mental projection*.

Excellent for cleansing the biomagnetic sheath* and for inducing relaxation, Mystic Topaz releases tension at any level and speeds up spiritual development where this has been laborious. Psychologically, Mystic Topaz helps in discovering inner riches.

Mentally, this stone assists in problem-solving, accessing the universal mind. Showing the influence you have had and knowledge gained through many life experiences, Mystic Topaz has the capacity to help you see both the bigger picture and minute detail, recognizing how they interrelate.

Mystic Topaz is an effective emotional support, stabilizing feelings and making you receptive to love from every source. This glittering stone realigns the meridians* of the subtle bodies*.

HEALING Works best at the subtle levels of being, but manifests health on all levels. Assists digestion and anorexia, restores taste, fortifies the nerves and stimulates the metabolism. Apply as a gem essence to the skin or for dimness of vision, but make the essence by the indirect method (see page 361).

POSITION Wear at the ears, neck and wrist.

NATROLITE

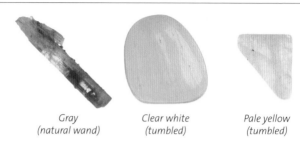

*Gray
(natural wand)*

*Clear white
(tumbled)*

*Pale yellow
(tumbled)*

COLOR	Clear white, gray or pale yellow
APPEARANCE	Long, lightly ribbed crystal or tumbled stone
RARITY	Rare
SOURCE	United States, Germany, Czech Republic

ATTRIBUTES Natrolite prepares and fine-tunes the nervous system to an influx of new vibrations, harmonizing it with the lightbody*.

Spiritually, pure white Natrolite can bring about a profound shift and stimulate metaphysical changes to channel high-level energy into the light and physical bodies, enabling living with full multi-dimensional awareness within a protective cloak for the awakened soul.

Mentally this stone assists in seeing the bigger picture and practicing holistic thinking from an illumined mind.

HEALING Works beyond the physical level of being, but supports the nervous system.

POSITION Hold in the left hand, grid (see pages 28–31), place over the third eye or soma chakra, or midway between soma and crown chakras.

NEPTUNITE

Crystals on matrix

COLOR	Black
APPEARANCE	Striated crystal in matrix
RARITY	Rare
SOURCE	California

ATTRIBUTES Neptunite has a natural affinity with the moon and the sea, relieving underwater environmental pressure. Spiritually, it helps in understanding the delusions, illusions and deceptions you place on yourself and others, especially in spiritual matters. Focusing and centering, it teaches how to sweep aside the veil and see into true reality. Psychologically, this stone is a comfort in seemingly intolerable situations, dissolving anger and resentment, and it shows why your soul chose to undergo an experience, assisting in clearing false beliefs that block forward progress.

HEALING Works beyond the physical level of being, but also cools temper tantrums.

POSITION Neptunite is fragile and best placed in the environment.

NOVACULITE

Raw

COLOR	White
APPEARANCE	Lustrous, translucent to opaque, waxy fine textured stone
RARITY	Reasonably easy to obtain
SOURCE	United States

ATTRIBUTES With its extremely fine and high energy, Novaculite hones the spirit and psyche. Spiritually, this stone facilitates angelic contact and multi-dimensional journeying*. Opening the crown and higher chakras, it aligns all the chakras to ground spiritual energy into the body. Creating an intense, strongly focused beam of energy, it is the ultimate cord-cutting tool. Novaculite slices through the ties that etherically link people together, taking them out at the root. Used at the chakras, it detaches these cords at exceedingly subtle levels and heals the site. At any level, it cuts through blockages and problems. It is extremely efficient used with Nuummite to clear ancient sorcery and spells. Follow it up with Tugtupite to bring unconditional love and forgiveness to heal the past.

196

Psychologically, Novaculite is helpful for obtaining a new perspective, especially on obsessive disorders as it pinpoints the underlying cause. It facilitates finding the gift in any situation no matter how traumatic. A placid and calming stone, Novaculite is beneficial for those who are in the depths of despair or the grip of mania.

Physically, due to its fine texture, Novaculite supports structure and elasticity in the body, particularly the skin, or in the environment. A useful conductor of electromagnetic energy, Novaculite is beneficial for the etheric body* and for clearing dis-ease* out of the etheric blueprint*. Novaculite performs etheric surgery on the subtle bodies*— the operation should be carried out by a qualified healer as the stone has a razor-sharp edge.

Environmentally, Novaculite can clear blockages in the earth's meridians* and repair the electromagnetic flow.

Reportedly boosting interstellar contact, this stone is said to assist in deciphering ancient languages. Enhancing personal magnetism, it is helpful to anyone who sells services to others, bringing buyer and seller together in harmony.

HEALING Helpful for cellular memory*, depression, obsessive disorders, warts, moles, chills, cellular structure and healthy skin.

POSITION Hold, grid (see pages 28–31) or place with care as the shards are sharp.

(*See also* Flint, pages 132–133.)

NUUMMITE

Polished slice

COLOR	Black
APPEARANCE	Opaque with scintillating flashes
RARITY	Becoming increasingly available
SOURCE	Greenland, Canada

ATTRIBUTES Nuummite is the sorcerer's stone and is powerfully protective against ill-wishing* and psychic manipulation. One of the oldest minerals on earth, it is an exceptional energy tool for those whose energies have evolved sufficiently to work with its intensity; it is particularly effective when shaped into a wand to pull out negative energy, imprints and implants*. Set Nuummite in silver and combine with Tugtupite especially for ritual working.

Spiritually, Nuummite assists in seeing beyond the outer façade, creating an inner landscape to be traversed. A protective stone, strengthening the auric shield* and effective against negative energies and sorcery, Nuummite helps traveling with stealth and sureness and is the perfect stone for lower-world* journeys* to retrieve a lost soul or child part. It shields from sight—and safeguards your car. This intense stone has an element of magic that must be used respectfully, with right intention, or else it rebounds. Activating the past-life and soma chakras, it opens and integrates all the subtle chakras, bringing about a profound shift in consciousness.

Karmically*, Nuummite assists in recognizing past-life contacts and highlights debts stemming from misuse of power, reminding you not to repeat patterns. Placed on the soma chakra, it draws karmic debris out of the physical and emotional bodies. With its strong electro-magnetic field and ability to reprogram cellular memory*, Nuummite quickly restores energy or power depleted by karmic debts and other causes, and clears blockages including those that are self-imposed.

Psychologically, by severing present-life embroilments that stem from past manipulation or incantations, Nuummite removes difficulties arising from another person's inappropriate protection or attempted guidance and dissolves defensive behavior patterns built against that manipulation. Having cleansed those experiences, Nuummite connects to your true self. Cutting through to your core, it reprograms your thoughts and insists that you be responsible for your own protection. Nuummite teaches respect and honor, demanding the fulfilment of obligations and promises that are relevant to life today and letting go those that are not.

Physically, this stone aligns the biomagnetic sheath* with the physical body, and removes any mental implants from extraterrestrial or magical sources in the present or any other life. Nuummite combines well with Novaculite to release curses, past-life imperatives* and the effects of sorcery and ill-wishing in any life. Novaculite provides spiritual guidance, cutting through ancient cords to outgrown mentors and the like. The combination is useful for psychic surgery on the

Nuummite with Tugtupite (polished, set in silver)

etheric blueprint*, cutting away all that is dis-eased due to past injury, trauma and actions. Use Nuummite for cutting and Novaculite to draw in purifying and revitalizing energy, healing and sealing where the dis-ease* was formerly sited. Adding Tugtupite brings in unconditional love and forgiveness. Set Nuummite in silver and combine with Tugtupite for ritual working.

HEALING Beneficial for insomnia, stress, degenerative disease, tissue regeneration, Parkinson's disease, headache, insulin regulation, the eyes, brain, kidneys and nerves. It strengthens the triple-burner meridian*.

POSITION Hold, grid (see pages 28–31) or place as appropriate. Wear constantly for protection against ill-wishing or psychic manipulation. It is particularly effective wrapped in silver.

(*See also* Tugtupite with Nuummite, pages 342–343.)

OLIGOCRASE

ALSO KNOWN AS OLIGIOCRASE

Raw

COLOR	White
APPEARANCE	Opaque or clear, bubbly stone
RARITY	Fairly easily obtained
SOURCE	Norway, Russia, Canada, Tanzania, India, France, United States

ATTRIBUTES Sunstone without yellowness, Moonstone without shimmer, Oligocrase facilitates the processing of emotions with the cycles of the moon, withdrawing to dream at dark moon and emerging to put ideas and insights into practice at full moon.

Psychologically, this stone breaks old patterns and habits, restoring trust and innocence, and works well at the north-west of the medicine wheel (see pages 368–375).

HEALING Balances fluids within the body, assisting lymphatic flow, and is beneficial for bones and fractures.

POSITION Hold, grid (see pages 28–31) or place as appropriate.

OPAL: **ANDEAN BLUE OPAL**

Andean Blue (raw)

COLOR	Greenish-blue
APPEARANCE	Opaque, slightly iridescent blue stone
RARITY	Easily obtained
SOURCE	Peru

ATTRIBUTES Andean Blue Opal promotes right action for the highest good. A useful journeying* stone enhancing receptivity, it induces mild hypnotic trance, enhancing divination and metaphysical gifts*. Spiritually, it stimulates communication from the heart as it smoothes the biomagnetic field*, enhancing connection with others. A karmic* healer, it cauterizes emotional wounds from any lifetime and supports inner serenity during stressful situations. By reminding of the need to heal the earth, it is useful for environmental healing and for those who transmute changing vibration through their physical or subtle bodies*.

HEALING Helpful for cellular memory*, water retention, muscular swelling; supports the heart, lungs and thymus.

POSITION Wear, hold, grid (see pages 28–31) or place as appropriate.

ADDITIONAL FORMS

Oregon Opal carries cosmic consciousness* and facilitates moving between dimensions, past-life exploration and karmic healing, showing how what is created in one life affects another. It searches out lies and delusions, both from other people and self-deception, revealing the truth. It releases old grief, trauma and disappointment, replacing these with joy and lightness. It cleanses the emotional body of baggage and amplifies the entire range of positive emotions, ensuring that you speak your emotional truth. Physically, this stone removes excess mucus.

*Oregon
(raw)*

Girasol (Blue Opal) enhances connections between members of a soul group* and shows where these are beneficial in present life. Indicating solutions to difficulties, especially where these could not be spoken about in the past, it brings untruths to light. Karmically, Girasol is useful when past-life experiences affect the present, especially as panic or phobias. It dissolves imprints on the etheric blueprint* and cellular memory is restored. Mentally, Girasol stimulates creativity, enhancing communication. An emotional comforter, it separates psychic impressions from your own hidden feelings. Assisting in understanding the deep causes of dis-ease*, it strengthens boundaries and teaches how to satisfy your emotional needs. Gridding* Girasol creates a quiet space in which to work and meditate. Physically, it helps iron assimilation, vision, fatigue, metabolism, hair loss and the lymph nodes.

*Girasol
(tumbled)*

PARAIBA TOURMALINE

Pink (raw)

Turquoise (faceted)

COLOR	Turquoise-blue, also pink or golden
APPEARANCE	Long-bladed transparent or opaque stone or faceted gem
RARITY	Rare and expensive (may be heat-treated)
SOURCE	Brazil, Nigeria, Mozambique

ATTRIBUTES Connecting to angels of truth and wisdom, Paraiba Tourmaline has a radiant heart energy that assists in stepping into infinite compassion for yourself and the planet. Linking to the turquoise flame* of pure, compassionate being, this stone invokes elevated states of consciousness and encourages service to humanity. This high-vibration* stone brings harmony and light into the darkest situations, helping in finding the gift of spiritual evolution at its heart. It encourages forgiveness at multi- and inner-dimensional* levels, setting you free from your karmic* past. Colored by copper, Paraiba protects against pollutants—physical, emotional, mental, spiritual or environmental—and is a powerful energy conduit.

Spiritually perfect for meditation and attuning to the Higher Self*, shielding the biomagnetic sheath*, aligning chakras and integrating the physical and light bodies, Paraiba sharpens intuition and opens clairvoyance*. Psychologically, it breaks old, self-defeating programs, replacing them with your present soul plan*. Assisting in living according to your aspirations, this stone identifies where you have strayed from your truth. Paraiba facilitates forgiving yourself and others and letting go. Bringing unfinished business to a conclusion, it provides closure on all levels. Having an affinity with sensitive people, Paraiba invokes tolerance of others, overcoming judgmentalism and fanaticism. It offers support to anyone who is overwhelmed by responsibility and encourages personal accountability.

Mentally, it assists the verbalization of thoughts and feelings. It calms the mind, removing extraneous thoughts. Clearing the throat chakra and facilitating communication from a higher plane, it filters information reaching the brain and clarifies perception, sharpens intellect and clears confusion.

Emotionally, this stone soothes fear, calms in stressful situations and assists in understanding underlying emotional states and interpreting exactly how you feel. Physically, it has a general tonic effect and is particularly beneficial for the eyes. It calms over-reactions of the immune system and auto-immune diseases.

HEALING Beneficial for sore throat, hayfever, eyes, jaw and teeth, stomach, arthritis, swollen glands and thyroid problems, cleansing organs, metabolism and hormone production.

POSITION Hold, grid (see pages 28–31), place as appropriate or on eyes.

NOTE Heat-amended Apatite or Fluorite is sold as Paraiba. Paraiba Fluorite is a powerful stone similar to Mystic Topaz.

PEACH SELENITE

Shaped

COLOR	Peach
APPEARANCE	Finely ribbed opaque stone
RARITY	Easily obtained
SOURCE	England, United States, Mexico, Russia, Austria, Greece, Poland, Germany, France

ATTRIBUTES Selenite is crystallized divine light, continuously radiating that light into your life to transmute your environment into sacred space. Symbolizing the transforming fires of the planet Pluto and the earthy wisdom of his wife Persephone, Peach Selenite is a regenerative stone that emits the dark light of the underworld rather than white light. It throws insight into your inner processes and enables accepting your shadow* and hidden self. It makes the perfect accompaniment for an evolutionary jump into expanded self-awareness and new life.

Spiritually, by affording deep insight into the cycles of birth, death and rebirth, this stone opens the priestess in every woman and is ideal for thanksgiving moon rituals at puberty or childbirth. A stone of emotional transformation, Peach Selenite is a powerful karmic* cleanser and healer, assisting in a life review to release ancient trauma.

Drawing out issues of abandonment, rejection, alienation and betrayal, no matter in what timeframe those occurred, Peach Selenite offers healing, forgiveness and acceptance.

HEALING Beneficial for puberty, menopause and any transition.

POSITION Hold or place as appropriate.

ADDITIONAL STONE
Selenite Phantom dissolves whatever has been overlaid on the soul core and connects to the true spiritual self and its overall evolutionary purpose. This stone clears mental and spiritual confusion and removes karmic entanglements—insights gained can be earthed into the physical body with the wider end of the Phantom. The point cuts through karmic debris, drawing it from the etheric body* and reprogramming cellular memory*. Useful for detaching entities* from the biomagnetic sheath* or for preventing external thoughts influencing the mind, this phantom dissolves emotional dis-ease* that has a karmic cause, acting as a symbol of rebirth and new life. Physically this stone is useful for cellular memory, spinal-column alignment and joint flexibility.

*Selenite Phantom
(natural point)*

Desert Rose dims your light while traveling and facilitates clandestine meetings. Psychologically, if you are caught in a self-imposed negative program* or belief system, Desert Rose releases it. Meditating with this stone transmutes ancient conflict into love. Teaching the art of receiving as well as giving love, Desert Rose controls emotional outbursts. An effective healer for the earth and disturbed earth-energy locations, Desert Rose connects to the protection of Mother Earth. Physically it helps the connective tissue and bones.

Desert Rose (natural formation)

THE ONE-WAY PORTAL

Laying a Selenite wand as a base, with an X-shaped cross over it of a long Chlorite Quartz point (such as Shaman Quartz or Green Phantom) and a Stibnite wand on top, creates a one-way portal that facilitates lost souls and entities* leaving the earth plane and prevents their return or reattachment. The Selenite creates a beacon of light, the Chlorite cleanses the energy and the Stibnite closes and guards the portal. It is very effective held over the higher crown chakras. Cleanse crystals afterward with a specialist etheric-level cleanser and wash your hands thoroughly after handling Stibnite as it is toxic.

PEARL SPA DOLOMITE

Natural formation

COLOR	Pale pink
APPEARANCE	Blades on a matrix
RARITY	Easily obtained
SOURCE	Spain, India, Italy, Britain, Switzerland, Namibia

ATTRIBUTES A stone of atonement, Pearl Spa Dolomite teaches that spirituality is a matter of inner balance, pragmatism and expression in the functional reality of the everyday world rather than something experienced 'out there' in another dimension. It assists in grounding* the awareness that you are a spiritual being who is currently on a human journey and assists in being more comfortable in incarnation, loving your physical body.

209

Psychologically, this serene stone overcomes feelings of loneliness, teaching the value in solitary contemplation and at-onement. It guards against nightmares, especially in children. Dissolving old patterns and negative behaviors, it encourages a spontaneous response to life rather than reacting as you have been taught you *ought* to do.

Mentally, by encouraging clarity and structured thought, Pearl Spa Dolomite slows a racing mind.

Emotionally, this stone ameliorates sorrow and negative emotions such as anger or resentment, creating a calm center. It ameliorates temper tantrums in children—or adults.

Physically, this stone is a useful detoxifier that stabilizes hyperactivity. Environmentally, Pearl Spa Dolomite enhances and harmonizes the effect of crystal combinations and grids*.

HEALING Supports the muscular, skeletal and reproductive systems, nails and skin, metabolism; helps weight loss and regulates appetite.

POSITION Hold, grid (see pages 28–31) or place as appropriate.

PRESELI BLUESTONE

Polished   *Raw*

COLOR	Blue-gray, blue-green
APPEARANCE	Mottled and flecked, granite-like; lustrous when polished
RARITY	Found at only one site
SOURCE	Preseli Mountains (Wales)

ATTRIBUTES Preseli Bluestone is an ancient stone of dreaming and far memory that forms the inner ring at Stonehenge in the English county of Wiltshire and which moves out of space and time to access multi-dimensions. With its powerful telluric electromagnetic charge, Preseli Bluestone opens a cosmic anchor* and attaches to the core of the earth, creating unshakeable inner-core energetic solidity to stabilize you through earth changes. It then aligns your energy to the galactic center* so that you are held suspended between the earth and the galaxy and can allow waves of energy to pass through your body to earth themselves in the planetary center. It also works as a shamanic anchor* for both lower- and upper-world* journeys*.

A unique British stone, spiritually Bluestone links to Merlin energy and the shaman in everyone. With a powerful connection with Mother Earth, it warns that whoever violates the earth violates themselves. Combined with chalk or Flint, Bluestone acts as a battery—generating, earthing and grounding spiritual energy and power, and enhancing psychic ability and metaphysical gifts*. A visionary stone for all past-life exploration, this stone specifically assists in tracking your Celtic heritage and links to Egyptian knowledge held deep within the stone. On the soma or past-life chakras, it is particularly useful for soul retrieval* and power retrieval, effortlessly reaching way back into the past. The perfect dreaming stone, it brings answers quickly and assists in accessing and integrating spiritual information.

Size matters with Bluestone—a small piece is exceedingly intense and larger pieces may need moving out of a bedroom at night to avoid over-stimulation. This stone is specifically directional—if you feel pressure or a headache develops, turn and face another direction when working with the stone or turn the stone. It can reset your internal or spiritual compass. This directional quality means that it channels the earth's electromagnetic forces and facilitates travel along telluric currents* or healing of the earth's grid. The stone links all the stone circles in the British Isles in an enormous energy spiral and then connects to other power centers around the planet. It shows the energetic geometric patterns encoded within circles and other sacred sites and facilitates reconnecting these where the energies have been violated or broken, whether deliberately or accidently. If power is being drawn from a sacred site for inappropriate purposes, Bluestone breaks the connection and protects the energy of the site.

Psychologically, Bluestone enhances willpower and courage, and gives enormous strength, enabling bearing hard knocks with equanimity—and understanding the lessons and gifts therein. It is an energy enhancer that also provides protection on all levels. This stone links the heart, thymus and throat chakras, enabling speaking your truth. Mentally, Bluestone focuses one-pointedly, clearing the mind of all trivia and creating a space into which knowledge arises intuitively.

Emotionally, Bluestone is a stabilizer, helping in leaving old attachments and feelings behind so that you can live calmly in the present moment.

Bluestone is an immensely physical stone, involving all the senses and balancing energy and, not surprisingly, it supports kinesiology and pyschometry. It has a strong connection with herbs and herbalism, especially plants grown on mountains. This stone can have opposite effects: sedating excess and revitalizing depletion. Bluestone enhances the ability to physically sense energy lines or the vibrations of crystals, or to attune to the subtle energies of the human body, such as acupuncture points. When walking the landscape carrying Bluestone, you are 'plugged in' to all that has happened there, but without attachment. This powerful stone assists in 'being in the moment'.

HEALING Has a benign effect on the throat and immune system, bringing the body's energies into balance.

POSITION Place on the soma or past-life (alta-major) chakras for dreaming and far memory, as appropriate for healing. Place under your pillow for dreaming. Remove or turn direction if a headache develops.

NOTE Bluestone is best purchased from suppliers who use natural shards of raw material. Some stones are more strongly directional than others.

PUMICE

Natural water-worn formation

COLOR	Light gray or beige
APPEARANCE	Light, holey as though bubbles have burst
RARITY	Easily obtained
SOURCE	Worldwide

ATTRIBUTES Not generally regarded as a crystal, Pumice is a powerful healer and absorber of negative energy. Placed over the thymus, it releases ancient pain held in the heart or gut, and heals ingrained emotional wounds, reprogramming emotional cellular memory*.

Psychologically, this stone scrubs off a suffocating coating of guilt, resentment or other negative energy that has traveled from the karmic* past or been imposed upon you in the present life, especially from childhood. It is also helpful when you suffer from a crippling sense of

214

inadequacy, no matter how much you may have hidden this from yourself. Like a serpent shedding its skin, peel away this coating by working all over the biomagnetic sheath* with the stone and then seal your biomagnetic sheath with Selenite or Quartz.

Psychologically, Pumice is particularly useful for abrasive people who have created a defence against the pain they carry, but who feel extremely vulnerable underneath a hard shell. This stone gently assists in letting go of protective barriers and accepting one's vulnerability, assisting trust and acceptance. It opens the ability to let other people in, encouraging intimacy of all kinds.

Physically, this stone assists toxin release especially during colonic hydrotherapy; after the treatment, holding Pumice cleanses negative energy from the therapist.

HEALING Assists the action of colonic hydrotherapy, detoxification, cellular memory and soothes irritable bowel syndrome (IBS).

POSITION Hold, grid (see pages 28–31) or place as appropriate. Leave in a healing or therapy room and cleanse frequently with salt water.

PURPURITE

Raw

COLOR	Purple
APPEARANCE	Vivid banded and veined metallic opaque stone
RARITY	Easily obtained
SOURCE	Namibia, Western Australia, United States, France

ATTRIBUTES An extremely effective stone for psychic protection, Purpurite stimulates enlightenment. Spiritually, by opening the higher crown chakras and linking them to the base, it stimulates unimpeded evolution, grounding* the resultant energy shift into functional reality.

Excellent for public speaking, Purpurite imparts clarity, focus and confidence to your thoughts and communication. It prevents interference with the transmission of your views.

216

Psychologically, Purpurite breaks old habits or attitudes that keep you caught in the past and lifts despair. Mentally, this stone increases alertness and receptivity to guidance and new ideas.

Physically a rejuvenating stone, Purpurite energizes the physical and mental bodies, overcoming tiredness and despondency at any level.

Environmentally, this stone facilitates house sales where adverse environmental or community interference is blocking a sale, particularly where past-life conflict has been recreated. Cutting the links between the group, it facilitates forward movement. It disperses negative energy from the environs, lifting curses or ill-wishing* and psychic interference, and imprinting positive energy. Equally helpful in any sale situation, program it (see page 358) to find a buyer quickly.

HEALING Useful for overcoming exhaustion, increasing stamina and rejuvenating; helps cellular memory*, bruises, bleeding, pustules, the cardio-thoracic system, blood flow and blood purification; stabilizes the pulse.

POSITION Hold, grid (see pages 28–31) or place as appropriate. Position between you and the source of psychic attack* or undue influence.

PYROPHYLLITE

Raw

COLOR	Pink
APPEARANCE	Fan-like crystals on a matrix
RARITY	Easily obtained
SOURCE	United States, Canada, Russia, Australia

ATTRIBUTES Pyrophyllite encourages psychological autonomy and assists if your boundaries are scattered, too diffuse or easily breached. If you cannot sense where you end and another person begins, or are easily swayed by others, holding Pyrophyllite on your solar plexus reinforces boundaries and shows how to say no.

Spiritually, this stone renegotiates promises, soul contracts or obligations that keep you entangled with another person, whether from the current life or another one in any dimension.

HEALING Assists indigestion, heartburn, over-acidity and diarrhea.

POSITION As Pyrophyllite is delicate, it is unsuitable to wear.

QUANTUM QUATTRO

Tumbled

COLOR	Blue-green-turquoise mix
APPEARANCE	Mottled opaque stone
RARITY	Easily available as tumbled stone
SOURCE	Namibia

ATTRIBUTES A combination of Shattuckite, Dioptase, Malachite and Chrysocolla on Smoky Quartz, Quantum Quattro prevents a healing crisis* or catharsis occurring as negative energies gently drop away. A stone of transformation, it has a dramatic effect on the energy field, strengthening the immune system and DNA, and activating 12-strand DNA healing*. Grounding* spiritual energies on to the planet and allowing information to pass freely from all levels of being, it is an important protection stone, absorbing negative energies and pollutants.

Spiritually, Quantum Quattro clears psychic vision and protects during channeling*, ensuring that the entity* does not take over the physical body. Aligned to the anticipated 2012 vibrational shift, this stone, when used with intention and sincerity, could bring about a better world. Meditate with it and clearly visualize the positive changes you wish to put in place to offset the negative expectations that abound around us. The combination symbolizes wholeness and peace.

Environmentally or physically, placed on an area of imbalance, this stone gently restores equilibrium. If one stone is placed on the third eye and another on the solar plexus, mind, body and emotions are balanced.

Psychologically, Quantum Quattro is particularly effective at healing the effects of grief—in a past or present life—and releasing heartache held within the physical body. It draws out deep feelings and psychosomatic causes, breaks unwanted ties and outworn patterns, and teaches how to take responsibility for your actions, thoughts and feelings. This stone removes hypnotic commands* and edicts against using psychic vision, clearing past-life curses and commands to secrecy. Supporting a positive attitude to life and instilling the ability to tune into one's resources, Quantum Quattro is especially helpful when you do not know what to do next, as it indicates direction. A strong mental cleanser and detoxifier, this stone releases the need to control others.

Emotionally, Quantum Quattro is a powerful healer for the heart and activator for the higher heart chakra. Drawing out negative emotions such as guilt from the solar plexus chakra, this stone reverses destructive emotional programming. Acting as a bridge to emotional healing, especially for the inner child*, clearing festering wounds and forgotten hurts, dissolving grief, betrayal and sorrow, it is extremely effective for healing the pain of abandonment. This stone teaches that difficulty in relationships is a mirroring of an inner separation from the self. Repairing that link and drawing in love at all levels, Quantum Quattro heals an emotional black hole that is desperate for love. This stone clears away perceptions as to how love ought to be and brings in a new vibration of love. It is beneficial to relationships that have become rocky, stabilizing and healing the home and personal interaction.

This tranquil and sustaining stone assists in accepting with serenity situations that are constantly changing, invoking great inner strength. Quantum Quattro enhances personal power and inspires creativity, promoting a concern for the environment and ecological solutions. Assisting elimination and detoxification on all levels, it brings in a positive vibration to fill the space. Quantum Quattro teaches how to leave behind anything that no longer serves a purpose. It protects the earth chakra below the feet and its grounding cord when in an area of disturbed earth energy. Alleviating ambivalence about being in incarnation, this stone assists in accepting the physical body and your sexual nature.

Tumbled

Quantum Quattro efficiently breaks the cycle of karmic* co-dependency that occurs within addictions or obsessive relationships. It helps carers or partners realize that they can neither 'do it for' the addict or partner, nor control their behavior. This stone assists standing by placidly while the other soul follows its journey, but also indicates when intervention would be positive.

HEALING A master healer; brings the body gently back into balance and acts as a general tonic. It is beneficial for intercellular structures, cell disorder, blood re-oxygenation, the lungs, pancreas, insulin and the thyroid, metabolism, T-cells and the thymus, Ménière's Disease, high blood pressure, pain, migraine, fatigue and shock. It lessens nausea and supports the liver, kidneys and digestive tract, alleviates PMT, overcomes addictions and stress. Beneficial for arthritis and ulcers, muscle strengthening, muscle cramps, infections and miasms*.

POSITION Hold, grid (see pages 28–31) around a bed or healing couch or place as appropriate. Use as an essence for headaches, burns and pain (see page 361).

221

QUARTZ WITH AJOITE

*Quartz with Ajoite
and Papagoite
(natural point)*

COLOR	Sea-green
APPEARANCE	Translucent phantom or colored patch
RARITY	Extremely rare
SOURCE	South Africa, United States

ATTRIBUTES A rare, exceedingly high-vibration* crystal attuned to the turquoise flame* of pure compassionate being, Ajoite wraps the soul in universal love. It takes you to the angelic realms while retaining contact with Mother Earth.

Spiritually, if your vibrations are in harmony with this stone, it brings about a profound shift, helping recognition of the multi-dimensional reality of your being. Drawing karmic* wounds or implants* out of the body, no matter at what level or from which timeframe they originate, this stone gently heals the resulting space with unconditional love, reframing* cellular memory*.

Psychologically, Ajoite resolves conflict through forgiveness and compassion for yourself and others. If you carry burdens inappropriately for others or consistently devalue yourself, Ajoite clears that pattern.

Purifying the emotional body, instilling infinite peace and creating environmental calm, this stone gently transmutes toxic emotions and old grief, replacing them with forgiveness and compassion. On the thymus, Ajoite dissipates stress, harmonizing the etheric blueprint* with the physical body, and attunes the body to perfect health.

HEALING Beneficial for cellular memory and cellular structures.

POSITION Hold or position as appropriate.

ADDITIONAL COMBINATIONS

Quartz with Ajoite and Papagoite (raw)

Ajoite with Papagoite effortlessly reaches interstellar dimensions and the enormity of your divine being. The rarest of minerals, Papagoite proffers infinite compassion and facilitates a return to original soul unity and grace. Transmuting sorrow and teaching that 'sin' is only separation from the divine, Ajoite with Papagoite instills deep serenity.

Ajoite with Shattuckite protects against electromagnetic smog* and psychic attack*. It enables remaining open spiritually, no matter how negative the environment or thoughts that surround you. Wearing this stone brings profound peace, centering you in your Self. In karmic healing, it releases need for reparation and frees the soul. Teaching the difference between atonement and at-onement, it offers total forgiveness and opens the karma of grace*. An excellent energy conduit, Ajoite with Shattuckite helps bowel blockages and constipation, assists cellular memory and overcomes stress-related illness.

Ajoite with Shattuckite (raw)

QUARTZ: **AMETHYST HERKIMER**

*Amethyst
(crystal on matrix)*

COLOR	Lilac-purple
APPEARANCE	Double terminated with inclusions
RARITY	Rare
SOURCE	United States, Himalayas, China

ATTRIBUTES Amethyst Herkimer is attuned to the violet flame* of transmutation and opens the highest spiritual connections. Spiritually, by fine-tuning the third eye, it is a powerful metaphysical tool that facilitates soul retrieval* from any lifetime, integrating disparate parts of the self and inducing deep soul healing. Aligning the incarnated soul with other soul dimensions, it reintegrates the soul as a vehicle for pure spirit. Used wisely by evolved souls, Amethyst Herkimer can bring enlightenment. It creates a powerful soul shield when journeying* or meditating, and purifies energy after spiritual or healing work.

Psychologically, Amethyst Herkimer facilitates creativity and attunement to the higher mind, releasing obsessions and ingrained behavior patterns. Emotionally, this stone is perfect for programming (see page 358) to attract your twinflame* and soul companions.

HEALING Works beyond the physical level of being to heal the soul.

POSITION Place on the heart or higher heart chakra, or as appropriate.

ADDITIONAL COLORS
'Citrine' Herkimer (yellow) transmutes poverty consciousness*, removing ingrained programs and beliefs that keep you mired in poverty no matter what their source, opening the way to abundance and enhancing motivation. A powerful cleanser and regenerator, this is an effective stone for enhancing earth energies and encouraging the ethical use of the earth's resources. A powerful protector for the biomagnetic sheath*, subtle bodies* and chakras, it realigns cellular memory* and connects the solar plexus and heart, bringing unconditional love into all emotions. Gridding* 'Citrine' Herkimer stimulates creative energy and encourages abundant fertility.

'Citrine' (natural formation)

'Smoky' Herkimer (gray/brown) aligns the earth and base chakras to ground spiritual reality. Useful for psychic clearing and detoxification, it protects against electromagnetic or geopathic pollution and draws its effects out of the subtle bodies, creating a protective shield for the body or, when gridded, for the environment. Aligned to the karma of grace*, this stone is an excellent accompaniment through death and beyond.

'Smoky' (natural formation)

Golden Enhydro Herkimer (natural formation)

Golden Enhydro Herkimer contains bubbles of liquid millions of years old and connects to All That Is*, bringing about deep emotional healing and transmutation. Attuned to the golden flame of the illumined mind, Golden Enhydro Herkimer goes straight to the ages-old wisdom of the Himalayas. This incredibly energetic stone aligns the solar plexus, third eye, crown and higher crown chakras with the soul star. A useful developer of spiritual gifts, it clears implants* and removes restrictions placed on spiritual sight in this or any other life.

A powerful healer for the solar plexus and karmic* emotional disturbances, Golden Herkimer cleanses the emotional body, creating emotional well-being. In those who have changed sex between incarnations, this stone eliminates resulting gender confusion or ambivalence.

Blue Herkimer with Boulangerite from Romania has a soft, gentle energy that brings joy to the heart and an innate sense of well-being. This stone abhors stagnation and pushes you forward into what you might be, at a pace you can accept. It is helpful for energy circulation within the body, particularly within less flexible components, decrystallizing blockages. Aligning and energizing the whole chakra system, this stone can stimulate the third eye when it has been forcibly closed in previous lives. Opening a new sense of vision, this stone transports you into a quiet space of inner contemplation and soul *knowing*.

Blue Herkimer with Boulangerite (natural formation)

QUARTZ: **AMPHIBOLE QUARTZ**

ALSO KNOWN AS ANGEL PHANTOM QUARTZ

Natural point

COLOR	Clear with white, yellow, red and peach inclusions
APPEARANCE	Phantoms, layers and 'wings' within clear or opaque Quartz
RARITY	Rare
SOURCE	Brazil

ATTRIBUTES Also known as Angel Phantom because of the inner wings and angelic vibration, Amphibole Quartz provides a connection to the highest level of spiritual experience, calling in your guardian angel and higher beings and bringing deep inner joy. It has an extremely gentle and calming energy.

Spiritually, placing Amphibole Quartz on the crown chakra activates all the higher crown chakras, opening a ladder up which awareness ascends to connect with your Higher Self* and, moving further up the vibrational scale, to attain the highest guidance.

Using this stone for introspection and insight, especially placed on the third eye, attunes to the wisdom of the universal mind, allowing a more detached perspective on life and on evolution. Gazing into its depths, you go to a space of deep universal love and are assisted in always acting from a place of love.

The phantoms and inclusions* within Amphibole Quartz can include red Hematite, a deeply stable stone that protects, grounds and dissolves negativity; white Kaolinite, which opens the inner ear; and yellow-peach Limonite, which stimulates and guards against psychic attack* or mental influence, making this stone a useful companion for spiritual journeying*. Phantoms symbolize the numerous lifetimes of the soul and take you traveling through multi-dimensions. They break up old patterns and assist in reconnecting to ancient wisdom held in your soul memory.

Environmentally, it has been suggested that Amphibole is the perfect workplace stone as it subtly shifts the energies to the highest possible and brings about cooperation and harmony. Triangulating three Amphiboles provides a perfect meditation or creative space.

HEALING Works best at the non-physical level of being.

POSITION Hold, grid (see pages 28–31) or place as appropriate.

(*See also* Phantom Quartz, pages 275–279; Limonite, pages 182–183.)

QUARTZ: **BLUE QUARTZ**

Tumbled

Natural crystals on matrix

COLOR	Blue
APPEARANCE	Clear blue Quartz or patches or threads included in Quartz
RARITY	Natural is rare
SOURCE	Worldwide

ATTRIBUTES Placed at the throat chakra, Blue Quartz reaches out to others and is of great assistance in understanding your spiritual nature.

Spiritually, this tranquil stone facilitates passing through a metamorphosis. Mentally, Blue Quartz reverses disorganization as it instills mental clarity and self-discipline. Calming the mind, it assuages fear, inspires hope and fires creativity.

HEALING Supports the throat, immune system, spleen, endocrine system and organs in the upper body; assists detoxification and depression, calming overstimulation. If rutilated, it is said to restrain premature ejaculation.

POSITION Hold, grid (see pages 28–31) or place as appropriate.

(*See also* Dumortierite, pages 121–122; Rutile, pages 318–319; Indicolite Quartz, below.)

ADDITIONAL FORMS
Indicolite Quartz (Blue Tourmaline included Quartz) has blue threads within a clear or cloudy white point and is a useful stone for stimulating out-of-body experiences and journeying*.

Spiritually, Indicolite Quartz transports you through high vibrations* and offers an overview of your lives, giving insight into the soul plan* for the present life. Psychologically, if you have been using revenge as an escape from past pain or attack as a defence against the possibility of being hurt, or are caught in similar destructive patterns, Indicolite Quartz frees you up to offer forgiveness and tenderness both to yourself and others.

Indicolite Quartz (natural point)

Emotionally, Indicolite Quartz releases blocked feelings and enables speaking about them. It ameliorates sadness, offering comfort and insight into the deeper causes and consequences of grief and loss. This beautiful stone teaches that no one ever mourns alone. It accesses a multitude of spirit guides and helpers who gather close to assist a soul who is dying, or one who will be left behind, through a difficult transition. It also reminds you that, while the body may die, love does not.

Indicolite Quartz also teaches that death occurs at the right time for the soul, no matter how inopportune it may appear. It says that the soul has learned its lessons or the karma of grace* has come into operation, gifts have been developed and the soul has headed home. And the stone is there to comfort those left behind.

Ideal for healers, this stone prevents negativity from sticking and assists in locating the site of dis-ease*—the crystal 'jumps' when it reaches the point of greatest disharmony. Place Indicolite Quartz anywhere there is dis-ease or congestion. Indicolite Quartz is beneficial for a chronic sore throat, cellular memory*, the pulmonary and immune systems, the brain, fluid imbalances, the kidney, bladder, thymus and thyroid, sinusitis, bacterial infections, the throat, larynx, lungs, oesophagus and eyes; also for soothing burns and overcoming insomnia and night sweats.

Blue Quartz with Lazulite has a profound and pure energy that brings about cosmic alignment and attunes to the bliss of the infinity of being. A useful stone for meditation and metaphysical gifts*, it creates an anchor into the divine and stimulates recognition of your own divine being. This stone is useful if you wish to know underlying causes of control freakery or addiction, bringing about in-depth healing of past or present life causes and creating unshakeable self-confidence. (*See also* Lazulite, page 173.)

Blue Quartz with Lazulite (raw)

QUARTZ: **BRANDENBERG**

Natural point

COLOR	Clear, purple, smoky brown, yellow
APPEARANCE	Bright clear point with phantoms or bubbles included
RARITY	Becoming more available but rising in price
SOURCE	Namibia

ATTRIBUTES Brandenberg has an exceedingly high vibration*. A powerful stone for spiritual alchemy, it connects to the immensity of your spiritual being and All That Is*. Attuned to the white flame* of pure consciousness and emanating infinite compassion, this stone is perfect for deep soul healing and forgiveness work.

Spiritually an effective aid to work at all levels, rapidly linking to multi-dimensions, this stone assists in looking inward or climbing the vibrational ladder to other dimensions. Brandenberg attaches a cosmic anchor* deep in the earth and at the center of the galaxy, ensuring an inner-core energetic solidity no matter what changes occur. Facilitating an objective viewpoint, it is useful when traveling to dimensions of which you could not otherwise retain consciousness awareness. This stone instills brainwave combinations that enhance meditation, regression and healing.

Although a hugely versatile crystal as each one carries the resonance of clear, smoky and amethyst vibrations, more than any other stone Brandenbergs are person-specific and task-related. When you find your particular stone, you *know*, but you may need several, as one could be attuned to earth healing*, another to soul or karmic* healing and so on. There are Brandenbergs that do everything and they may be tiny or huge—size has no relevance, it is the resonance that counts. Call your Brandenberg to you in the spiritual dimension before seeking the physical stone.

This stone is a gatekeeper that protects against psychic attack* and alien invasion, and repels negative energy, calling in positive light. It holds a light when working in shadows or underworld, especially during soul- or child-parts retrieval* and facilitates purification and integration of those parts into your present self. Placed on the soma, soul star or stellar gateway chakras, Brandenberg attunes to your core spiritual identity, facilitating true self-reflection and consciousness activation. On the heart seed chakra, it assists travel to the between-life state* to ascertain your soul plan* for the current lifetime, identifying forks in the road where a conscious choice was needed. It shows how to return to your original soul plan if you have deviated and how to release outgrown soul imperatives*. On the past-life chakras, Brandenberg heals the imprints and effects of trauma in previous lives, no matter in what dimension those lives were lived. On the third eye, this stone removes blockages to spiritual or psychic sight and accesses guidance from the purest source.

Brandenberg works by restoring to its perfect energetic state the etheric blueprint* from which your physical body was formed by taking it back to the highest vibration and attuning to All That Is: the original, perfect blueprint before time began. The healing, often instantaneous and profound, filters into the mental, psychological, emotional and physical bodies, restoring balance on all those levels.

A Brandenberg clears the higher heart chakra and opens the throat so that spiritual truth is spoken with unconditional love and compassion. It quickly disconnects a previously made mystic marriage or any relationship that has resulted in intertwining at the higher chakras.

Physically, this stone accelerates convalescence and restores vitality by taking you into the most perfect energetic state possible.

HEALING A master healer that supports recovery from illness and depletion and restores vitality; helpful for concussion and immune deficiencies, chronic fatigue, limbic brain function and multi-dimensional cellular memory* healing. It ameliorates dental pain.

POSITION Place or hold as appropriate.

SPECIFIC COLORS
Smoky Amethyst Brandenberg visibly combines Amethyst and Smoky Quartz, either as phantoms or body color. It is the finest tool available for removing implants*, attachments*, spirit possession or mental influence. This is the stone *par excellence* for conscious transformation or transition, especially through death.

Smoky Amethyst (natural point reversed scepter)

Smoky Brandenberg is the perfect stone for earth healing, taking the earth grid back to its perfect blueprint, restoring the earth's chakra and meridian* systems, and sending the healing deep into the earth to restore the Earth Mother herself. This stone cleanses and re-attaches your cosmic

Smoky (natural point)

anchor. If you took on a dis-ease*, physical or psychiatric condition or traumatic circumstances for reasons of karma or soul growth—or for restitution—Smoky Brandenberg facilitates understanding the gifts you seek. It helps in facing the remainder of your current life with equanimity and joy, knowing that your situation is exactly right for spiritual evolution.

Amethyst Brandenberg is an excellent stone for any matters of the heart as it takes you into the transmutational violet flame of unconditional love and divinity at the center of the universe. Being bathed in this love brings about profound healing. Past-life heartbreak or imperatives toward soulmates are dissolved by an Amethyst Brandenberg, setting you free to call in your twinflame* in the present incarnation, whether as an inner marriage between your masculine and feminine qualities, or as an outer-world alliance that totally supports who you are in your fullness and spiritual being.

Amethyst (natural point)

'Citrine' Brandenberg is a rare and special crystal attuned to the golden flame of the illumined mind. It opens soul abundance and spiritual joy, teaching how to fully appreciate life as an enlightened and truly empowered soul incarnated on the earth.

Chlorite Brandenberg (green inclusions) is attuned to the viridian flame of spiritual heart purification and is a deep soul cleanser and etheric purifier, preparing the lightbody* for full embodiment.

'Citrine' (natural point)

QUARTZ: BUSHMAN RED CASCADE QUARTZ

Natural formation

COLOR	Orange-red on white
APPEARANCE	Small red crystals cascading down a larger point
RARITY	Rare, one site only
SOURCE	South Africa

ATTRIBUTES The color in Bushman Red Cascade Quartz comes from Limonite, which creates a powerful energetic charge attuned to the vermilion flame* of the spiritual will that draws on deep reserves of physical and emotional energy. If you feel depleted, physically or spiritually, this vigorous drusy stone quickly refreshes, taking you to a high energetic state, but needs to be used with caution as the energies may be too much to handle unless you are skilled in assimilating crystal energy. In those who are sensitive, it can bring on a manic episode—or inspire creativity—so use under the guidance of a qualified healer.

Psychologically, Bushman Quartz improves creativity. Mentally, this stone enhances intellectual skill and efficiency, instilling persistence and encouraging positive action; you can program Bushman Quartz (see page 358) to bring about a favorable legal outcome.

Emotionally, Bushman Quartz works well with Smoky Quartz to purify negative emotions and release ingrained behavioral patterns of lethargy or apathy. It awakens the personal will, aligns it to the Higher Self* and shows the way forward, acting as a spur to soul growth.

Physically, by stimulating the base and sacral chakras, Bushman Red Cascade invigorates and adds fecundity and zest to your life.

This stone works well in the south of the crystal medicine wheel (see pages 368–375) to bring about a rebirth and assist the soul in coming comfortably into incarnation with a fully functioning spiritualized will aligned to its soul plan*.

HEALING Supports vitality, vigor and blood flow; strengthens blood vessels and muscles.

POSITION Hold, grid (see pages 28–31) or place as appropriate.

(*See also* Drusy Quartz, pages 250–251; Orange River Quartz, pages 272–273.)

QUARTZ: CANDLE QUARTZ

White (natural point)

Red (natural point)

COLOR	White, gray, reddish brown, yellow
APPEARANCE	'Melted wax' down a core crystal
RARITY	Easily available
SOURCE	Madagascar, Brazil, worldwide

ATTRIBUTES A light-bringer for the planet and those assisting the earth to change vibration, Candle Quartz brings your guardian angel closer. Meditating with this stone highlights your soul purpose and focuses your life path toward service. Enhancing intuition, this is a scrying* stone for the planet or personal illumination. A stone of spiritual alchemy, a large Candle Quartz attracts abundance and is helpful when working in a group as it radiates love to and on behalf of the group, creating group harmony. It helps in putting ancient knowledge into practice, and brings totems and power allies closer. It belongs in the south of the medicine wheel (see pages 368–375), the place of the past, emotions and heart. Restoring trust and innocence, it brings healing to a hurt child within and assists incarnating more fully within an aura of unconditional love, heals the ancestral line* and karmic* inheritance.

Psychologically, Candle Quartz dissipates feelings of oppression and despair, creating tranquillity and confidence in an illumined mind that sees beyond the confines of everyday circumstances. Emotionally, it teaches that you are never truly alone, connecting to the core of divine love in your inner being. It helps in developing emotional independence and inter-dependence, showing when it is beneficial to rely on and share with a partner in a mutually supportive situation and when to stand alone. It assists your partner in not feeling isolated when you practice emotional autonomy and, if necessary, assists in leaving with loving grace a partnership that no longer serves.

Physically, this stone helps feeling good about your body and is useful if physical incarnation is difficult. It shows how the physical body is damaged by emotional or mental distress, and heals the heart.

HEALING Supports the conversion of carbohydrates and nutrients and insulin regulation. It clears headaches caused by a blocked third eye.

POSITION Grid (see pages 28–31), wear or place as appropriate.

SPECIFIC COLORS
'Smoky' Candle Quartz instills clarity and assists in looking within to find your truth. It is perfect for journeying* through death and rebirth and for cleansing energy.

Pink Candle Quartz is an efficient heart opener, activating the higher heart chakras and the compassionate heart.

Red Candle Quartz is sometimes called 'Celestial Quartz' (see page 242).

QUARTZ: **CATHEDRAL QUARTZ**

ALSO KNOWN AS LIGHTBRARY, THE ATLANTIS STONE

Smoky (natural formation)   *White (natural formation)*

COLOR	Clear, white, yellow, smoky-gray
APPEARANCE	Multi-terminated Quartz
RARITY	Easily obtained
SOURCE	Brazil

ATTRIBUTES Containing the Akashic Record* and the wisdom of ages, Cathedral Quartz is a 'light library' giving access to all that has occurred on earth and in the celestial realms, and holds the story of your soul's path throughout time and beyond. Perfect for linking to your Higher Self and facilitating spiritual evolution, it can be read to ascertain your plan for the current incarnation, soul purpose and imperatives*.

Spiritually, this stone gives an objective overview of lifetimes in all dimensions, showing why you have chosen the lessons and co-created the reality you now experience. Facilitating communication with guides and advisers, this stone clarifies karma* and dharma. The gift in the most

240

traumatic of experiences becomes visible when tuning into this stone and it provides support through crisis, challenge and spiritual revolution.

Mentally, Cathedral Quartz assists attunement to the universal mind and facilitates evolution of consciousness by raising thought to a higher vibration*, opening the illumined mind. It amplifies the effects of other crystals, and acts as a receptor and transmitter for group thought, raising it to a higher vibration. Physically, Cathedral Quartz is excellent for pain. A useful 'preventative', held at the first sign of invasion of the body by bacteria or viruses or over the site of a physical disturbance or emotional dis-ease*, it provides relief.

HEALING Offers rapid healing for minor conditions and acts as an anti-viral. It is excellent for pain relief.

POSITION Place over pain, grid around bed (see pages 28–31) or hold.

SPECIFIC COLORS
Smoky Cathedral Quartz provides deep soul cleansing and purification. It draws off negative energies and ingrained patterns, replacing them with light, illuminating how experiencing an opposite, apparently negative, condition or emotion assists in developing positive traits such as compassion, empathy and love for one's self.

Citrine Cathedral Quartz is useful when you have experienced emotional or physical lack, especially ingrained poverty consciousness* from several lives. It goes back to the problem's core, dissolves the underlying belief and replaces it with a positive outlook, fills you with light and love, and teaches how to express spiritual and physical abundance and joyfulness throughout your life and lives.

Citrine (natural formation)

QUARTZ: **CELESTIAL QUARTZ**

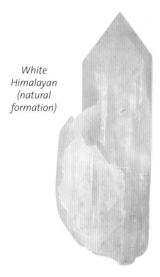

White Himalayan (natural formation)

White Madagascan Candle Quartz, otherwise known as Celestial Quartz (natural point)

COLOR	White, gray or red
APPEARANCE	Fissured and etched clear crystal, or tiny crystals or waxlike coating on a core point
RARITY	Rare
SOURCE	Madagascar, Himalayas

ATTRIBUTES Celestial Quartz is another stone over which confusion reigns. Some 'Celestial Quartz', which may be white, gray or red, is from Madagascar, also known as Candle Quartz, while another 'Celestial Quartz', found in the Himalayas, looks like Nirvana Quartz, but does not reach quite the same high vibration*. Each type holds a distinctly

242

different energy and has varied ways of facilitating energy shifts, but each frees up an adherence to the karmic* level of being, leading to awareness of the grace that, ultimately, when sufficient work has been done, sets the soul free and takes it into an experience of All That Is*. Both act as a 'reader' for the Akashic Record*, pinpointing the soul's purpose in incarnating. At that point, the celestial energies are brought into, experienced and expressed within the everyday physical world, bringing about profound earth healing*.

Madagascan Red or Smoky 'Celestial Quartz' has a more grounded energy than white and assists people who have only a toehold in incarnation to take up residence in the physical body, integrating it more firmly with the lightbody* and making earth a comfortable place. It contains information on how coming earth changes might manifest. A useful stone for earth and environmental healing, it realigns, repairs and re-energizes the earth's meridians* and kundalini* force. This stone works particularly well in the south of the crystal medicine wheel (see pages 368–375), assisting the soul to come into physical incarnation while maintaining full spiritual awareness. It is also extremely effective in grids* for earth healing or repair of the earth's meridian system.

HEALING Both types of Celestial Quartz work mainly beyond the physical level of being to heal the soul. Red 'Celestial Quartz' brings vitality into the body, restructuring cells, and Smoky Celestial detoxifies.

POSITION Hold or position as appropriate. Madagascan Celestial Quartz is particularly effective gridded (see pages 28–31) around a healing couch or to create a sacred space.

(*See also* Candle Quartz, pages 238–239.)

243

QUARTZ: **CHINESE CHROMIUM QUARTZ**

Heat-amended formation

COLOR	Green
APPEARANCE	Bubbly coating on points and 'tubes'
RARITY	Fairly easily obtained
SOURCE	Manufactured

ATTRIBUTES Chinese Chromium Quartz is created by superheating Quartz with Chromium so that it fuses on the surface. An insightful stone to meditate with to find out exactly what underlies a breakdown in the pancreas and reveal the psychosomatic causes of diabetes, it often indicates that the incarnating soul feels that the sweetness has gone out of life. Pinpointing the control mechanisms in which you have become stuck, Chinese Chromium Quartz gives clarity about what is needed to bring life back into balance and reconnect to joy, the crystal suggesting what would bring back that sweetness—and exactly how this will occur. In the meantime, Chinese Chromium Quartz provides understanding and companionship, teaching that all you need is within your self.

Emotionally, facilitating independence and centering in your heart, Chinese Chromium Quartz helps in realizing that no one else is required for, or provides, your happiness. That is up to you.

Physically, Chromium has traditionally been used to heal the pancreas and associated blood-sugar imbalances and conditions. In those who feel drawn to this stone, it regulates metabolism and stimulates the immune system. If you have mercury toxicity or other heavy-metal overload, Chinese Chromium Quartz works homeopathically to mobilize the metals out of your body.

HEALING Assists in heavy-metal toxicity, blood-sugar imbalances, diabetes, chronic fatigue, weight regulation and hormone deficiencies.

POSITION Hold, grid (see pages 28–31) or position as appropriate. Tape over the pancreas.

QUARTZ: **CHINESE RED QUARTZ**

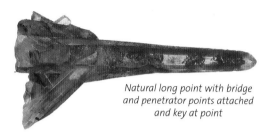

*Natural long point with bridge
and penetrator points attached
and key at point*

COLOR	Red
APPEARANCE	Coated or included Quartz point
RARITY	Easily obtained
SOURCE	China

ATTRIBUTES Naturally coated or included* Chinese Red Quartz
promotes healing and reconciliation at a personal, family or collective
level. Spiritually, this stone induces a feeling of being put through
purifying flames to burn away karma*, leaving the soul ready to start
anew. This stone fosters forgiveness and teaches that the apparent
mistakes of the past were learning situations that help humankind
grow in understanding and move forward in their evolution. It eases the
pain of racial conflict and encourages forgiveness for the perpetrators.
Chinese Red Quartz also points to the fact that, at a higher level,
race and religion are an illusion that is transcended in the oneness
and unity of spirit.

Psychologically, this stone assists in finding the gift in every situation, bringing clarity to the positive lessons within a life challenge and illuminating the soul plan* for the present lifetime. It shows how, by experiencing a lack of a particular quality in the outer environment, the soul creates that quality in the inner being. Combine Chinese Red Quartz with Tibetan Blackspot to reconcile differences and bring a profound inner peace.

Emotionally, Chinese Red Quartz is useful for overcoming profound despair and restoring life-force and vitality to the body. This stone induces perseverance and overcomes frustration, bringing in joy. By promoting self-forgiveness, Chinese Red Quartz ameliorates the physical manifestation of negative emotional states of inner rage, anger and festering resentment that lie behind arthritis and diseases of the auto-immune system, such as lupus, and provides the motivation to recover from ME.

Environmentally, Chinese Red Quartz is used by earth healers and stabilizes the planet, including the oceans and mountains. The stone is also helpful in business and in enhancing financial security.

Natural point

HEALING Supports oxygenation of the blood and organs of the body, enhances energy, eases swelling and inflammation in arthritis and auto-immune diseases. Recharges the base and sacral chakras.

POSITION Place as appropriate.

NOTE An artificial Chinese Red Quartz created from Hematite is also available, but the properties are weaker.

QUARTZ: **DREAM QUARTZ**

ALSO KNOWN AS EPIDOTE IN QUARTZ

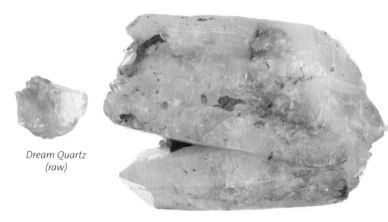

Dream Quartz
(raw)

Epidote inclusions in Quartz (raw)

COLOR	Green
APPEARANCE	Dark streaks or translucent stone
RARITY	Reasonably easily obtained
SOURCE	Columbia (Dream Quartz), Bulgaria, Austria, France, Russia, Norway, United States, South Africa (Epidote in Quartz)

ATTRIBUTES Epidote in Quartz appears in two forms: dark streaks on a matrix* or the light green Dream Quartz that has a more refined vibration. People tend to have strong reactions to this stone, loving it or intensely disliking it.

Spiritually, those who resonate with this stone find it extremely peaceful—a gateway to deep meditative states and inter-dimensional travel, conducive to insightful lucid dreaming, promoting dream recall, and a useful tool for dreaming up a new future. Placed on the soma or past-life chakras to activate past-life memories, Dream Quartz gives protection while journeying*, and cleanses and reframes traumatic experiences. The Epidote component is strongly protective.

Those who do not resonate with the stone may need to question why they have an aversion to it and exactly what is being stirred up—indicating perhaps a deeply entrenched attitude or limiting behavior pattern that needs transcending. It may also indicate that they are, for the moment, incapable of living out their dream, and pinpoint the changes needed before allowing themselves to dream once more.

Epidote crystals in Quartz (raw)

Psychologically an opener for the higher heart and mind, this hopeful stone rejuvenates and gives you the courage to break free from limiting patterns and bounce back after enormous setbacks, adding a new impetus to soul growth.

HEALING Helpful for bruises, sprains, pain and dissolving stones and crystallizations of joints or granulation in organs.

POSITION Hold, grid (see pages 28–31) or place as appropriate. Place under the pillow to induce lucid dreaming.

(*See also* Epidote, pages 125–126.)

QUARTZ: **DRUSY**

*Smoky and white
Drusy Quartz (raw)*

COLOR	White, orange, blue, brown, gray
APPEARANCE	Tiny crystals on a matrix
RARITY	Easily obtained
SOURCE	Worldwide

ATTRIBUTES Drusy Quartz carries the energy-enhancing qualities of Quartz but these, in most forms, are scaled down to a gentler vibration so that the core energy is more easily assimilated, especially if the Drusy Quartz is coating another crystal such as Danburite or Elestial Quartz. Red Drusy Quartz such as Bushman Cascade, however, has a highly energetic charge while Smoky Drusy Quartz gently detoxifies.

Spiritually teaching how to savor all the experiences of life, Drusy Quartz revitalizes and remotivates at the spiritual level of being and assists in releasing self-imposed limitations. It is the perfect stone for creating harmony and restoring equilibrium.

HEALING White Drusy Quartz is said to work well for periodontal disease; Orange Drusy Quartz revitalizes and overcomes lethargy.

POSITION Hold, grid (see pages 28–31) or place as appropriate.

(*See also* Drusy Danburite, page 115; Bushman Red Cascade Quartz, pages 236–237; Youngite, pages 351–352.)

SPECIFIC COLORS AND FORMS

Orange Drusy Quartz is ideal for the bed-ridden or those with chronic illness—and for carers. Facilitating offering and receiving help, it fosters harmony and encourages a show of thankfulness and appreciation on both sides. This form increases compassion and instills the ability to laugh at life in difficult circumstances. Kept in your pocket, Orange Drusy Quartz energizes your whole body. It cleanses, realigns and invigorates the base and sacral chakras and activates kundalini* flow.

Blue Drusy Quartz invokes spiritual protection and helps in nurturing yourself during the grief process, opening awareness of the spiritual companionship available if only you ask. It is the perfect stone for total immersion in the joy of being.

Drusy Quartz on Sphalerite is a powerful mental-energy cleanser that clears feelings of isolation or alienation, supports the nervous system and reduces environmental disease. Sphalerite discerns truth from deception, particularly in channeled* information and protects those in the public eye. Alleviating homesickness, it is a perfect anchor for those for whom the earth is not their natural home and assists in realigning to a differently gendered physical body from that of previous lives, rebalancing male-female energies.

Drusy Quartz on Sphalerite (natural formation)

QUARTZ: ELESTIAL QUARTZ

*White
(natural
formation)*

COLOR	Clear, smoky, amethyst, pink, yellow
APPEARANCE	Multi-terminated, enfolded and layered crystal often with internal windows and phantoms
RARITY	Easily obtained
SOURCE	Brazil, worldwide

ATTRIBUTES Elestial Quartz sets you on your soul's path. Spiritually, it links to the divine and higher planes and opens metaphysical gifts*. An extremely high-vibration* stone for spiritual evolution, it opens the soul star and higher crown chakras, bringing down a flow of divine energy through the chakras. Perfect for creating and holding a sacred space in which to live, work and love, each color has specific properties. It takes you into other lives to understand your karma* or deep into your self to understand the evolutionary processes. Instilling trust in the universe, it facilitates powerful karmic release, bringing about core soul healing.

Psychologically a stone of change and transformation, it works as an emotional catalyst. Dissolving confusion, blockages and fear, it opens the way to necessary change, which may happen abruptly and unexpectedly. Physically, it is useful for balancing polarities and restructuring.

HEALING Aids multi-dimensional cellular healing, regeneration; rebuilds etheric blueprint*, restoring brain cells after drug or alcohol abuse.

POSITION Hold or grid (see pages 28–31) as appropriate.

ADDITIONAL COLORS AND FORMS

Smoky Elestial Quartz is an outstanding purifier and detoxifier, pulling negative energy out of the environment or the self and replacing it with protective, vibrant light. An exceptional earth healer*, this stone transmits energies along the earth's meridians* to cleanse and revitalize the power points of the planet. Protecting against geopathic stress* or psychic invasion, Smoky Elestial Quartz is particularly efficient for gridding* to create safe space. Alternatively, hold Smoky Elestial over your dantien* and picture the energy enfolding the space and the individual or group within it.

Karmically, Smoky Elestial draws past life trauma or dis-ease* out of your present-life physical body, reframes* it, heals the etheric blueprint and the subtle energy bodies* and assists the soul in understanding the gift in the experience. Cleansing and healing the ancestral line* of trauma and emotional pain, Smoky Elestial provides multi-dimensional cellular memory* healing. This intense stone takes you back into past lives to reclaim power, purify negative karma and be released from anyone who has enslaved you in their power, no matter when that may have been. Emotionally, it releases karmic enmeshment* and dissolves magical rituals that no longer serve.

Physically, this stone resets the body after severe pain and facilitates multi-dimensional cellular healing. Smoky Elestial resonates with the earth and base chakras and bridges all chakras up to the soul star, enhancing energy flow along the chakra line. Grid or hold Smoky Elestial to heal the earth, prevent nightmares, relieve depression, improve concentration and guard against the effects of X-rays or radiotherapy. Hold over the site of pain.

Smoky (natural formation)

White Elestial Quartz opens the stellar gateway chakra and is attuned to the white flame* of pure consciousness. It is an exceptional elevator and integrator of vibrational energies, bringing the spiritual into the physical dimension. It purifies earth energies, brings ley lines into balance and is an excellent gridding stone for creating sacred space.

Amethyst (natural formation)

Amethyst Elestial Quartz opens all higher crown chakras. Attuned to the transmutational violet flame, this extremely powerful healing stone stimulates the pineal gland and opens a connection to spiritual guides and helpers and stellar beings. Dispersing negative energy, it provides reassurance and calm. Assisting multi-dimensional cellular healing and brain integration, it ameliorates the effects of drugs or alcohol, releasing addictive patterns and soul imperatives*. Smoky Amethyst Elestial Quartz is extremely useful in spirit-release work or death-midwifery. It is particularly effective when gridded around the room in which the work is done.

Smoky Amethyst (natural formation)

Rose Elestial Quartz is an exceptional heart healer attuned to the pink flame of unconditional and compassionate love. It releases the effects of karmic heartbreak, removes emotional burdens and sets you free to love again. Taking you into the universal heart, it helps in remembering that everything is love. In this place there is no karma, no karmic debt, no soul imperatives, no guilt or imbalances. Combined with Smoky Elestial, it grounds universal love and elevates consciousness. It heals abandonment and rejection, and teaches that you are always in relationship with the divine within.

Rose (natural formation)

QUARTZ: **FADEN QUARTZ**

Natural formation

COLOR	White
APPEARANCE	Clear flat crystal with distinctive thread-like line
RARITY	Easily available
SOURCE	Worldwide

ATTRIBUTES Faden Quartz has fractured during its growth and healed again—forming a visible line—and this crystal unifies the self, too, encouraging fragmented soul parts* to reintegrate. Symbolizing the silver cord* tethering the etheric body* to the physical during out-of-body experiences, this stone provides protection during journeying*. Placed on the soma chakra, Faden Quartz reels the soul back to the body and can activate the upper portion of a cosmic anchor*.

Spiritually, Faden Quartz provides a link to the Higher Self*. Helpful during past-life regression and for entering the between-life state*, it provides an overview of soul lessons and root causes of dis-ease*.

Psychologically, if you are undergoing intense internal trauma, Faden Quartz gives you the strength to carry on.

Emotionally, Faden Quartz helps to heal broken trust in relationships and teaches how to have both emotional autonomy and be intimate with another person. Uniting personal love with the divine, it encourages loving yourself from within your own heart. Inducing emotional stability and harmonizing extremes, this stone calms the emotional body when placed on the solar plexus.

By bridging gaps, this crystal harmonizes the energies of a group or family, particularly if the intention is to overcome conflict or heal a break. Promoting communication during the healing process when working at a distance, Faden Quartz connects healer and patient. It enhances self-healing and personal growth, purifies the biomagnetic sheath* and harmonizes chakra energy flow, opening all, but especially the crown and past-life, chakras.

Environmentally, Faden Quartz efficiently grids* areas of unstable earth or physical energy to regain equilibrium.

HEALING Supports the healing of breaks and fractures, cysts and encrustations, and back pain. Bringing stability at all levels, it assists cellular memory* and inner alignment.

POSITION Grid (see pages 28–31) or place as appropriate.

QUARTZ: **FAIRY QUARTZ**

White (natural formation)

COLOR	White or grayish
APPEARANCE	Long opaque point with tiny crystals forming raised lines
RARITY	Fairly easily obtained
SOURCE	South Africa, Mexico

ATTRIBUTES Fairy Quartz links to the faery kingdom, and to planetary and earth devas*. Spiritually, it assists in unraveling family myths and ancestral or cultural stories in which you are locked, reframing* them where appropriate. Fairy Quartz draws out emotional or physical dis-ease*, removes emotional pain and introduces healing energy into the body, especially that of a child. It harmonizes the home environment and quietens children after nightmares. This stone is perfect for programming (see page 358) to support your creative inner child*.

HEALING Detoxifies tissues, draws off pain, stabilizes vertigo.

POSITION Place, hold or grid (see pages 28–31) as appropriate or use as a wand.

(*See also* Spirit Quartz, pages 300–303, and Fairy Wand Quartz, page 311.)

QUARTZ: **FENSTER QUARTZ**

ALSO KNOWN AS WINDOW QUARTZ

Natural formation

COLOR	Clear white
APPEARANCE	Windows within a Quartz crystal
RARITY	Easily obtained
SOURCE	Worldwide

ATTRIBUTES Fenster Quartz is an efficient tool for transmitting healing light and for high-vibration*, multi-dimensional energy work. The internal windows of this stone open on to another world, stimulating clairvoyance* and inner-sight.

Spiritually, Fenster Quartz throws light on the workings of your soul and its history. Ask to be taken to the dimension where your soul knowledge is stored to reveal the purpose you had when first incarnated. Wait quietly for the knowledge to make itself known and ask how it is to be used in your present incarnation. Check out whether you have any soul imperatives* overlaid on your original purpose; if so, allow them to dissolve.

Psychologically, Fenster Quartz helps in healing dysfunctional patterns and letting go of outgrown emotions. Karmically*, throwing light on past-life or childhood causes of addiction, it assists in removing them, letting go the desperate desire for more that lies behind obsessions and compulsions of all kinds. Particularly helpful for examining the mental and emotional constructs underlying obsessive-compulsive disorders, Fenster Quartz breaks the cycle of co-dependency that occurs within addictions. It help carers or enablers realize that they can neither 'do it for' the addict, nor control an addict's behavior.

Physically, Fenster Quartz reprograms cellular memory* and assists the body to find its optimum functioning. It is helpful for any kind of muscular twitch.

HEALING Beneficial for the eyes and overcoming addictions, eating disorders, obsessive-compulsive disorder, tics and Tourette Syndrome.

POSITION Place or grid (see pages 28–31) as appropriate.

QUARTZ: **ICE QUARTZ**

ALSO KNOWN AS GLACIAL ETCHED QUARTZ

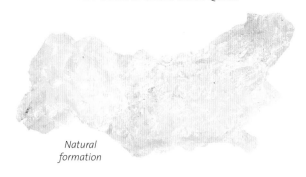

*Natural
formation*

COLOR	White
APPEARANCE	Pure white crystal that is fissured and etched
RARITY	Rare
SOURCE	Pakistan

ATTRIBUTES Ice Quartz, often labeled Glacial Etched Quartz, looks and feels similar to Nirvana Quartz but is less intense. It resonates with the energy of the recently discovered celestial body Sedna and the Inuit myth of the goddess who, after being thrown out of a kayak by her creator-god father, had charge of the creatures of the sea.

Spiritually, this gentle stone is a useful intermediary when the energy of Nirvana Quartz is too overpowering for the level of awareness so far attained. Attuning to it quietly shifts barriers, opens consciousness and gives a glimpse of exciting possibilities but does not overwhelm, giving you time to adjust and unfold at your own pace. An expert on right timing, Ice Quartz is a useful stone to hold if you wish to know why

260

something has not come to fruition. It shows the gift in patient waiting. Holding Ice Quartz takes you into profound stillness, aligning to the inner divine and the immensity of being. When the time is right, you become aware of the call to be all that you are—and of the means to make the journey.

A karmic* emotional healer that assists in releasing victim mentality or victimization and anything from past lives that is emotionally entangling, Ice Quartz helps in stepping off the karmic treadmill of relationships. Emotionally, it unblocks frozen feelings and shows how to let go. This stone teaches emotional independence and autonomy, bringing about the realization that you alone are responsible for creating and maintaining your sense of well-being and happiness, and releasing dependence on any external source, including a partner or loved one. Ice Quartz also shows that aloneness is not loneliness and that there is value in solitariness and isolation, opening the way to finding solace in being with your Self.

Psychologically, Ice Quartz helps in letting go of control mechanisms that have historically made you feel safe from hurt. Encouraging a release of the need to do it your way, this stone opens you to a new relatedness to yourself, others and the world, and introduces the world of conscious choices.

HEALING Works beyond the physical level of being to heal the soul, but is helpful for frozen shoulder and arthritis.

POSITION Hold or grid (see pages 28–31) to create a sacred space.

NOTE Combine Ice Quartz with Nirvana Quartz (see pages 270–271) at the soul star and higher crown chakras to step high-vibration* energy down for gentle assimilation.

QUARTZ: **KUNDALINI QUARTZ**

Natural point

COLOR	Greenish or brownish-yellow
APPEARANCE	Clear points around larger point
RARITY	Becoming more easily obtainable
SOURCE	Congo

ATTRIBUTES A natural citrine, Kundalini Quartz raises the kundalini* energy up the spine from the base chakra to the crown, cleansing all chakras as it passes through and opening higher chakras to the soul star and beyond. Held over the head, it creates a cosmic orgasm that takes you into the heart of creation to become a co-creator, an experience which it then grounds into functional reality. The perfect crystal for tantric sex, Kundalini Quartz draws abundance and creates passion on all levels.

HEALING Unblocks the reproductive system and increases libido.

POSITION Grid (see pages 28–31), place at the earth, base and soul star chakras or hold over the head.

262

QUARTZ: **LEMURIAN SEED**

*Clear (natural long point,
self-healed in center)*

COLOR	Clear, smoky, pink, tangerine, yellow, blue
APPEARANCE	Long point, deeply etched horizontal striations on alternate faces, often frosted.
RARITY	Rare
SOURCE	Brazil, Russia, Tibet, Arkansas (United States), Zambia

ATTRIBUTES Perfect tools for lightworkers*, Lemurians hold a blessing of unconditional love for the earth as we enter a profound vibrational shift. They remind lightworkers to attend to their evolution as well as facilitating that of others. Ascended like a ladder, accessing inner- and multi-dimensional states, they teach that we are many-dimensioned beings and give an objective view of prior lifetimes. Piercing illusions of separateness in physical incarnation, they remind that healing is re-membering our spiritual selves and time is an illusion of physical incarnation, showing how to move beyond into All That Is*.

Ideal to grid* for angelic contact, Lemurians open a stargate, anchoring ancient wisdom into the present. Reawakening to spiritual training and healing abilities, they consciously reconnect past knowledge. In past-life therapy, accessing before dis-ease* or destructive emotional patterns set in, they facilitate recovery of inner perfection. Excellent for chakra balancing and clearing, Lemurian wands remove karmic* debris and soul imperatives*. Activating higher resonances* of each chakra and integrating with the lightbody*, Lemurians facilitate deep communication between physical and subtle levels of being, grounding vibrational shifts into the physical.

Mentally, Lemurians teach that thoughts are creative and take on form and, harnessed to right intent and self-belief, manifest full potential. To re-enter a significant dream or to obtain clarity and insight and for conscious dreaming or dreaming up a new reality, sleep with one under your pillow.

In a medicine wheel (see pages 368–375) or gridded (see pages 28–31), especially when activated with Elestial Quartz, Lemurians open a multi-dimensional healing space and powerful energy portal taking in past, present and future, through which any part of soul evolution can be accessed and transformed. Use Lemurians with Smoky Elestials to anchor high-vibration* energy and activate a cosmic anchor* for the lightbody. Combines well with Hanksite to cleanse and purify Lemurian negative energies (may be cathartic), transforming into positive memories.

HEALING Like a laser, Lemurians cut out the dis-eased or outworn, opening new energy channels in the subtle and physical bodies.

POSITION Hold or place as appropriate.

SPECIFIC COLORS

'Smoky' Lemurian is an efficient karmic cleanser, freeing from the past and assisting understanding exactly how misuses of power in previous lives—as victim or perpetrator—created a karmic net that held you in a

'Smoky'
(tabby point)

'Pink',
(natural point)

'Citrine'
(natural point)

dense vibration. Teaching wise use of power, this stone creates an empowered soul able to operate multi-dimensionally with full awareness and shows that by courageously embracing darkness and facing our shadow*, we appreciate light.

'Citrine' Lemurian brings spiritual abundance, accessing gifts and skills from the past in any dimension to work in your present environment. Attuned to the golden flame* of the illumined mind, it shows how to rebalance the earth's grid to facilitate shifting into an abundant earth.

'Tangerine Dream' Lemurian rectifies karmic and soul imbalances and amends the etheric blueprint* to accommodate the higher vibrational needs of the lightbody. This Lemurian has an accelerated energy pattern that offers profound change and activates soul-based creativity.

'Tangerine Dream' (natural point)

'Pink' Lemurian is strongly heart-centered, attuned to the pink flame of unconditional, compassionate love, removing emotional and karmic debris from the heart chakra and emotional body, taking it to a purer vibrational state and bringing in universal love. It removes emotional ties and dissolves misused or abused heart-energy imprints from Lemuria or Atlantis, facilitating emotional independence in your present life. It activates the lightbody heart chakra.

'Blue' Lemurian offers an overview of lives and why you incarnated again. Stimulating journeys* through multi-dimensions to insight needed for the service you offer, Blue Lemurian is ideal for healers, as negativity does not stick. It assists diagnosis and locating the site of dis-ease, 'jumping' at the point of greatest disharmony, which it dissolves and infuses with light.

'Blue' (natural point)

QUARTZ WITH LEPIDOLITE MICA

Natural soulmate formation

COLOR	White and silvery
APPEARANCE	Delicate flakes within Quartz
RARITY	Fairly easily obtained
SOURCE	Worldwide

ATTRIBUTES This shamanic combination heightens intuition and the ability to act on this in a practical manner. Deepening unconditional love, it distinguishes between true spirituality and delusions, illusions and wishful thinking. Heightening energetic responses to acupuncture and acupressure, Quartz with Mica identifies and seals energy leakage and transmutes negative energy in the chakras or biomagnetic sheath*. It teaches how to manifest what you most desire.

HEALING Helpful for eating disorders, motor skills and macular degeneration.

POSITION Hold, place or grid (see pages 28–31) as appropriate.

(*See also* Shaman Quartz, pages 287–288.)

QUARTZ: **LILAC QUARTZ**

Raw

COLOR	Lilac
APPEARANCE	Opaque to clear Quartz
RARITY	Rare
SOURCE	South Africa

ATTRIBUTES A higher resonance* of Rose Quartz, Lilac Quartz stimulates metaphysical gifts* and facilitates inter-dimensional travel, taking meditation to a new high.

Spiritually, this stone of self re-membering and heightened self-awareness enables recalling all dimensions of consciousness, integrating the vast spectrum of your spiritual self. Resonating with the heart to higher crown chakras, Lilac Quartz brings about profound emotional and multi-dimensional healing.

HEALING Beneficial for brain-frequency disharmonies and cellular regeneration.

POSITION Hold, grid (see pages 28–31) or place as appropriate.

QUARTZ: **MORION QUARTZ**

Natural formation

COLOR	Black with white encrustations
APPEARANCE	Quartz point covered with encrustations
RARITY	Medium
SOURCE	Russia, Spain, South Africa, Switzerland, China, Romania, France, Kazakhstan, Himalayas

ATTRIBUTES Morion Quartz is a naturally irradiated (but not radioactive) dark Quartz often covered with encrustations of Dolomite, Pyrite or Feldspar with efficient shielding properties, especially when used in traveling or lucid dreaming. Spiritually, by enhancing psychic vision, it reconciles dualities, bringing together yin and yang, masculine and feminine, earth and sky and taking you into a place of non-duality. As a wand, Morion pulls negative and stagnant energy out of the body, the encrustations re-energizing according to their properties: Pyrite creates an energetic shield and the psychological motivation to move forward and Dolomite assures the soul that it is safe in incarnation.

Psychologically, Morion overcomes the effects of stress and helps in exploring your shadow energies* and finding their gift, imparting the courage to overcome obstacles and to find trust once again, and supporting self-esteem and inner confidence. A peaceful and grounding* stone, Morion is a gentle healer for damaged emotions or heartbreak, enfolding you in a feeling of safety and calm that enables walking your path with equanimity. Physically, Morion promotes self-healing and detoxification. Environmentally, this stone is a powerful earth healer with a strong connection to Mother Earth. Morion is an energetic detoxifier for areas of natural radiation or nuclear power stations, spent-fuel dumping grounds, electromagnetic smog* and radon gas. It is helpful where sea or river water has become polluted with radiation and neutralizes sick building syndrome.

HEALING Supports radiation therapy and removes toxicity; beneficial for osteoporosis, broken bones, teeth, back, hip and leg pain, and for circulation, digestion and metabolism.

POSITION Hold or place as appropriate. Place under the pillow for lucid dreams. Grid (see pages 28–31) as appropriate and cleanse regularly.

ADDITIONAL FORM
White Morion is a rare formation of white Quartz covered with Calcite and Pyrite encrustations. This high-vibration* stone brings about spiritual alchemy. It invites the presence of angelic beings and higher helpers into your life, provides profound guidance and clarity, and assists in re-membering your soul. A pair of black and white Morions brings about perfect energetic balance and creates an exceedingly high-vibration meditation or healing space.

White Morion (natural formation)

QUARTZ: **NIRVANA QUARTZ**

ALSO KNOWN AS HIMALAYAN GROWTH INTERFERENCE

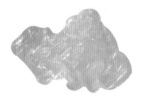

White (natural
formation)

Pink (natural
formation)

COLOR	White, pink, lilac-purple
APPEARANCE	Crevassed, jagged, multi-faced clear crystal resembling ice
RARITY	Rare
SOURCE	Himalayas

ATTRIBUTES A powerful spiritual-alchemy crystal, Nirvana Quartz is an exceedingly high-vibration* stone attuned to the white flame* of pure consciousness that facilitates spiritual illumination, opens the soul star chakra and grounds those energies into the earth. Amplifying the flow of ascension* and spiritual energy into the physical and subtle bodies*, Nirvana Quartz integrates the lightbody*.

Spiritually, this stone facilitates a shift into the enlightenment of inner Nirvana—bliss states of pure illumined mind combined with unconditional love of all that exists, experienced within the human body. Standing at the interface of consciousness and matter, mind and body, spirit and soul, past and future, human and divine, Nirvana Quartz feels like crystallized divine consciousness. It holds a wisdom that

270

brings about a profound shift in awareness and a rapid acceleration into accepting your spiritual destiny as a universal being. It removes any barriers to spiritual or psychological growth and awakens undreamed of and unformed potential, although it may provoke an acute healing crisis* that requires other stones as the soul sheds its karma*, soul imperatives* and deepest illusions to attune to its true purpose and realize its awesome possibilities. Teaching that we truly create our reality, this stone vastly expands our vision of what that reality could be.

Nirvana Quartz creates a bridge to channel energy through an intermediary between a healer and a third person unknown to the healer. Particularly useful for spirit-release work where a friend or relative acts as the intermediary, it reminds that spirit attachment is one situation where informed consent is not mandatory as the soul rarely chose to allow the entity* to attach. Additional stones may be needed to seal the biomagnetic sheath* against re-invasion.

HEALING Works beyond the physical level of being to open the enlightened mind.

POSITION Hold or position as appropriate, especially on the soul star chakra. Combine with Ice Quartz in grids (see pages 28–31).

SPECIFIC COLORS
Pink Nirvana Quartz is attuned to the divine feminine and goddess energy, opening the higher heart chakra to an influx of divine love and reminding you that all is love.

White or Purple Nirvana Quartz is attuned to the divine masculine and assists in integrating your inner male and female to move beyond gender into pure spirit.

Purple (natural formation)

271

QUARTZ: **ORANGE RIVER QUARTZ**

Twinflame or soulmate

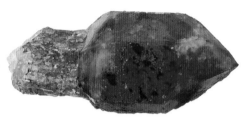

Scepter

COLOR	Orange, red and brown
APPEARANCE	Colored inclusions or patches in or on Quartz
RARITY	Rare, one site only
SOURCE	South Africa

ATTRIBUTES Laid down in clearly defined layers incorporating Hematite, this highly energetic stone revitalizes all levels of being and is attuned to the vermilion flame* of the spiritual will. Adding zest to life at every level, Orange River Quartz draws the creative life force from the earth up into the earth chakra and takes it up the chakra line, activating the creativity of the base and sacral, to the crown and soul star. It is excellent for recharging the base and sacral chakras.

Spiritually, if you have lost your soul purpose or motivation, this stone realigns with your Higher Self* and helps in accepting the life path you have laid down for yourself.

Psychologically, if you have lost your capacity for enjoyment, Orange River Quartz restores it to the full, opening you both to give and receive pure pleasure.

One formation shown opposite is a scepter*, a tool for multi-dimensional healing, conferring power and spiritual authority. It aids regaining and owning spiritual power, but any Orange River Quartz assists in overcoming karmic* misuse or abuse of power, experienced as perpetrator or victim. Helping in reconnecting to your personal will and aligning that to the guiding will of the Higher Self, if you gave away your power in the present or any other life, this stone assists in reclaiming it and using it wisely and well in the service of your soul.

The other formation is a tantric twin* which, if you are emotionally prepared, calls in your twinflame*, creating a mutually supportive, unconditionally loving relationship and allows the memory of painful past relationships to fall away, re-energizing your emotional life. It may also call a soulmate to continue lessons or unfinished business.

Physically, this stone is an efficient healer, realigning the meridians* of the body and encouraging energy flow in the organs via purified and re-energized blood.

HEALING Supports the blood, liver and spleen, regulates blood flow, increases the strength of red corpuscles and stimulates the immune system and reproductive organs.

POSITION Hold, grid (see pages 28–31) or place as appropriate.

(*See also* Bushman Red Cascade Quartz, pages 236–237.)

QUARTZ: **OURO VERDE QUARTZ**

Raw

COLOR	Olive to yellow-green
APPEARANCE	Slightly oily or cracked olive-green Quartz
RARITY	Easily obtained (artificially enhanced with gamma rays)
SOURCE	Brazil

ATTRIBUTES With strong energy that never requires cleansing or recharging, Ouro Verde Quartz gives powerful protection. Spiritually, by showing you the deeper meaning of life, this stone facilitates the viewing of potential future events with wisdom from the past, which leads to more constructive choices. Psychologically, it strengthens the character and assists in manifesting your full potential. Ouro Verde detects psychological, environmental and emotional triggers for illness.

HEALING Assists the healing of tumors, herpes and allergies; beneficial for peripheral circulation, Raynaud's disease, anaphylactic shock; protects against radioactivity and radon gas. If you have an adverse reaction, replace with natural Smoky Quartz.

POSITION Hold, grid (see pages 28–31) or place as appropriate.

QUARTZ: **PHANTOM QUARTZ**

*Natural double-
terminated point*

COLOR	See below
APPEARANCE	Ghostly or solid triangles within clear Quartz
RARITY	Most Phantoms easily obtained
SOURCE	Worldwide

ATTRIBUTES Symbolizing the many lifetimes of the soul, a Phantom facilitates broader spiritual awareness and assists with transitions. Taking you traveling through multi- or inner-dimensions*, it strips away the layers to reveal your spiritual core. Karmically*, Phantom Quartz assists in accessing the Akashic Record*, recovering repressed memories and reframing* or renegotiating past contracts, facilitating visits to the between-lives state* to discover your current soul plan* and to release outdated soul imperatives*. Smoothing transitions of all kinds, it shows what your next step could be.

Psychologically, a Phantom reconciles your shadow* and reveals the gifts it holds. Physically, this stone activates healing ability and facilitates healing the physical body through amendments to the etheric blueprint*. Environmentally, it stimulates healing for the planet, realigning detrimental landscape patterns.

HEALING See individual colors, below.

POSITION Hold, grid (see pages 28–31) or place as appropriate.

SPECIFIC COLORS

White Phantom speeds the transmission of light and information between higher realms and the earth, opening the recipient to receive healing across huge distances and unbounded time. This stone can perform etheric surgery and remove impacted layers of karma, opening the way for multi-dimensional cellular memory* healing to occur and the karma of grace* to operate. Particularly useful for contacting guides and stimulating clairaudience*, it enhances meditation, releases ingrained patterns and is beneficial for hearing disorders.

White (natural point)

Amethyst Phantom facilitates accessing the pre-birth state* and the plan for your present lifetime, assisting evaluation of the progress made with soul lessons for your current incarnation. This stone brings about multi-dimensional cellular healing and is particularly useful for understanding the dis-eases* that lie behind psychiatric illnesses.

Amethyst (natural point)

Green Phantom acts on the earth, base, solar plexus, heart and third eye chakras to keep you grounded and protected, creating a psychic shield. Chlorite-included Green Phantom rapidly absorbs negative energy and toxins and clears a build-up of negative energy anywhere in the body or environment. This stone assists with the removal of energy implants, accessing their source in this or any other life (use under the guidance of an experienced therapist). A large Chlorite Phantom placed point down in the lavatory cistern energetically cleanses the house. Green Phantom ameliorates panic attacks, stabilizes bi-polar disorder and helps with self-realization. Some Green Phantoms formed from

Green (natural point)

other minerals create a powerful healer that accelerates recovery. Green Phantom facilitates angelic contact and clarifying clairaudient communication. It alleviates despair and helps you feel supported.

Yellow Phantom is an intellectually-attuned stone that assists the mind in recalling and reorganizing memories and thought patterns, acting as a link to the higher mind. The inclusion* is Limonite, a stone that stimulates intellectual activities of all kinds. This phantom removes mental attachments or influences* from this life or any other. It unites the third eye, crown, past-life and solar plexus chakras to bring insights into the emotional and psychological effects of previous experiences and the reason why the soul chose to undergo these.

Yellow (natural point)

Orange Phantom, Carnelian included, strongly energizes and rejuvenates, activating and harmonizing the solar plexus, third eye, heart and sacral chakras to enhance creativity. Orange Phantom is helpful in overcoming an addictive personality, ending the constant search for even more and focusing on recovery. The paler-colored Phantom enables journeying* to contact your Higher Self* and to access who you truly are. Once you have reconnected to this vital sense of Self, your insights can be put into practice in everyday life.

Orange (natural point)

Reversed Orange Phantom forms when Carnelian fuses around Quartz and offers insight into one's inner workings and the true meaning of life. Carry this stone for long-term sustenance and vitality. Pinpointing the site and subtle cause of dis-ease, Reverse Orange Phantom enables taking control of your life.

Reversed Orange (natural point)

Red Phantom is an inclusion of Limonite, Hematite and/or Kaolinite. Useful for healing breaks in the biomagnetic sheath and removing

energy implants, this Phantom re-energizes the lower chakras and synthesizes these with the solar plexus to release emotional pain or past-life trauma and heal emotional dysfunction. Red Phantom is particularly useful for encouraging creativity. By allowing you to feel what was blocked out and repressed in childhood in order to survive, it reconnects to your joy, healing your inner child*—additional stones may be required. This stone imparts tranquillity to your mind and energizes the physical body. Chinese Red Phantom, formed from Hematite, overcomes despair and restores the life-force and vitality to the body. This Phantom induces perseverance and overcomes frustration. Used by earth healers, it stabilizes the planet. Enhancing financial security, it is helpful in business.

*Red
(natural
point)*

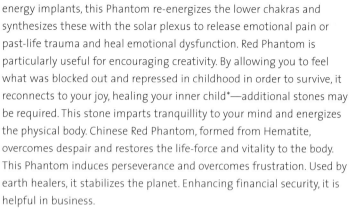

Blue Phantom enhances telepathic communication between people or earth and the spiritual realms. This stone facilitates multi-dimensional travel, knowledge-retrieval and divination. In making you feel a part of the perfect whole, this stone helps in reaching out to others with compassion and tolerance. Blue Phantom is helpful for ameliorating anger and anxiety. It supports the throat, endocrine and metabolic systems, and the spleen and blood vessels.

*Blue
(natural
point)*

Smoky Phantom activates the past-life chakras and assists in retrieving and reframing traumatic memories. A useful entity* remover, Smoky Phantom Quartz takes you back to your original soul group*, linking into the purpose of the group's incarnations. It assists in identifying and attracting members of your soul group in the present life to fulfil your karmic or spiritual task and teaches that experiences cannot be judged from an earthly perspective. If negative energies or imperatives have intervened in your group purpose, a Smoky Phantom removes these, taking the group back to its original intention. The Phantom goes to

*Smoky
(natural
point)*

before a problem or pattern originated to reconnect to a state of wholeness and harmony.

Pink Phantom promotes peace and self-love. It assists empathetic communication between friends or lovers; or you and a spirit guide or Higher Self. This stone facilitates accepting life as it is—and making changes, when appropriate, that enable finding fulfilment. If two healers are working at a distance, it provides a strong link, stimulating telepathy and providing spiritual protection. It is beneficial for overcoming restriction, abandonment, betrayal or alienation and supports the heart and assists lupus and auto-immune diseases.

Pink (natural point)

Desirite is white with orange, brown, white and blue Phantoms. Resonating to the master number 44, the number of metamorphosis, Desirite assists transmutation on all levels and a re-cognition of the interweaving of the divine with the spiritual. Its different-colored Phantoms form a ladder for ascension*. Dubbed the 'as above so below stone', it reflects physical and spiritual reality. Rubbing your thumb up the crystal takes you into profound meditative states. Strongly grounding*, this stone moves to a high vibration*, each level being accessed successively, the first linking to Native America and Lemuria, and the second to Egypt. Perfect for angel and Ascended Master* work, Desirite accesses lives far back in the history of the planet. Although a powerful healing tool for those who are attuned to it, Desirite does not work well as part of a healing layout; it is best used alone or to realign and rebalance after a healing session. Desirite works beyond the physical to clear old soul patterns, the core cause of hearing disorders, and to create multi-dimensional cellular healing. See also the properties of the individual colors of Phantom Quartz, as this stone synergizes the energy of them all.

Desirite (natural point)

QUARTZ: PINK CRACKLE QUARTZ

*Heat-amended
natural point*

COLOR	Pink-color infused (and see opposite)
APPEARANCE	Clear Quartz crystal crackled and crazed inside
RARITY	Easily obtained
SOURCE	Artificially amended Quartz

ATTRIBUTES Although Crackle Quartz has been superheated and color-infused, it carries life-enhancing and energy-expanding qualities. Promoting fun and joy in life, it appeals particularly to children or to the inner child* in everyone, and the full color range creates a useful chakra set for children.

Psychologically, this stone insists that you be responsible for your feelings, recognizing that they arise inside your self and that only you can opt for inner joy and happiness rather than relying on other people to provide this. Emotionally, Pink Crackle Quartz is particularly helpful for healing an abused or emotionally damaged child, gently drawing out the pain and replacing it with love. It links the solar plexus chakra with the heart, bringing unconditional love into the emotional center. Healing a broken or damaged heart center, this stone teaches the emotional independence that arises when you no longer worry about what others may think and cease to follow external instructions as to how you *should* feel, relying instead upon how you *are* internally. Physically, this stone helps to recharge; it is a useful adjunct to Reiki* healing, facilitating contact with your Higher Self*.

Lilac (tumbled)

HEALING Supports cellular memory*, brittle bones, compound fractures and anxiety; helpful for pain experienced during flying.

POSITION Hold, grid (see pages 28–31) or place as appropriate.

Blue (tumbled)

SPECIFIC COLORS

Lilac Crackle Quartz assists spiritual development. It gently breaks open crystallized beliefs, promoting a change of attitude and new perceptions on the spiritual pathway.

Green (tumbled)

Blue Crackle Quartz assists in making yourself heard and facilitates communication, overcoming speech and hearing problems, and ameliorates breathing difficulties.

Green Crackle Quartz helps to earth and comfort an ungrounded person or someone who feels uncomfortable in their body due to physical abuse or dislike of physical incarnation.

Yellow (tumbled)

Yellow Crackle Quartz assists with healing mental abuse and authoritarianism, assuring the child within that it is OK to believe in yourself and your perceptions. It heals a broken mind or cracks open a closed one to encompass new possibilities.

Orange or Red Crackle Quartz is useful for stimulating creativity and the playful child within.

Orange (tumbled)

QUARTZ: **PRASIOLITE QUARTZ**

Natural

Tumbled

COLOR	Leek green
APPEARANCE	Translucent to clear Quartz
RARITY	Natural is rare; most Prasiolite is created by heat-treating Amethyst
SOURCE	Brazil, United States, Sri Lanka, Madagascar, Finland, Russia, Namibia

ATTRIBUTES A stone of transformation, Prasiolite acts as a bridging stone between the frequencies of earth and those of higher realms so that energy passes in either direction into the heart and soul of the wearer. Placed on the earth chakra, it draws nurturing and creative energy from the earth into the heart to feed the soul. On the crown chakra, Prasiolite draws the highest frequencies of spirit into the higher heart chakra.

Spiritually, this stone is useful for contact with your Higher Self*; meditating with it assists in embodying that energy and projecting it into everyday life, grounding* and manifesting your spiritual purpose. If you have difficulty recognizing the innate divinity of yourself or everyone else, wear Prasiolite over your heart. Prasiolite is useful for upper-world* shamanic journeying*. Going into deep connection with

All That Is*, it assists in unwinding ancestral patterns* in the south-east of the medicine wheel (see pages 368–375), meeting the spirits of your ancestors and those of the planet. In ancestral line* or past-life healing, Prasiolite rejigs the etheric blueprint* for your present life, pinpointing significant karmic* connections and the gift or karmic justice in traumatic situations.

Emotionally, this stone protects the spleen chakra from energy depletion, reversing a 'put-upon' or martyred disposition or a feeling that you have to give your all to someone or something else, deeply depleting your energies in the process. Prasiolite supports those with a needy disposition to find an inexhaustible energy source and confidence within themselves through their connection to the Earth Mother and Celestial Father, activating a cosmic anchor*. This stone assists those who are ready to leave the planet in doing so with dignity and full awareness, having expressed all that they wished to say before they leave.

HEALING An effective heart healer; supports spleen function, blood cells and the digestive and immune systems.

POSITION Place or position as appropriate. To correct energy depletion, wear over the spleen chakra, under the left armpit or over the base of the sternum.

ADDITIONAL STONE
Mariposite, a dense, marble-like bright green and white Quartz, helps in adapting to new situations and in developing a more flexible personality. A stress-reducer that stabilizes energies, it lessens exhaustion and reduces fears. This is a supportive stone for craftspeople and self-expression. (*See also* Seriphos Quartz, page 286.)

Mariposite (tumbled)

QUARTZ: **SATYALOKA QUARTZ**

Yellowish-white (polished)   *Gray (polished)*   *Yellow (polished)*

COLOR	Clear, white or yellowish-white
APPEARANCE	Translucent or opaque crystal with inclusions
RARITY	Easily obtained but increasingly expensive
SOURCE	Southern India

ATTRIBUTES Attuned to the white flame* of pure consciousness, this exceedingly high-vibration* stone is spiritually enhanced by monks from Satyaloka, South India, who infuse the stone, already containing energy from a sacred mountain, with spiritual light before sending it into the world. Their intention is that this truly holy stone will bring about a shift into planetary consciousness, opening the way for higher consciousness to manifest on the earth and enlightenment for all. Opening the illumined mind, this stone is an excellent tool for facilitating a vibrational shift, whether at a personal or planetary level, and for bringing about profound, holistic spiritual healing. The stone resonates with the crown chakra of the earth, opening and aligning the crown and higher crown chakras of the physical and subtle bodies*.

Facilitating an instantaneous download of spiritual insight as to what is required to move spiritual evolution forward, this stone may take time to process. Placed on the crown chakra, it facilitates spiritual awakening or a shift into immediate enlightenment that is lived out on the earth. Placed on the soma chakra, it activates the lightbody*; placed on the third eye, it induces spiritual visions and connects to guidance from an immensely high vibration. Satyaloka Quartz sets up a powerful resonance in your inner being that activates the intelligent interface between the soul and the physical being, allowing this to direct your way forward. Each stone assists in the way that is right for its user. It may adjust or amplify energies, open channels and pathways at a soul, multi- or inter-dimensional level or bring about a profound shift of attitude. Satyaloka Quartz is a supportive companion for those who experience the loneliness of the spiritual path, reconnecting with the divine within everything and especially yourself.

HEALING Amplifies the energy of other healing stones and infuses the physical and subtle bodies with transformational energy rather than working directly on the physical level of being, effecting multi-dimensional vibrational healing.

POSITION Meditate with the stone on the crown chakra or place as appropriate.

COMPANION STONE
Satyamani Quartz complements Satyaloka Quartz, uniting the divine masculine and feminine energies and further facilitating enlightenment, and it is attuned to the golden flame of the illumined mind. Satyamani and Satyaloka work in harmony with Nirvana Quartz and are particularly effective triangulated around the subtle bodies with Nirvana Quartz at the higher crown chakras (especially the soul star chakra).

Satyamani Quartz (polished)

QUARTZ: **SERIPHOS QUARTZ**

ALSO KNOWN AS HEDENBERGITE

Natural formation

COLOR	Apple to olive green
APPEARANCE	Blade shaped, with leaf-like overlays
RARITY	Rare (form of Hedenbergite, one location only)
SOURCE	Seriphos Island (Greece)

ATTRIBUTES Seriphos Quartz performs etheric surgery, cauterizing etheric blueprint* wounds, removing cysts and encrustations. Ideal for prosperity rituals, it connects to nature, making you feel at home on earth and in the body. Facilitating transitions of all kinds, it harmonizes extremes. Activating an intuitive ability imbued with love and fostering creativity, it stimulates mental clarity and indicates a new life path. A powerful healer, Seriphos Quartz opens and stabilizes the heart and heart seed chakras and is effective for releasing negative energy and earth healing*.

HEALING Supports the immune and endocrine systems.

POSITION Hold, grid (see pages 28–31) or place as appropriate.

QUARTZ: **SHAMAN QUARTZ**

Natural formation

COLOR	White with green and/or orange-brown inclusions
APPEARANCE	Clear crystal with internal layers, phantoms and canyons
RARITY	Fairly easily obtained
SOURCE	Brazil

ATTRIBUTES Shaman Quartz is a powerful journeying* crystal that induces trance, visionary experience and soul healings. Traversing its inner landscape allows you to bridge the worlds and journey through multi-dimensions and timeframes. Shaman Quartz contains different minerals that assist communication with the spirit realm: Chlorite Shaman Quartz has strong associations with Mother Earth and facilitates healing journeys through nature; Chlorite assists with self-realization, provides support and cleanses the past; visionary Fluorite provides protection and discernment; protective Rutile enhances out-of-body journeying and pinpoints the karmic* cause of a dis-ease*; Hematite dissolves negativity, and grounds and harmonizes body, mind and spirit; while Mica heightens the connection to your spiritual self, sharpens intuitive perception and gets to the bottom of things.

Shaman Quartz high in Chlorite works well in the north-west of the medicine wheel (see pages 368–375), the place of habits, patterns and routines. Clearing cellular memory* and healing the present-life ancestral line*, it opens the way for changes in your life and the family. Showing how innate patterns were formed and passed down the family, and how you have carried the ancestral pattern through your life, it teaches how to have compassion for yourself and the family, find the gifts and break away to set future generations free.

Mentally, Shaman Quartz with Rutile is helpful for problem-solving or obtaining answers. Set out your problem in your mind, gaze into the stone and ask to journey to see the solution. Be aware that you may hear rather than see the response and that it could be presented as a later, external signal.

Environmentally, by absorbing negativity and environmental pollutants, Shaman Quartz clears a build-up of stagnant energy anywhere in the subtle bodies* or environment. This stone removes energy implants*, accessing their source in any lifetime.

HEALING Works best on the subtle levels of being rather than the physical, but is a useful anti-viral held over the thymus at the first sign of cold or flu.

POSITION Hold or place as appropriate.

(*See also* Green Phantom (Chlorite) Quartz, pages 276–277; Rutile, pages 318–319; Quartz with Lepidolite Mica, page 266.)

QUARTZ: **SHIFT CRYSTAL**

Natural formation

COLOR	White or colorless
APPEARANCE	Multi-faceted, bladed and indented with inner spaces
RARITY	Rare and may be confused with Nirvana Quartz
SOURCE	Russia, Pakistan, Brazil

ATTRIBUTES Shift Crystal literally shifts you into a new space and accelerates spiritual growth, although other stones may be needed to assimilate the changes. Spiritually, this stone takes you to a place of wild abandon, leaving behind everything that fetters or restricts you, opening to a peak experience of bliss and ultimate creativity. The perfect stone for meditation, manifestation and dreaming-up, you need to be ready to accept whatever it offers, as there is no going back and the effects can be dramatic, traumatic and overwhelming—it frequently, virtually instantaneously, shifts you on to your soul path*, opens healing potential and clears the evolutionary way forward. Whatever is outworn, outgrown or no longer serves in your life, at any level, falls away under the influence of this catalytic stone.

When you are ready for such a profound change, meditate with the crystal for 20 minutes, asking to be shown the way forward. Sleep with the stone under your pillow and place it under your chair or wear it during the day. Be receptive to signals from the universe and make the choice to respond appropriately.

Psychologically, one of the most profound lessons that a Shift Crystal teaches is that of emotional independence and personal autonomy. It brings about the realization that you alone are responsible for creating your well-being and happiness. Such a sense is an inner state that is not dependent on any external source, including a partner or loved one. Only you can maintain it.

Physically, Shift Crystal greatly amplifies Reiki* healing, strengthening healer and patient, and carries the symbols during and after a session or reprograms cellular memory*.

HEALING Works beyond the physical level of being to bring about soul evolution and multi-dimensional cellular healing.

POSITION Hold or use over the heart, higher heart, third eye, crown and higher crown chakras.

NOTE 'Shift Crystals' from Brazil have energy similar to Nirvana Quartz.

QUARTZ: **SIBERIAN QUARTZ**

Purple (man-made)

COLOR	Blue, green, purple, gold
APPEARANCE	Bright, clear Quartz
RARITY	Easily obtained
SOURCE	Artificially created Quartz

ATTRIBUTES Regrown in Russia from natural Quartz combined with chemicals to produce the vivid colors, Siberian Quartz has a powerful vibration but differs in its effect according to the color and the chakra with which it resonates.

HEALING See individual colors, below.

POSITION Wear, hold, grid (see pages 28–31) or place as appropriate.

SPECIFIC COLORS
Purple Siberian Quartz resonates with the crown and higher crown chakras. A powerful stimulant for the third eye and higher crown chakras, it brings about mystical states of consciousness. Working beyond the physical, this is a stone for the spiritual magician, assisting

in co-creating or dreaming up your reality, and in keeping centered and grounded during ritual or spiritual working.

Blue Siberian Quartz is a mystical stone that unites the throat, third eye and crown chakras to bring about intense visionary experiences, uplifting the spirit and instilling deep peace. It opens the subtle and physical bodies to receive an influx of cosmic consciousness*. On the third eye, the crystal stimulates psychic vision and telepathy and enhances communication. It assists in speaking your truth and facilitates being heard. Psychologically, the vibrant color lifts stress and depression. Physically, it is beneficial for throat infections, stomach ulcers, inflammation, sunburn and a stiff neck or muscles.

Blue (man-made)

Green Siberian Quartz resonates with the heart and higher heart chakras and carries a strong love vibration to heal the heart and emotions. Creating prosperity and abundance, it is a beneficial stone in matters of health, love and money. Psychologically, this stone harmonizes disputes or meetings between people who have opposing points of view. Physically, it is beneficial for the heart, lung conditions and altitude sickness.

Green (man-made)

Gold Siberian Quartz stimulates the solar plexus, releasing emotional blockages and increasing will power and the ability to bring creative vision into positive manifestation. It connects the mind with the emotions, throwing light on psychosomatic health conditions and offering healing possibilities.

Gold (man-made)

QUARTZ: **SICHUAN QUARTZ**

Natural double-terminated point

COLOR	Clear
APPEARANCE	Clear Quartz, may have black spot inclusions, often double terminated
RARITY	Easily obtained
SOURCE	China, Himalayas

ATTRIBUTES Energetically combining Herkimer and Tibetan Quartz, and carrying an extremely high vibration* that integrates spirit and matter, Sichuan Quartz connects the third eye and crown chakras and rapidly opens psychic and inner vision to bring about an illumined mind.

Spiritually attuned to the white flame* of pure consciousness, this stone enhances telepathy and soul communication and clears chakra blockages. Karmically* beneficial and insightful if held by a healer or past-life therapist while working with a client, Sichuan Quartz accesses the Akashic Record*, putting you in touch with ancient Chinese or Buddhist wisdom. In karmic healing, it highlights the past-life reasons for dis-ease* or karmic lessons in the present life, illuminating the gifts within the experience and breaking outgrown connections.

Emotionally, Sichuan Quartz is particularly helpful for breaking the patterns that lie behind dependent or co-dependent relationships and it pinpoints the causes of psychosomatic disease. Helpful in ascertaining the psychological patterns that underlie eating disorders, it brings about deep healing of the biomagnetic sheath* and the etheric blueprint* from which the present physical body devolved. It instigates profound physical healing, but may need support from other stones.

Sichuan Quartz is usually a double-terminated stone that radiates or absorbs energy at both ends simultaneously. These crystals are useful in healing as they absorb negativity and break ingrained habits, which assists in overcoming addictions. Sichuans integrate previously blocked parts of the self. During healing, Sichuan Quartz harmonizes the subtle bodies* with the physical and bridges energy gaps along the chakra line, assisting in centering within your Self. This rarified and yet earthed Quartz has a strongly grounded* energy that passes into the body and the personal self, restructuring cells and boundaries.

HEALING Realigns energy meridians* and stimulates cellular memory*, bringing about multi-dimensional healing.

POSITION Position or hold this stone as appropriate, especially along the chakra line.

NOTE Black Phantom or Spot Quartz from Virginia and Arkansas carry similar energy to Sichuan Quartz. (*See also* Herkimers, pages 224–226.)

QUARTZ: **SMOKY AMETHYST QUARTZ**

Natural formation

COLOR	Purple and smoky brown
APPEARANCE	Often included as a phantom or distinct patch within a point
RARITY	Sometimes difficult to obtain
SOURCE	Worldwide

ATTRIBUTES Smoky Amethyst Quartz is an extremely useful combination for soul healing and protection. Smoky Amethyst assists in contacting the highest possible spiritual energies and then grounds that spiritual energy into the body. This is the perfect stone for clearing entities*, unwanted influences or attachments* of any kind, especially when held at the third eye, as the Smoky Quartz heals and seals the biomagnetic sheath* and calls in beneficial influences to protect the soul once the spirit has been sent to the light by the Amethyst. Protecting against psychic attack*, inappropriate prayers or thought forms* and guarding against alien invasion, Smoky Amethyst repels negative energy, calling in positive vibrations.

Emotionally, by contacting guides and angelic helpers, this stone assists disconnection between those who have previously made a mystic marriage and are still intertwined at the higher spiritual chakras.

Physically, Smoky Amethyst amplifies and directs sound healing, creating a two-way flow of energy. The combination is beneficial for a wide range of conditions.

HEALING Combines the healing properties of Smoky Quartz and Amethyst, but works effectively at the soul and subtle levels. It supports the endocrine system and hormone production; helps the metabolism, the cleansing and eliminating organs, the assimilation of minerals, the re-absorption of water and fluid regulation, and the digestive tract, regulating flora and parasite removal; aids the immune system and reproductive system; helps the heart, lungs, respiratory tract, abdomen, back, hips, legs, skin, muscle, nerves, nerve tissue, cellular disorders, hearing disorders; boosts libido and concentration; benefits pain-relief and helps cramp, headaches, bruises, swellings, burns and other injuries, insomnia, nightmares, fear, depression, stress and geopathic stress*; guards against X-ray exposure.

POSITION Grid (see pages 28–31), hold or place as appropriate.

NOTE If the combined stone is not available, use individual Smoky Quartz and Amethyst.

QUARTZ: **SMOKY CITRINE QUARTZ**

Natural point

COLOR	Yellow and brown
APPEARANCE	Dark brownish-yellow patches in a clear crystal
RARITY	Rare
SOURCE	Worldwide

ATTRIBUTES Enhancing metaphysical abilities* and grounding* them in everyday functional reality, Smoky Citrine removes blockages from your spiritual path. This stone does not hold negative energy or need cleaning. Reframing* vows such as celibacy and removing detrimental attitudes from the past, Smoky Citrine clears beliefs and thought forms* that keep you mired in poverty, opening the way to abundance. Purifying the etheric blueprint*, it aligns the earth chakra with the solar plexus chakra and assists in moving out of circumstances, or an environment, that does not allow expansion.

HEALING This stone works beyond the physical level of being to clear the subtle bodies*.

POSITION Grid (see pages 28–31) or position as appropriate.

QUARTZ: **SMOKY ROSE QUARTZ**

*Smoky crystals on
rose matrix*

COLOR	Pink and gray-brown
APPEARANCE	Opaque or clear pink Quartz with Smoky points or inclusions
RARITY	Rare
SOURCE	South Africa, South America

ATTRIBUTES Useful for cleansing the heart and higher heart chakras and aligning to the Earth Mother, this gentle stone keeps your environment pure. The Smoky portion pulls negative energy out of the environment or the body and transmutes it. It creates a protective shield, and the Rose Quartz portion then fills the inner space with pure unconditional love. This is the perfect stone to place on an altar or in the center of the medicine wheel (see pages 368–375). Activating a cosmic anchor*, the Smoky portion of the stone anchors your energy in the earth's core and the Rose portion aligns it to the galactic center*, creating an inner-core energy solidity that enables riding out earth-energy changes and perturbations.

A useful journeying* stone that takes you into the heart of divine love, Smoky Rose Quartz is the perfect companion for anyone who suffers from fear of death or dying, for which it should be placed by the bed or under the pillow.

Psychologically, Smoky Rose Quartz dissolves resentment and draws out the effects of abuse, filling the heart with unconditional love and providing a protective shield to allow healing to continue.

Emotionally, Smoky Rose Quartz cleanses negative emotions and heals heartbreak from any lifetime, replacing it with unconditional love for yourself and others. It opens you to intimacy and creates a space in which a soulmate* or twinflame* manifests.

Physically, Smoky Rose Quartz is one of the finest stones for cleansing and healing the heart, removing blockages, stabilizing blood pressure and improving the flow of blood and lymph to all the organs, which it purifies and re-energizes.

HEALING Supports the heart and the cleansing organs of the body.

POSITION Hold, grid (see pages 28–31) or place as appropriate.

NOTE If the combined stone is not available, use individual Rose and Smoky Quartz.

QUARTZ: **SPIRIT QUARTZ**

*White
(natural
point)*

*Flame Aura
(alchemicalized point)*

COLOR	White, yellowish-brown, purple, lilac or gray-brown; some artificially colored
APPEARANCE	Tiny drusy crystals covering a long point
RARITY	Easily obtained
SOURCE	South Africa

ATTRIBUTES Spirit Quartz is an exceptionally spiritual stone that takes the energetic properties of Quartz to another level. This uplifting stone radiates high-vibration* energy in all directions while the core crystal tightly focuses healing that reaches multi-dimensions and reprograms cellular memory*. Carrying the gifts of the spirit and enhancing metaphysical abilities*, this stone opens the crown and higher crown chakras, aligning and purifying the entire chakra system.

Spiritually, this stone facilitates out-of-body journeying*, assists the ascension process*, activates the lightbody* and facilitates multi-dimensional spiritual and cellular healing. Encouraging insightful

dreams, it is helpful in all metaphysical work, especially for reframing*
the past. Carrying the vibration of universal love, this crystal heals and
rejigs the etheric blueprint* for the present life. Pinpointing significant
karmic* connections and the gift or karmic justice in traumatic
situations, it promotes self-forgiveness. A stone of non-duality that
perfectly balances and blends male and female, yin and yang, Spirit
Quartz facilitates the transition between different brainwave states,
facilitating combination states and stimulating heightened awareness
and psychic perception. A useful aid to rebirthing, this stone purifies
and stimulates the subtle energetic bodies.

Spirit Quartz assists at death, guiding the soul through different
dimensions of the afterlife to the highest possible vibration and into
the hands of those who are waiting to welcome it home. It provides
comfort to those who are left behind, and is useful for obtaining an
overview of any situation. Placed in the south-east of the medicine
wheel (see pages 368–375) or used in meditation or regression, Spirit
Quartz takes you to meet the spirits of your ancestors and those of the
planet—program it (see page 358) for ancestral healing, especially for
reframing the past.

Group-oriented Spirit Quartz is particularly useful for those who give
service, especially as part of an organization, as it synthesizes group
efforts and brings about productive harmony. Facilitating spiritual or
healing groups, it provides insights into problems experienced within a
community or a family and can be programmed to alleviate these. Spirit
Quartz cleanses other stones and enhances their energy in a healing
layout. It stabilizes earth energies.

Psychologically, Spirit Quartz heals discord, instilling patience and
overcoming obsessive behavior, offering insights into the cause.
It assists with an effective but gentle psychological, mental and
emotional detox.

HEALING Offers multi-dimensional healing and rejigs cellular memory. It is beneficial for detoxification, fertility and skin eruptions.

POSITION Hold or place as appropriate. Grid (see pages 28–31) around the bed of a dying person to assist transition.

SPECIFIC COLORS

'Amethyst' (natural point)

'Amethyst' Spirit Quartz (lilac) opens the higher crown chakras, aligning to the infinity of being and bringing about transmutation of prior misuses of spiritual power. Bringing about multi-dimensional healing, including soul parts* not currently in incarnation, this compassionate stone facilitates transition to other states of being. It assists a soul facing death and offers immense support and comfort throughout a terminal illness. 'Amethyst' Spirit Quartz is the perfect carrier for flower or gem essences to gently dissolve karma, attitudes and emotions that would be detrimental if taken into the next world. An effective tool for spirit release, it encourages a trapped soul to move toward the light, attracting guides for the journey. Holding the stone enables a practitioner to safely journey wherever may be necessary to release the soul and to ascertain whether there is anything that the soul needs to complete before it moves on.

Aqua Aura Spirit Quartz, created from gold bonded to Quartz, brings about profound soul healing and reintegration, realigning soul fragments* from many lifetimes. Setting you free from limitations, it encourages manifesting your highest spiritual potential.

Aqua Aura (natural point)

'Citrine' Spirit Quartz (yellow) works through the earth and solar plexus chakras, helping in standing centered in your power and directing your life from that place. This stone purifies intent and is particularly useful for accessing true abundance while paradoxically releasing dependence on, or attachment to, material things. Promoting self-awareness, it purifies and cleanses the biomagnetic sheath*. In business, it focuses goals and plans. In grids*, 'Citrine' Spirit Quartz protects a house against electromagnetic smog* or geopathic stress and heals disturbed earth energies. It is helpful for conflict-resolution and sending forgiveness to those you feel have wronged you, or to ask for forgiveness for yourself or a world situation.

'Citrine' (natural point)

Flame Aura Spirit Quartz, created from Titanium (Rutile) and niobium alchemically coated on to Quartz, is a powerful initiation tool, bringing about a profound multi-dimensional energy shift, drawing kundalini* energy up the spine and through the subtle bodies*. It adjusts its effect to provide what each soul needs for its evolution and harmonizes all the rays and planets on an astrological chart. It assists in 'reading' people at an energetic and subtle level. (*See also* Rutile, pages 318–319.)

'Smoky' Spirit Quartz (gray) activates and aligns the base chakra with the third eye, grounding spiritual insight into everyday life. Strongly protective with powerful cleansing properties, it assists integration. A most effective psychopomp* conveying a soul safely to the next world, it cleanses the subtle bodies, removing karmic and emotional debris, and reprograms cellular memory, ensuring a good rebirth. Beneficial for any work that entails visiting the underworld or exploring the subconscious mind, it cleanses and releases deeply held emotions and states of dis-ease* or traumatic memories, including those that have passed down the ancestral line*. Such work should be carried out under guidance as it may induce catharsis. This stone stabilizes and purifies environmental imbalance or pollution, no matter what the cause.

'Smoky' (natural point)

303

QUARTZ: **STAR HOLLANDITE QUARTZ**

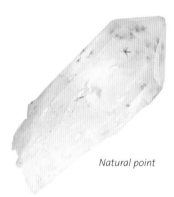

Natural point

COLOR	White
APPEARANCE	Tiny six-pointed stars included within a Quartz point
RARITY	Rare
SOURCE	South Africa and worldwide

ATTRIBUTES Spiritually, Star Hollandite takes you into the oneness of all things and ultimate stillness. A stone for contacting star beings, star lore or universal wisdom, Star Hollandite views the origins of ancient Egypt and the intervention of the star people in its development—as well as your place within that experience—dissolving any karma* that may remain.

Psychologically, Star Hollandite helps to disperse tension and anxiety and supports rational thought. Drawing off negative energy at the physical and mental levels, it creates calm acceptance and inner watchfulness. This stone helps in realizing the breadth of your being and offers the solace of knowing that you are not alone in the universe. Holding this stone calls in a guide or helper or allows you to visit the stars for comfort and advice.

The stars within the crystal are Geothite, a mineral that attunes to the notes of the earth and stars, bringing deeper contact with earth energies. Resonating to 44, the number of metamorphosis, Geothite facilitates clairaudience* and metaphysical abilities*. Powerfully attuned to the healing power of nature, it enhances dowsing abilities. Contacting the devas* and the *anima terra*, soul of the earth, this stone makes you more sensitive to subtle energies and the energetic currents within the earth and the human body.

Environmentally, Star Hollandite facilitates a 'fine-tuning' of the energy meridians* of the planet and reactivates power points set in place by the ancients.

HEALING Works mostly beyond the physical level of being, but see Geothite.

POSITION Hold or grid (see pages 28–31) as appropriate.

(*See also* Geothite, pages 142–143.)

QUARTZ: **STARSEED QUARTZ**

Natural point

COLOR	White
APPEARANCE	Deeply etched on alternate faces or may have drusy Quartz encrustations on alternate faces
RARITY	Rare
SOURCE	Worldwide

ATTRIBUTES Accessing the wisdom of the ancient civilizations of Lemuria, Atlantis and Egypt, and their connection with the star people, Starseed is the perfect crystal for stellar and inter-dimensional communication. Engraved with indentations that act like a star map, Starseed assists you during meditation in discovering which star your spirit is associated with and your earth mission. It re-attunes to your star group and the collective purpose of the group, ameliorating home-sickness. It can break the ancestral-line patterns* that hold you in thrall, allowing you to be fully your Self.

306

Spiritually, this crystal carries the energy of Green Tara, Buddhist goddess of compassion, and takes you to a Shamballa-like state, incorporating exceptional clarity and pure form within an infinity of being. There is nothing to do in this state except to *be*.

Psychologically, this crystal highlights forks in the road and shows that apparent mistakes carry the seeds of soul growth, shifting you from the perspective of the personality to that of the soul. As with all etched crystals, Starseed can be read to rediscover ancient knowledge and the soul's purpose in incarnating in the present life.

In karmic* or physical healing, Starseed Quartz connects to the blueprint* that controls the etheric blueprint and realigns to your optimum pattern.

In conjunction with Sugar Blade Quartz, Starseed awakens the third eye, soma, soul star and stellar gateway chakras and activates the unmanifest, bringing your heart and soul into unity. It provides profound healing for metaphysical abilities* blocked in previous lives.

HEALING Works beyond the physical levels of being by realigning the etheric blueprint to the original, pure blueprint, so that it manifests physical perfection.

POSITION Hold or grid (see pages 28–31) as appropriate.

NOTE Combine Starseed Quartz with Sugar Blade Quartz for maximum effect.

QUARTZ: **STRAWBERRY QUARTZ**

Raw

Tumbled

COLOR	Pink
APPEARANCE	Clear to opaque Quartz or inclusions within Quartz
RARITY	Rare (may be manufactured)
SOURCE	Russia

ATTRIBUTES Assisting in living consciously and joyfully in the moment, Strawberry Quartz teaches you how to find humor in all situations and bring divine love into everything you do. Natural Strawberry Quartz makes a potent gem essence (see page 361) for bringing love into the heart. Sprayed as an essence or gridded* around a room, it creates a harmonious, loving environment and wraps you in a cloak of love, wherever you may be.

Spiritually insightful, this stone enables the discovery, during meditation, of why the circumstances of your present incarnation were chosen and the karmic* gifts you brought to it.

308

Psychologically, Strawberry Quartz lessens the restrictions you place upon yourself and assists in reprogramming false beliefs, bringing in a positive view. This stone has an intense energy that assists both dream-recall and understanding the message a dream holds. Stabilizing connections between the physical and the subtle bodies*, Strawberry Quartz brings to light hidden causes of current situations, especially when these are self-created. It enhances self-esteem and reduces anxiety, replacing it with tranquillity.

Mentally, by facilitating clear thinking, Strawberry Quartz calms an agitated mind and gives a more objective perspective.

Emotionally, this stone brings joy and happiness into your life, teaching you how to no longer rely on others for positive feelings. Relieving tensions in an existing relationship, it encourages romance.

Physically, Strawberry Quartz facilitates the flow of divine love through all the cells of the body, bringing them into equilibrium and imparting a sense of well-being.

HEALING Heals anxiety and supports the heart.

POSITION Hold, grid (see pages 28–31) or position as appropriate.

NOTE Strawberry Quartz may be artificially manufactured, which lessens but does not completely negate the intensity of its action.

QUARTZ: **SUGAR BLADE QUARTZ**

Raw

COLOR	White
APPEARANCE	Long blades on the side of Drusy Quartz
RARITY	Rare
SOURCE	South Africa

ATTRIBUTES Having a particularly strong resonance with the soma and soul star chakras and the Higher Self*, Sugar Blade Quartz helps to attune to the extraordinary breadth of your core spiritual identity and reflect this out to the world.

Spiritually, this formation carries the life-force energy of All That Is* and a hologram of your multi-dimensional self. It aligns to and engages with the Higher Self and the infinity of being, and assists in choosing a life direction, showing which door to open to the future and which to close on the past.

A stone for extraterrestrial contact, Sugar Blade Quartz puts you into mental communication with star people to access the teachings of our neighbors in the universe. To know which star you hail from, place

Sugar Blade Quartz on the soma or stellar gateway chakra to assist your journey* home and help bring back conscious awareness of whatever you discover.

Used in conjunction with Starseed, Sugar Blade Quartz awakens the third eye and soma chakras and activates the unmanifest, bringing heart and soul into unity. This stone provides profound healing for metaphysical abilities* blocked in previous lives, opening clairvoyance* and psychic vision.

Psychologically, this stone is particularly useful for those who feel that the earth is not their home planet and who have loose boundaries, as it makes physical incarnation more comfortable and protected by grounding* the lightbody* into the physical.

HEALING Works beyond the physical level of being to heal the lightbody.

POSITION Place or hold as appropriate. To encourage spaceship landings, grid around a suitable site.

ADDITIONAL STONE

Fairy Wand Quartz, from Mexico, which is similar to Spirit Quartz, has a strong connection with the faery realm and is useful for inner-dimensional* travel. A reversed Quartz scepter, shown here, transmits healing energy, cleanses it and returns it to the healer. Scepter Fairy Wand Quartz frees the mind from false illusions and brings it a point of stillness. Used with care by someone who has reached a high level of initiation, it heals incomplete initiations or completes one that failed in the past. Assisting in finding the gift in every experience, it calls together a soul group* to complete its mission. (*See also* Fairy Quartz, page 257.)

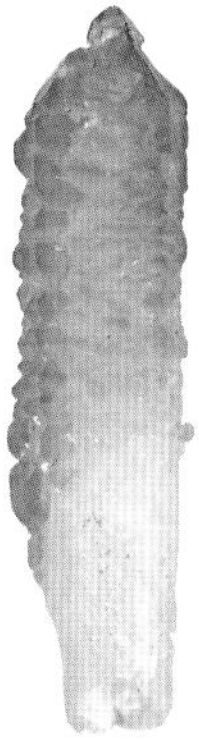

*Fairy Wand
Quartz
(reversed scepter)*

QUARTZ: **TANZINE AURA QUARTZ**

Natural point

COLOR	Lilac-blue (and see below)
APPEARANCE	Coated Quartz point
RARITY	Becoming more easily obtained
SOURCE	Artificially amended Quartz

ATTRIBUTES Alchemicalized from gold and indium, Tanzine Aura Quartz brings multi-dimensional balance and profound spiritual interconnection. Attuned to the transmutational violet flame, it opens and aligns the soul star and highest crown chakras and draws cosmic energy into the physical body and to earth. This stone takes you into a centered state of 'no-mind' that enhances sensual enjoyment of the world.

Emotionally, Tanzine Aura provides deep spiritual comfort, dissolving emotional blockages and replacing these with unconditional love and the sense of being part of a greater soul group* supporting each other in learning from life's challenges—a group chosen prior to incarnation for gifts they bring. Physically, Tanzine Aura Quartz has a powerful regulatory effect on the pituitary, hypothalamus and pineal glands, bringing physical equilibrium. Indium assists assimilation of minerals, supporting optimal metabolic and hormonal balance, resulting in physical and mental well-being. Believed to be anti-carcinogenic, it energetically reactivates an inactive thyroid.

HEALING Beneficial for metabolism, migraine, mineral assimilation, insomnia, attention-deficit hyperactivity disorder (ADHD), the immune system, pneumonia, convalescence, depression, inflammation, thyroid fibromyalgia, lupus, diabetes, vision, glaucoma, the urinary tract, blood pressure, circulation, the pancreas, spleen and liver.

Apple Aura Quartz (natural point)

POSITION Wear constantly at throat. Hold, grid (see pages 28–31) or place as appropriate.

SPECIFIC AURA QUARTZES

Apple Aura Quartz, nickel on Quartz, protects the spleen worn over the base of the sternum or taped over the spleen chakra. It cuts drains on multi-dimensional energy and overcomes psychic vampirism*. It severs ties with previous partners or mentors who retain a powerful mental or emotional hold despite physical separation.

Flame Aura Quartz (natural point)

Flame Aura Quartz, Titanium (Rutile) and niobium on Quartz, is a powerful initiation tool. It brings about a multi-dimensional energy shift, drawing kundalini* energy up the spine and through the subtle bodies*, adjusting its effect to provide what each soul needs for evolution. Harmonizing planets on an astrological chart, it assists in 'reading' people at an energetic and subtle level.

Opal Aura Quartz (natural point)

Opal Aura Quartz, platinum on Quartz, facilitates total union with the divine and cosmic consciousness*. Signifying hope and optimism, Opal Aura is a crystal of joy. Purifying and balancing all

chakras, it opens deep meditative awareness. By integrating the lightbody* into the physical dimensions, it grounds* new vibrations.

Rose Aura Quartz, platinum on Quartz, makes a powerful connection to universal love and produces a dynamic energy that works on the pineal gland and heart chakra to transmute deeply held doubts about self-worth and give the gift of unconditional love of your Self. It imbues the whole body with love, restoring cells to perfect balance, and links base, sacral, heart and third chakras to bring passion into the heart.

Rose Aura Quartz (natural point)

Tangerine Sun Aura Quartz, iron and gold on Quartz, opens a blocked or unawakened third eye—especially in a six-sided form. It heals the third eye and soma chakras after psychic trauma or restriction. Deeply supportive for spiritual exploration and facilitating visualization and profound insight by connecting to higher spiritual forces, it grounds spiritual vision and manifests in everyday life.

Psychologically, Tangerine Sun makes you more responsive, uplifting the spirit, and imparts the ability to face life's challenges with equanimity and cheerfulness. Mentally, Tangerine Sun analyzes and categorizes, aligning clarity, insight and perspective with strength. Emotionally, Tangerine Sun disperses dark moods and lightens emotional troughs, bringing emotional balance. It unites base, sacral and solar plexus chakras, cleansing energetic flow and stimulating creativity, particularly when blocked by criticism or disapproval.

Tangerine Sun Aura Quartz (tumbled)

Physically, Tangerine Sun imparts abundant energy and stabilizes the link between the physical and subtle bodies. With strongly penetrative powers, it enters every cell of the body, recharging and invigorating cell function and imparting great physical and psychological strength, and enhances sexuality. It supports and oxygenates the blood, liver and spleen and overcomes anaemia.

314

QUARTZ: VERA CRUZ AMETHYST

Natural points in companion formation

COLOR	Very light lavender
APPEARANCE	Light and clear; may have phantoms
RARITY	Rare
SOURCE	Mexico

ATTRIBUTES An extremely high-vibration* stone attuned to the transmutational violet flame, ethereal Vera Cruz Amethyst works with the etheric blueprint* and subtle DNA* to bring about profound inter-dimensional cellular healing. An effective stone for purification, particularly at the spiritual level, it removes imprints and attachments of all kinds. A protective stone, it facilitates safe out-of-body experiences and spiritual journeying*.

Spiritually, this particular Amethyst instantly takes you into a beta-brainwave state, facilitating meditation, trance and divination skills. When held to the soma or third eye chakras, it dreams a new world into being. A powerful tool for shamanic working at high levels, when placed on the soul star chakra this stone accesses the vibratory planes where souls meet and merge in oneness. Vera Cruz Amethyst activates and cleanses all the chakras, especially the third eye and crown or higher crown chakras, and aligns them to the lightbody* through the soul star.

Psychologically, it is useful for understanding and reframing* the causes of addictions, and in particular assists spiritual obsession, especially within the subtle bodies* or stemming from a past-life cause. Vera Cruz is helpful in breaking the cycle of co-dependency that occurs within addictions. It helps carers and enablers realize that they can neither 'do it for' the addict, nor control an addict's behavior. This stone assists in standing back, loving unconditionally and allowing the other soul to take its own journey. It breaks a dependency on being the 'care-taker'—needing to be needed—or being the one who is 'cared-for', a karmic* dynamic that underlies co-dependent relationships. Vera Cruz teaches that addictions are a search for the wholeness and immersion in spirit that communication with the divine brings about. Facilitating the expansion of self that the addict seeks in a more constructive way than is possible with drink, drugs or any other dependency, this stone helps the soul to express its gifts fully.

HEALING Works beyond the physical level of being to heal the lightbody, but effects profound cellular healing and supports in overcoming addictions.

POSITION Hold or grid (see pages 28–31) as appropriate.

RED FELDSPAR WITH PHENACITE

Raw

COLOR	Red and white
APPEARANCE	Opaque stone with clear inclusions and crystals
RARITY	Rare combination
SOURCE	Madagascar, Russia, Zimbabwe, United States, Brazil

ATTRIBUTES This 'kick-ass stone' gets things moving and reminds that spiritual evolution does not have to be taken too seriously. Raising self-awareness and the ability to love unconditionally, it changes your reality, grounding spiritual insight into physical expression. It accesses the Ascended Masters* and Akashic Record*. In dreamwork, it explores the deepest implications and brings a fruitful outcome. Psychologically, by encouraging letting go of the past and ingrained patterns, this stone reprograms cellular memory*, opening a more dynamic way of being.

HEALING Useful for repatterning the etheric blueprint* and cellular memory; beneficial for skin and muscular problems.

POSITION Hold to third eye, grid (see pages 28–31) or place.

RUTILE

ALSO KNOWN AS TITANIUM

Rutile in Quartz with Rutile crystal in center

COLOR	Reddish orange-brown
APPEARANCE	Metallic crystalline, often fine included needles
RARITY	Easily obtained
SOURCE	Africa, Australia

ATTRIBUTES Rutile imparts an ethereal vibration to any crystal in which it is included*, enhancing out-of-body journeying* and angelic contact through its attunement to the divine. Nevertheless, it is not an airy-fairy crystal when accelerating spiritual growth; it goes immediately to the heart of a matter and insists you deal with it.

Spiritually, Rutile fine-tunes intuition, pinpointing possible pitfalls in your path before you find them and highlighting the most productive choices to make. Often found included within Quartz (Angel's Hair), it integrates higher vibrations* into the lightbody*.

Psychologically, Rutile heals psychosomatic dis-ease*, going directly to the root of a problem. It pinpoints karmic* causes of chronic illness and reprograms cellular memory*. Placed on the sacral chakra or dantien*, Rutile counteracts sexual problems that have a past-life cause, bringing the reasons for those conditions into conscious awareness for reframing* and release. (Guidance from a qualified therapist assists the process.)

Emotionally, Rutile stabilizes relationships of all kinds by creating emotional fidelity and grounding* higher chakra connections.

Environmentally, Rutile holds the earth's grid stable, restoring its cellular memory*, and is extremely useful in healing grids*. It radiates power down the song-lines of the earth. This stone strongly activates the earth section of a cosmic anchor*, holding you aligned between the earth's core and the galactic center* and enabling you to ground high-vibrational energy downloads* and pass them on to the earth. If included in Quartz, this stone also opens the galactic portion of the cosmic anchor.

A powerful cleansing crystal, Rutile protects and purifies the biomagnetic sheath*, bringing it into balance with the physical body.

HEALING Beneficial for lactation, cellular memory, elasticity of blood vessels, cell regeneration, bronchitis, premature ejaculation, impotence, frigidity and inorgasmia.

POSITION Hold, grid (see pages 28–31) or place as appropriate. Place a hand's breadth beneath the navel for sexual healing and on the earth chakra to activate a cosmic anchor.

SCAPOLITE

Blue (shaped)

COLOR	Blue, gray, yellow, purple, violet
APPEARANCE	Shiny, striated opaque or translucent crystal
RARITY	Certain colors are rare
SOURCE	Madagascar, United States, Norway, Italy, Mexico

ATTRIBUTES A stone of self-discipline stimulating independence and achievable goals based on objective mental planning rather than wish-fulfilment, Scapolite overcomes inertia and self-sabotage, induces transformation and provides the clarity to see what is needed.

Psychologically, this stone clears scapegoating, no matter how subtle, blocking any outside influence that is sabotaging your life. It enables speaking to an inner saboteur or scapegoat, ascertaining what role that figure believes it has in your life—usually something you have outgrown that is no longer appropriate—and aligning the figure to assist your current lifeplan. Scapolite then propels you out of spiritual inertia and into dynamic action.

Mentally, Scapolite is useful for effecting conscious change. It frees up the left side of the brain, increasing analytic ability. This is the perfect stone to carry if you have dyslexia. Emotionally, Scapolite removes self-blame. It rejigs the emotional blueprint*, clearing the effects of old emotional trauma.

Physically an effective unblocker, Scapolite facilitates the release of 'stuck' energy from the body, especially in the legs and veins.

HEALING Assists post-operative recovery and stimulates cellular memory* and calcium assimilation. It is said to unblock varicose veins, cataracts and glaucoma, assist with bone disorders and the shoulders, calm restless eyes and overcome incontinence.

POSITION Hold or position as appropriate.

SPECIFIC COLORS
Blue Scapolite is extremely calming, cutting through confusion and assisting in going deep within the Self to find the source of problems from this or another life.

Purple (raw)

Purple Scapolite is an extremely high-vibration* stone that takes you back to a state of oneness that wipes out soul memory of being alienated, scapegoated or sabotaged, clearing past life patterns and inner voices that may be sabotaging your life now. This powerful stone lifts your awareness out of the mire and assists evolution.

Yellow (raw)

Yellow Scapolite clears mental sabotage, manipulation and thoughts such as 'I'm not good enough' that hold you back from achieving your full potential, enabling taking decisions from an objective perspective. Physically, it calms hyperactivity.

SEPTARIAN

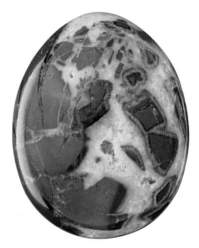

Shaped egg

COLOR	Yellow and gray
APPEARANCE	Cracked, 'mud'-filled fissures and nodules lined with gritty stone
RARITY	Easily obtained
SOURCE	Australia, United States, Canada, Spain, England, New Zealand, Madagascar

ATTRIBUTES Bringing together the qualities of Calcite, Aragonite and Chalcedony, Septarian encourages taking care of the earth—the gray concretions found on the stone connect to devic* energy. This stone focuses the healing vibrations within drumming and chanting circles, and can be used to enhance the cohesiveness of any spiritual group.

Useful for Neuro Linguistic Programming (NLP), Septarian assists in repatterning and reprogramming, and directs the practitioner to the most appropriate tools.

Spiritually, Septarian harmonizes the emotions and intellect with the higher mind to bring illumination.

Mentally this joyous stone provides support while you incubate ideas and assists in manifesting them, inculcating patience, tolerance and endurance. Conversely, if you have ideas but never put them into practice, it concretizes your creativity. Septarian is a useful support during public speaking as it assists in making each individual within an audience feel that they are being personally addressed. Septarian also enhances your ability to communicate within a group.

Emotionally nourishing and calming, Septarian is a useful tool for self-nurturing and for caring about others. Healers can meditate with Septarian for insight into the cause of dis-ease*. This stone is extremely helpful in focusing the body's healing ability and facilitates flexibility of physical movement.

Physically, Septarian detects and rebalances blockages in the body— it is often found in an egg-shaped nodule that confines and shapes energy physically. If the stone has a pointed end, it is a useful reflexology or acupressure tool. Septarian eggs make perfect 'hand comforters' to use in times of stress.

HEALING Beneficial for seasonal affective disorder (SAD), self-healing, skin disorders, cellular memory* and metabolism; reduces swelling and growths. It supports the intestines, kidneys, blood and heart.

POSITION Hold, grid (see pages 28–31) or place as appropriate.

SHIVA LINGAM

Shaped

COLOR	Red and beige or gray
APPEARANCE	Smooth, opaque phallic shape
RARITY	Natural ones are rare
SOURCE	India; may be artificially shaped and polished

ATTRIBUTES Symbolizing the Hindu god Shiva's union with his consort Kali and activating the base and sacral chakras, a Shiva Lingam raises and controls kundalini* energy. It is perfect for facilitating spiritual evolution through tantra or sexual magick. A symbol of sexuality and potent male energy, this stone has been sacred for thousands of years. It facilitates the union of opposites, such as masculine and feminine or body and soul, and is excellent for sexual healing.

Imparting psychological insight, Shiva Lingam facilitates looking within to release all that you have outgrown. This stone is particularly useful for emotional pain that arises from early childhood, especially from sexual abuse, as it reinstates trust in male energy and in your own male qualities and can draw a sexual-healing partner to you.

Suitably programmed (see page 358), a Shiva Lingam severs subtle etheric sexual connection after a relationship has ceased and removes hooks from the vagina or uterus, re-energizing the base chakras and opening the way for a new relationship. It is the perfect stone for creating a self-loving ritual to reclaim femininity and female power.

HEALING Beneficial for overcoming sexual mortification or abuse, infertility, impotence, inorgasmia and menstrual cramps. It stimulates the electrical flow in systems of the body and subtle meridians.

POSITION Hold, grid (see pages 28–31) or place as appropriate.

SPECTROLITE

Polished

*Polished
(red flash)*

COLOR	Greenish with vivid flashes of aqua-blue, orange, yellow, green and red
APPEARANCE	Dull until light sets off the iridescence
RARITY	Easily obtained but expensive
SOURCE	Finland, Canada, Russia, Mexico, Portugal, New Zealand

ATTRIBUTES A higher resonance* of Labradorite, Spectrolite enfolds the soul in a cloak of protection in any realm.

Spiritually, this highly mystical stone raises consciousness and facilitates multi- and inter-dimensional journeying*. Holding profound esoteric wisdom, Spectrolite takes you into other lives, removing psychic debris from previous disappointments or ill-wishing* and strengthening your trust in the universe. A stone of transformation, it prepares body and soul for ascension*. Wearing it prevents energy leakage or vampirization of the biomagnetic sheath* or spleen chakra, especially by a discarnate spirit. Enhancing psychic vision, this stone filters the third eye and deflects unwanted energies or information from impinging on you. Spectrolite removes other people's projections*, including thought forms* hooked into the biomagnetic sheath, soma chakra or third eye.

Psychologically, Spectrolite banishes insecurities and fears, and brings out your strengths. Mentally, Spectrolite balances analysis and rationality with inner sight. Emotionally, this stone increases empathy and acceptance of individual difference and shows why people choose to evolve through challenging lifescripts.

HEALING Helpful for insomnia caused by psychic or mental overload.

Bytownite (tumbled)

POSITION Hold, place or wear as appropriate. (Raw Labradorite is more appropriate for gridding).

ADDITIONAL FORMS

Bytownite (Golden Yellow Labradorite) accesses the highest levels of consciousness and facilitates metaphysical gifts* and visualization, opening a blocked third eye. By expanding the mental body and attuning to higher wisdom, Bytownite detaches you from the undue influence of others and treats co-dependency—or an enabler unable to let someone learn their life lessons or who unconsciously wants to prolong dependency. Useful for overcoming indecision, this stone works on the etheric blueprint* to assist the stomach, spleen, liver, gall bladder and adrenal glands.

Bytownite (raw)

Violet Hypersthene (Velvet Labradorite) has a gentle, grounding*, protecting and strengthening energy, drawing in spiritual power to surround you with light. It is the perfect accompaniment to lower-world* journeys on the crystal medicine wheel (see pages 368–375). On occasions Hypersthene can provoke a powerful cathartic detox of negative energy or make you face your deepest fears.

Violet Hypersthene (polished)

SPECULARITE

ALSO KNOWN AS SPECULAR HEMATITE

Shaped and polished

COLOR	Silvery blue
APPEARANCE	Dark and sparkling like a night sky
RARITY	Easily obtained
SOURCE	United States, Canada, Italy, Brazil, Switzerland, Sweden, Venezuela, Africa

ATTRIBUTES A higher resonance* of Hematite, Specularite assists in manifesting your unique spirit on earth, identifying where your particular talents can best be used. Protective and grounding*, this stone activates a cosmic anchor*, earthing high-frequency spiritual energies into the functional reality of the everyday world and lifting the vibration of subtle* and physical bodies so that they efficiently receive those energies. Useful in earth healing*, Specular Hematite counteracts electro-magnetic energies.

HEALING Beneficial for haemoglobin, anaemia and blood.

POSITION Hold, grid (see pages 28–31) or place by a computer to harmonize it and the physical body.

STIBNITE

Natural wand

COLOR	Silver
APPEARANCE	Metallic, needle-like fans and blades that tarnish, often wand-like
RARITY	Easily obtained
SOURCE	Japan, Romania, United States, China

ATTRIBUTES Uniting the base, sacral, soma and solar plexus chakras and forming a perfect holding space, Stibnite creates an energetic shield around the physical body and is a useful stone for journeying* as it protects during travel and then brings the soul home to the physical body.

Spiritually, when used as a wand with focused intention, this stone separates out the pure from the dross and is an efficient tool for releasing entity* possession or negative energy. Used wisely, it can attract all you desire, but ensure that this is what you really need for your highest good.

Psychologically, this stone shows you the gold in your center, recognizing your gifts, and assists in finding the value in the most difficult experiences.

Shamanically, Stibnite carries the energy of Wolf, facilitating journeying with this perceptive power animal to explore the north of the medicine wheel (see pages 368–375).

Emotionally, Stibnite assists in eliminating tentacles from clingy relationships that penetrate the subtle* or physical bodies, especially after physical separation. It assists in tie-cutting rituals and past-life releases and is particularly useful in situations where you find it difficult to say no to a former partner—although having cut a tie may stimulate a situation that tests if the cutting is complete and you can indeed stand your ground. If so, hold the crystal and focus your awareness to ensure success.

HEALING Helpful for cellular memory*, the oesophagus and stomach and for dissolving rigidity, cold sores and infection.

POSITION Hold, grid (see pages 28–31) or place as appropriate.

NOTE See also page 208 for the one-way portal. As Stibnite is toxic, wash hands thoroughly after use and make the gem essence by the indirect method (see page 361).

STICHTITE

Raw

COLOR	Lilac, purple
APPEARANCE	Waxy, opaque layers
RARITY	Easily obtained
SOURCE	United States, Tasmania, Canada, South Africa

ATTRIBUTES Encouraging you to manifest your true self and live in accordance with your soul contract for the present life, Stichtite facilitates the movement of kundalini* energy up the spine to the heart. It is a powerfully protective stone.

Psychologically, by assisting in keeping your mind, opinions and emotional awareness acutely tuned, Stichtite teaches how negative emotions and ingrained attitudes affect your well-being, supporting while you reframe these. This stone can ameliorate and throw light on the emotional issues that underlie eating disorders and food cravings or allergies.

Physically, Stichtite is a stone of resilience and recovery, supporting convalescence and reprogramming neural pathways in the brain to counteract degenerative dis-ease*.

If you or a child need to take a different path, Stichtite is the perfect tool and it is helpful for indigo children* with hyperactivity, attention-deficit hyperactivity disorder (ADHD) or similar dis-eases. A beneficent stone to keep in your pocket if you live alone, Stichtite provides companionship and has a calming influence on the environment.

HEALING Beneficial for ADHD, skin elasticity and stretch marks, headaches, hernia, teeth and gums, Parkinson's and dementia. It calms the digestive and nervous systems and stabilizes blood pressure and brain chemistry.

POSITION Hold, grid (see pages 28–31) or place as appropriate. For ADHD, keep in a pocket.

(*See also* Atlantasites, pages 59–60.)

SUPER SEVEN

ALSO KNOWN AS MELODY STONE, SACRED SEVEN

Raw

COLOR	Deep purple, orange, red and brown
APPEARANCE	Clear to opaque swirling crystal with several colors visible
RARITY	Rare and apparently mined out, but new sources are opening up (may be Super Five or Six)
SOURCE	Brazil, United States

ATTRIBUTES Super Seven combines the spiritual and protective qualities of Amethyst, the cleansing and grounding ability of Smoky Quartz and the energy-amplifying properties of Quartz with Rutile, Goethite, Lepidocrocite and Cacoxenite. The smallest piece of Super Seven carries the vibration of the whole, whether or not all the minerals are present, reminding that you are a child of earth and the stars.

Spiritually, this high-vibration* stone is a spiritual powerhouse with exceptional clarity. Said to be shifting the vibratory level of the planet

Natural slice

and everything upon it, it brings in the Aquarian Age. Many pieces of Super Seven contain a spiritual being attuned to the highest sources of guidance and inspiration so that you do not need to go anywhere to obtain guidance. Meditating with Super Seven is a heavenly experience and it is a useful stone to carry flower or gem essences (see page 361) for distant healing.

This stone supports and heightens the vibration of other crystals in its vicinity. Activating all the chakras and the subtle bodies* and aligning them to the highest spiritual vibrations*, it activates spiritual gifts and enhances metaphysical working of all kinds. It heals physical, intellectual and spiritual dis-ease* and brings the soul back into communication with the divine, reminding us that we, too, are part of a whole that is much more than the brotherhood of humanity. Emotionally, this is a soothing and nurturing crystal.

Environmentally, small Super Seven points are available that are extremely effective for healing the planetary grid*, stimulating self-healing or opening to new spiritual realities. Particularly effective for grids*, these points pull stagnant energy out of the body, or remove areas of disturbed earth or community energy, and are particularly useful where there is fear of terrorist activity or racial unrest, as they instill peace and a sense of communal safety and interconnection.

HEALING Extremely useful for harmonizing the body, stimulating the body's natural healing system and healing cellular memory*. It supports the immune system, skin and bones.

Small point

POSITION Hold, grid (see pages 28–31) or place as appropriate. For earth healing*, grid into the ground.

TANZANITE

Natural

Polished

Shaped

COLOR	Lilac-blue
APPEARANCE	Bright faceted gem or slightly opaque stone
RARITY	Easily obtained but expensive
SOURCE	Tanzania (may be artificially created)

ATTRIBUTES A stone of transmutation through the violet flame*, Tanzanite has extremely high vibrations* linking to the angelic realms, spirit guides, Ascended Masters* and Christ consciousness*. It helps in entering altered states of consciousness with ease and in living consciously in the eternal now.

Spiritually, this stone facilitates inner and outer journeying*, metaphysical abilities* and profoundly deep meditation. Tanzanite opens subtle chakras on the biomagnetic sheath*, linking to the soul star in order to access and ground the next level of spiritual evolution into the physical plane. Connecting to the Akashic Record*, this stone

335

facilitates multi-dimensional cellular and karmic* healing so that the soul is ready for ascension*.

Psychologically helpful in ascertaining your true vocation, Tanzanite is beneficial for over-worked people, harmonizing fluctuations of energy and assisting in taking time for yourself.

Emotionally, this stone overcomes depression and anxiety, replacing it with trust and poise. It is the perfect stone for resolving the head-heart dilemma, teaching how to live from a compassionate heart with an illumined mind.

Tanzanite jewelry should be worn with care as it may over-stimulate sensitive people. If it induces uncontrolled psychic experiences or mental overload from unwanted telepathy, remove and replace with an appropriate protection stone, such as Hematite, Banded Agate or Smoky Quartz.

Shaped

HEALING Beneficial for reprogramming cellular memory*, past-life healing, the hearing and calming the mind; supports the hair, skin, head, throat, chest, kidneys and nerves.

POSITION Wear, hold, grid (see pages 28–31) or place as appropriate.

TIFFANY STONE

ALSO KNOWN AS BERTRANDITE, PURPLE PASSION, OPALIZED FLUORITE, PURPLE OPAL

Slice

COLOR	Deep purple, blue, pink, green, orange and yellow
APPEARANCE	Swirls of crackled color
RARITY	Extremely rare
SOURCE	One mine in Utah (United States)

ATTRIBUTES Tiffany Stone is an extremely rare and complex gemstone of beryllium and other minerals formed from volcanic ash pressurized for over 2,000 million years. Collecting the mineral is banned, so it is becoming expensive as stocks decline, but some beautiful jewelry is available. Beryllium is one of the lightest but strongest minerals and, spiritually, high-vibration*, high-energy Tiffany Stone enhances intuition and metaphysical gifts*, opening the higher crown chakras and

337

connecting to multi-dimensions and the highest of guidance. Assisting in interpreting channeled* material, this stone is useful for integrating the lightbody* into the physical realm, supporting the soul as it does so.

Psychologically, Tiffany Stone encourages persistence and following the soul's path wherever that might lead. Emotionally, it encourages becoming more open and receptive. Tiffany Stone removes blockages and, by bringing out emotional strength, assists transitions of all kinds. It fills the heart and higher heart chakras with unconditional love. This stone also encourages decluttering at every level.

Mentally, Tiffany Stone enhances clear thought and mental acuity, supporting academic study. It enables communicating and cleansing feelings that have formerly been hidden or of which you feel ashamed.

Physically, it has excellent electrical and thermal conductivity, allowing energies to flow freely. It assists the flow of energy in the meridians*, releasing blockages, energizing and cleansing the chakra system. It stimulates libido and the flow of sexual energy, earning itself the name 'Purple Passion', and is useful for tantric practices.

HEALING With its high Fluorite content, Tiffany Stone is said to strengthen bones and ligaments; it is beneficial for tendonitis, arthritis and osteoarthritis.

POSITION Grid (see pages 28–31) or place as appropriate. If wearing, use in polished form.

NOTE Beryllium is toxic; use the stone in polished form and prepare the gem essence by the indirect method (see page 361).

TUGTUPITE

ALSO KNOWN AS REINDEER BLOOD

Polished

Raw

COLOR	Pink, white, crimson (on exposure to heat or ultra-violet light) with black
APPEARANCE	Translucent or opaque, mottled and veined
RARITY	Rare but available as jewelry
SOURCE	Greenland, Canada, Russia

ATTRIBUTES A stone of integration, Tugtupite bridges the compassionate heart with the illuminated mind and anchors unconditional love in the world. It teaches the power of self-love—without which it is not possible to value yourself or another, to give or receive love or to know intimacy. An exceedingly peaceful stone aligned to the pink flame of pure love, Tugtupite has the rare quality of tenebrescence, meaning that on exposure to sun or ultra-violet light, or on being worn or held, its white or pale pink color deepens to crimson. It fluoresces bright red under ultra-violet light.

Inuit legend says that Tutu, a reindeer girl, went into the mountains to give birth and where her precious, life-giving blood fell, Tugtupite was formed. The Inuit also say that this stone awakens forgotten love and intensifies libido and lovers' passion, causing the stone to glow fiery red. One of the best stones for opening and cleansing the heart chakras, especially the heart seed, this stone signifies romance, passion and fertility. It deepens and expands love, bringing an unconditional quality to all relationships, and aligns and integrates all the chakras with the heart and higher heart chakras so that love is expressed through every act and thought.

Spiritually, when placed over the higher heart chakra of someone whose vibrations have been raised sufficiently, Tugtupite acts like a shaman blowing into the chakra to awaken the dormant channel that connects the compassionate heart to higher states of consciousness. It literally accesses a new level of love to facilitate the vibrational shift and the birth of the lightbody* in the everyday world.

A strongly protective stone that equips you to face difficult situations with equanimity and fearlessness, Tugtupite acts as a liver-defender to block other people's rage or resentment (place under the right armpit) as it neutralizes anger and cuts off inappropriate tugs on your heart strings (wear over your heart). It draws out and transforms your own anger into creative energy and is the perfect stone to assist recovery from a 'psychic mugging'. This stone also clears hooks from any organ of the body—especially the pancreas and stomach—attached to a needy outside source and is particularly effective when used with Nuummite to cut cords from past lives. Tugtupite removes the effect of old relationships and clears the biomagnetic sheath* of the residual effects of psychological or physical abuse. Used for spirit-release in cases of emotional attachment, it encourages forgiveness for yourself and others involved.

Psychologically, Tugtupite promotes forgiveness, compassion and unconditional love, especially of yourself, and promotes the ability to give of oneself without falling into sacrifice or martyrdom. It also

Shaped

340

strengthens conscience and assists in resolving ethical dilemmas. The soft energy of Tugtupite is perfect for ameliorating anxiety and stress and releases poverty consciousness*, bringing abundance on all levels.

Mentally, Tugtupite facilitates a tuning into universal consciousness, bringing increased clarity and breadth of vision to the illumined mind. Tugtupite teaches emotional independence and autonomy, bringing about the realization that you alone are responsible for creating and maintaining your well-being and happiness, and that this is not dependent on any external source, including a partner or loved one. This stone protects from emotional blackmail, providing the strength to cut loose and overcome outside interference. Keep this stone close to your heart as it assists emotional honesty and intimacy. It may take you through a deep emotional catharsis, releasing the grief of the ages for the planet and yourself. Tugtupite reminds you how to love, gently clearing away any blockages, opening your heart and enfolding it in unconditional, universal love. Love then blossoms in your life.

Environmentally, this is the perfect stone to send unconditional love to the world, healing war zones and sites of ethnic conflict.

HEALING Purifies blood, stabilizes blood pressure and heals the heart; regulates metabolism and hormone production; increases fertility. Lifts depression or seasonal affective disorder (SAD).

POSITION Place over the heart or under the right armpit for protection, or as appropriate. Tugtupite is particularly effective worn constantly over the higher heart chakra.

Polished

NOTE Avoid harsh abrasives or salt. Synthetic Tugtupite is now being manufactured, but has few healing qualities.

341

TUGTUPITE WITH NUUMMITE

Combined stone (raw)

COLOR	Pale yellowish matrix with flashes of pink, red and black
APPEARANCE	Mottled and speckled
RARITY	Rare
SOURCE	Greenland

ATTRIBUTES This powerful combination brings together the loving strength of Tugtupite with the awesome protective power of Nuummite, creating an impenetrable shield that, paradoxically, both facilitates and assimilates vibrational change. Assuring, 'I'll stick with you whatever', this combination offers psychological strength and protection from within your heart against outside influence of any kind and assists in healing heartbreak and abandonment.

Psychologically, this combination is particularly helpful for reversing the effects of an unsafe or deprived childhood, whether that was from physical, emotional or mental abuse or benign neglect. Offering a sense of paternal safety that facilitates fathering yourself, and anchoring that deep in your core, this combination assists in standing in your compassionate heart imbued with unconditional love and forgiveness for all concerned.

An extremely effective spirit-release tool where a discarnate spirit or incarnate parent is tugging at the heart strings trying to retain emotional control allegedly 'for your own good', this combination is also helpful when prayers are being said that interfere with your autonomy. Tugtupite encourages forgiveness and insightful communication and Nuummite severs old connections so that unconditional love flows into your heart and provides a shield. Particularly useful when you are in victim mode, teaching how to become a strong survivor instead, the combination helps to explain why the connection and manipulation are no longer relevant and assures the other person that you are now strong enough to stand up for yourself. This combination gets in touch with the love at the center of the universe, expressing that to everything within it. It dissolves the effects of sorcery in the present or any other life, creating a protective shield around your heart.

HEALING Works best at the subtle levels of being to release emotional wounds and to cut off from the past. When held, it instills a profound feeling of safety and the ability to cope.

POSITION Hold or position as appropriate. Wear for as long as possible over the heart. Grid in a Star of David in the environment (see page 31) to facilitate vibrational change in the earth's energy field.

NOTE If the combined stone is not available, use individual Tugtupite (see pages 339–341) and Nuummite (see pages 198–200) stones placed together.

343

URANOPHANE

Raw

COLOR	Orange-yellow
APPEARANCE	Hair-like crystals carried on a matrix
RARITY	Rare
SOURCE	Zaire, Germany, United States, Czech Republic, Germany, Australia, France, Italy

ATTRIBUTES This radioactive crystal is not for prolonged use or general healing. Under the supervision of a suitably qualified practitioner it can support nuclear-based medicine and radiation therapy and acts as a homoeopathic catalyst, releasing karmic*, environmental and soul damage caused by previous radiation. Uranophane subtly realigns the vibrations of the biomagnetic sheath* so that the energy shifts are assimilated into the physical and etheric bodies*.

HEALING Said to be useful for tumors and radiation damage.

POSITION Grid (see pages 28–31) and place with caution around the subtle bodies*. Keep wrapped in foil with Malachite alongside.

USSINGITE

*Lavender-violet
(raw)*

COLOR	Lavender-violet, purple, pinky-beige, dark red
APPEARANCE	Mottled opaque stone
RARITY	Rare
SOURCE	Greenland, Russia, Canada

ATTRIBUTES Ussingite is a color-specific stone, the light, bright violet and purple forms being high-vibrational* and the murky pinky-beige carrying a much denser vibration with a completely different effect.

Spiritually, ethereal violet Ussingite emanates serenity and vibrates at the frequency of spiritual purification. By opening an expanded state of awareness and forming an access point to celestial crystals in other dimensions, violet Ussingite instantly creates a vibrational shift in the frequency of the subtle bodies*, awakening the lightbody* and bringing it into alignment with the Higher Self*. This color opens the higher crown chakras and spiritual vision, and acts as a communicator with the angelic realms and spirit guides so that actions are guided by spiritual wisdom and people are irresistibly attracted to you. The deeper

Purple (raw Russian)

and denser Russian purple Ussingite takes you traveling through multi-dimensions and, although it does not reach the highest frequencies of ethereal violet Ussingite, it brings some high frequencies into form.

Pinky-beige Ussingite awakens the unawakened soul, but conversely, in those who have made the vibrational shift, pulls back to a denser vibration, closing the connection with higher frequencies. With an unawakened soul, it brings about a shift that is sufficient for the soul to realize that work is required to rectify karmic* deficiencies, ingrained beliefs—no matter how spiritual these may appear—and behaviors that are holding it back from spiritual progression. However, pinky-beige Ussingite cannot assist that soul in instantly shifting to the highest vibrations.

Pinky-beige (shaped)

Pinky-beige Ussingite facilitates emotional independence and autonomy, stimulating the realization that you alone are responsible for creating and maintaining well-being and happiness. All Ussingite assists in clearing the ties to anyone on whom you are over-dependent or co-dependent.

Deep red Ussingite dissolves blockages in the base and sacral chakras, neutralizing old anger, and awakens these chakras to an inflooding of

kundalini* energy that creates a level of profound sexual sharing and personal creativity not previously available to the soul. If a stone combining violet and red is placed on the dantien*, it purifies, re-energizes and attunes to the universal kundalini force.

Deep red (tumbled Russian)

HEALING Works best beyond the physical vibration to heal the soul and the lightbody; supports the liver and blood purification and stabilizes blood pressure.

POSITION Wear or place as appropriate.

COMBINATION STONES
Ussingite with Tugtupite is a useful combination to open and protect the heart seed chakra at the base of the breastbone. It clears past-life connections and outgrown soul contracts, facilitating lodging the Higher Self energies within the heart and linking it to the pink flame of universal heart. Use to support the soul in anchoring itself fully in incarnation.

Ussingite with Tugtupite (raw)

Ussingite in Sodalite enhances the ability of Sodalite to harness logic to intuition and anchor the higher mind into the physical, enabling you to view matters from the perspective of an illumined mind. It highlights and removes any ingrained spiritual beliefs that no longer serve you.

Ussingite in Sodalite (raw)

VIVIANITE

Raw

COLOR	Deep green or blue (tarnishes on contact with air)
APPEARANCE	Small, transparent or metallic clusters or blades in matrix; crystals are sometimes bent
RARITY	Can be expensive
SOURCE	Germany, United States, Brazil

ATTRIBUTES Vivianite works with the third eye to sharpen intuition and to act as a guide during travel through the multi-dimensional planes of reality. Spiritually, it accesses your core soul purpose and assists in seeing what has formerly been obscured. A layered stone, it is helpful for working on several levels at once as the energy goes out in waves. If anyone has been hampering your vision, Vivianite clears the veils from your eyes and enables true seeing. Use it to recognize what you have been refusing to see in yourself or in others and to heal inner sight. This stone can also assist in coming to terms with having seen the unseeable or the unacceptable.

Vibrant Vivianite is a useful auric cleanser as it pulls out excess stimulation and negative energy, replacing it with peace and calm. This stone reverses the spin of the crown chakra if required, creating a base note and connecting to the subtle body of the earth to hold you gently in incarnation. This stone is the perfect adjunct to healing visualizations and to ritual working at a distance as it brings the souls together to enhance the effect.

Psychologically, Vivianite assists with dreamwork, reworking a dream creatively to provide healing and insight. This stone assists in setting and attaining realistic goals and imparts the strength to carry on through adversity, making life appear stimulating and challenging rather than dreary. If you continually make emotional projections* or harbor illusions about the future, Vivianite encourages being in the moment.

Emotionally, Vivianite is helpful for uncovering your deepest feelings and things you deny to yourself, integrating your shadow*. If your relationship needs a shake-up, Vivianite brings about revitalization.

Physically, it is an excellent healer for chronic eye conditions. Environmentally, as the crop-circle stone, Vivianite links into earth energies and assists in reading crop markings and contacting the energy behind the patterns. To integrate crop-circle energy into your life, meditate with Vivianite in the center of a circle or gaze into a photograph of a circle.

HEALING Beneficial for eyes, especially iritis, conjunctivitis or cataracts; assists spinal alignment, the heart, liver, memory, vitality, cellular memory*; removes free-radicals; aids the assimilation of iron.

POSITION Hold, grid (see pages 28–31) or place as appropriate. If healing eyes, ensure the eye is closed and place the stone on a sterile tissue.

WAVELLITE

Raw on matrix

COLOR	Green
APPEARANCE	Pearly, vitreous, roseate or radial crystalline needles
RARITY	Not easily obtained
SOURCE	United States, Bolivia, Britain

ATTRIBUTES Wavellite accesses deep core issues or a different perspective before allowing answers to rise gently into awareness. Assisting in easily managing challenging situations, it clears trauma or abuse arising from present or previous lives from the emotional body, facilitating deep soul healing, and provides an overview of attitudes that led to dis-ease*, reframing* cellular memory*. Physically, this stone maintains health and well-being.

HEALING Benefits energy flow from the biomagnetic* to the physical bodies and cellular memory: good for blood flow, white-cell count and dermatitis.

POSITION Hold, grid (see pages 28–31) or place as appropriate.

YOUNGITE

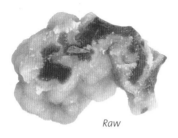

Raw

COLOR	Orange-brown and white
APPEARANCE	Tiny drusy crystals over a jasper matrix
RARITY	Largely mined out
SOURCE	United States

ATTRIBUTES A combination of Brecciated Jasper and Drusy Quartz, Youngite is a shamanic stone that accesses different planes of consciousness, taking you to a space without thought where souls meet and merge.

Spiritually, it links to multi-dimensions, supraconsciousness and All That Is*. Youngite was traditionally said to be the perfect stone for spiritual warriors and leaders as it lights the way forward and offers the courage to stand up and be counted.

The Brecciated Jasper component of this stone heals mental stress, centers the mind and heightens mental agility and rational thought, strengthening intellectual capability in difficult circumstances, while the Drusy Quartz component enhances the ability to laugh at the most traumatic of events.

Psychologically effective for all inner-child* work, Youngite reconnects to the joyous, innocent child that lies within everyone and releases the creative possibilities that child offers. Healing wounds from childhood and beyond, especially those held in the base and sacral chakras, it is helpful in soul-retrieval* as it gently coaxes back childish soul fragments that split off through trauma, joy, forward projection or wishful thinking.

HEALING Works best beyond the physical level of being; excellent for inner-child healing and ameliorating mental stress.

POSITION Hold, grid (see pages 28–31) or place as appropriate.

ZEBRA STONE

Polished slice

Raw

COLOR	Black, white, brown, pink, green
APPEARANCE	Whorls, contour lines and bands of opaque stone
RARITY	Fairly rare
SOURCE	Madagascar, South Africa, India, Brazil

ATTRIBUTES An efficient grounding* stone, Zebra Stone keeps you connected to the earth during spiritual working. It teaches how to fully inhabit your body, with your feet firmly on the ground. Shaking out apathy or disinterest, it fills you with zest for life and remotivates you toward goals.

Emotionally, this stone overcomes depression and anxiety. It provides powerful stimulation for artistic creativity.

HEALING Brings vitality to the body and supports the blood; beneficial for bones and lymphatic flow.

POSITION Hold, grid (see pages 28–31) or place as appropriate.

ZIRCON

Orange (raw)

COLOR	Yellow, green, brown, red, orange
APPEARANCE	Faceted gem or translucent, often double-pyramid
RARITY	Not all colors are easily available
SOURCE	Australia, United States, Sri Lanka, Ukraine, Canada (may be heat-treated to enhance color or be artificially produced)

ATTRIBUTES In ancient times Zircon was used to protect against robbery, lightning, bodily harm and disease. Each color resonates with a different chakra. Promoting unconditional love for yourself and others, it harmonizes your spiritual nature with the earth and brings physical and subtle bodies* into alignment. It assists in recognizing that you are a spiritual being on a human journey, and highlights the oneness from which all souls originated. This stone of psychological insight brings together opposites and instills stamina and tenacity of purpose.

Mentally, Zircon enhances clear thinking and helps separate the significant from the unimportant. Overcoming racism and prejudice, it teaches the brotherhood of humanity and clears from the emotional body the imprint of discrimination, victimization, homophobia and misogyny in this or any other life.

Emotionally, Zircon teaches constancy. Known as a stone of virtue, traditionally it was a test for celibacy. Overcoming jealousy and possessiveness, it promotes letting go of old love and opening to new.

HEALING Beneficial for synergy, sciatica, cramp, insomnia, depression, bones, muscles, vertigo, the liver, menstrual irregularity.

POSITION Hold, grid (see pages 28–31) or place as appropriate.

NOTE Zircon may cause dizziness in those who wear pacemakers or are epileptic. Cubic Zircon has considerably diluted powers.

Brown (raw)

SPECIFIC COLORS
Brown Zircon is useful for centering and grounding* as it opens the earth chakra.

Red Zircon lends vitality to the body, particularly during periods of stress. Adding power to rituals for creating wealth, it activates the base chakra and libido.

Red (raw)

Orange Zircon is an efficient talisman for use during traveling as it protects against injury. This stone increases beauty and guards against jealousy. It stimulates the sacral chakra and creativity.

Yellow Zircon assists in attracting success in business and love and heightens sexual energy. It lifts depression and makes you more alert. This color activates and cleanses the solar plexus chakra.

Green Zircon attracts abundance and stimulates the heart chakra.

QUICK REFERENCE

In this section you will find essential information for working with your crystals, including how to cleanse and activate them, chakra associations and diagrams of physical and subtle anatomy for efficiently positioning crystals, plus details of the crystal medicine wheel. The Glossary helps with unfamiliar terms, including crystal shapes. There is a comprehensive index to help you find exactly the right stone for your needs. Instructions on how to finger dowse will also help you to select appropriate stones.

These pages will also show you how to make a gem essence, if you don't already know how to do so. Gem essences are an excellent way to use crystal energy. Sprayed around a room, rubbed on the wrist or over an organ, or used as instructed by a qualified crystal healer or essence therapist, these gentle energetic essences work subtly to effect change, usually at an emotional or psychological level but they are also efficient space clearers and energy enhancers.

AWAKENING CRYSTALS

Crystals only work when they have been activated. But first they need purifying—and afterward they will require regular cleansing to keep them working at optimum efficiency.

CLEANSING YOUR CRYSTAL

If your crystal is not soluble, friable or layered, hold it under running water for a few minutes and then place in sunlight or moonlight for a few hours to re-energize and recharge it. Delicate crystals can be cleansed in raw brown rice, or with sound, light or a smudge stick. Salt can be used if the crystal is not layered, friable or delicate. Carnelian cleanses and recharges other crystals if stored with them. You can also buy purpose-made crystal cleansers.

ACTIVATING YOUR CRYSTAL

Hold your crystal in your hands, concentrate on it and say out loud, 'I dedicate this crystal to the highest good of all who come into contact with it.' If you would like to 'program' the crystal for a specific purpose, state clearly what that is.

STORING YOUR CRYSTAL

As delicate stones can easily be damaged, it is sensible to keep them in a bag when they are not in use or on display. If you do display stones, remember that strong sunlight quickly fades colors.

CHOOSING YOUR CRYSTAL

You can either choose a crystal to which you are instantly attracted, look up a crystal's properties to ensure it does what you require or use a pendulum to dowse or the finger-dowse technique (see page 360).

The quickest way to cleanse your crystals is to wash them under running water for a few minutes.

HOW TO FINGER DOWSE

Finger dowsing harnesses your innate bodily intuition to choose exactly the right crystal for your needs or to answer questions.

1 Begin by looping your thumb and finger together as shown.

2 Slip your other thumb and finger through the loop and close together. Hold over a crystal or photograph. Ask your question.

3 Pull steadily. If the loop breaks, the answer to your question is no. If the loop holds, the answer to your question is yes.

MAKING A GEM ESSENCE

As crystals work by resonance, the vibration is easily transferred into spring water, making a gem essence. First cleanse your crystal (see page 358), then place it in a clean glass bowl. Cover with pure spring water. (If the crystal is toxic, layered, soluble or fragile use the indirect method, placing it in a clean glass bowl, then placing this bowl in the bowl of water.) Leave in the sun or moonlight for 6–12 hours. Remove the crystal. Add two-thirds brandy or cider vinegar as a preservative. Bottle in a clean glass bottle—this is a mother tincture and needs further dilution.

USING THE GEM ESSENCE

To dilute the mother tincture before use, add seven drops of mother tincture to a small glass dropper bottle, top up with one-third brandy to two-thirds water if taking by mouth or putting on the skin. If using as an eye drop, do not add alcohol or vinegar at any stage. Sip at regular intervals, rub on the skin or bathe affected parts. A few drops of gem essence can be added to a spray bottle of water and spritzed around your home or workspace, or added to your bath.

Place the crystal in a clean glass bowl with spring water.

Bottle in a clean glass bottle with two-thirds brandy or cider vinegar.

PHYSICAL AND SUBTLE ANATOMY

Knowing exactly where the internal organs and the subtle chakras, blueprints* and energy meridians of the body are positioned makes placing crystals for maximum effect an easy task.

PHYSICAL ANATOMY

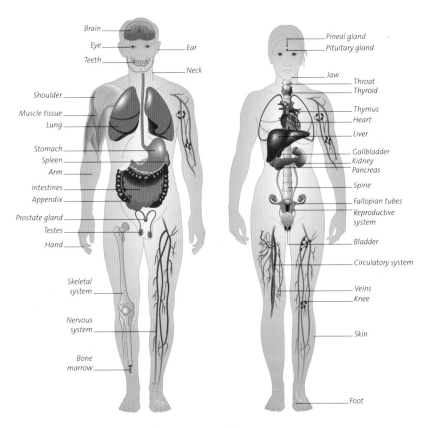

Brain
Eye
Teeth
Ear
Neck
Shoulder
Muscle tissue
Lung
Stomach
Spleen
Arm
Intestines
Appendix
Prostate gland
Testes
Hand
Skeletal system
Nervous system
Bone marrow

Pineal gland
Pituitary gland
Jaw
Throat
Thyroid
Thymus
Heart
Liver
Gallbladder
Kidney
Pancreas
Spine
Fallopian tubes
Reproductive system
Bladder
Circulatory system
Veins
Knee
Skin
Foot

SUBTLE ANATOMY: CHAKRAS AND BLUEPRINTS

1 HIGHER EARTH CHAKRA Above the feet; linkage point to earth's etheric field

2 EARTH CHAKRA Between the feet; linkage point to the earth

3 BASE CHAKRA At the perineum; sexual and creative center

4 SACRAL CHAKRA Just below the navel; the other sexual and creative center

5 SOLAR PLEXUS CHAKRA At the solar plexus; emotional center

6 HEART SEED CHAKRA At the base of the breastbone; site of soul remembrance

7 SPLEEN CHAKRA Under left armpit; potential site of energy leakage

8 HEART CHAKRA Over the physical heart; love center

9 HIGHER HEART CHAKRA Over the thymus; center of immunity

10 THROAT CHAKRA Over the throat; center of truth

11 PAST-LIFE OR ALTA-MAJOR CHAKRA Just behind the ears; stores past-life information

12 THIRD EYE CHAKRA Midway between eyebrow and hairline; center of insight

13 SOMA CHAKRA At the hairline above the third eye; center of spiritual identity and consciousness activation

14 CROWN CHAKRA At the top of the head; spiritual connection point

15 HIGHER CROWN CHAKRA Above the crown of the head; linkage point for spirit

16 SOUL STAR CHAKRA About 1 foot above the crown of the head; linkage point for the spiritual and subtle bodies* through which higher energies can be grounded or physical vibrations can be raised

17 STELLAR GATEWAY CHAKRA Above soul star chakra; cosmic doorway to other worlds

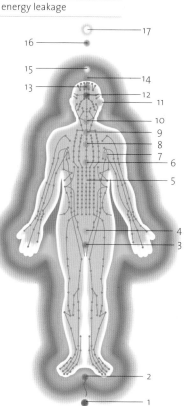

CHAKRA ASSOCIATIONS

CHAKRA	COLOR	POSITION	ISSUE
HIGHER EARTH AND EARTH	Brown	Below feet	Material connection
BASE	Red	Base of spine	Survival instincts
SACRAL	Orange	Below navel	Creativity and procreation
SOLAR PLEXUS	Yellow	Above navel	Emotional connection and assimilation
HEART SEED	Pink	Base of breastbone	Soul remembrance
SPLEEN	Light green	Under left arm	Energy leaching
HEART	Green	Over heart	Love
HIGHER HEART	Pink	Over thymus	Unconditional love

POSITIVE QUALITIES	NEGATIVE QUALITIES
Grounded, practical, operates well in everyday reality	Ungrounded, no sense of power, cannot operate in everyday reality, picks up negativity
Base security, sense of one's own power, spontaneous leadership; active, independent	Impatience, fear of annihilation, death wish, violence, anger; over-sexed or impotent, vengeful, hyperactive, impulsive, manipulative
Assertive, confident; fertility, courage, joy, sexuality, sensual pleasure, acceptance of sexual identity	Low self-esteem, infertility, cruelty, inferiority, sluggishness, emotional hooks or thought forms; pompous
Empathetic; good energy utilization, organization, logic, active intelligence	Poor energy utilization, emotional baggage, energy leaching; lazy, overly emotional or cold, cynical, taking on other people's feelings and problems
Remembrance of reason for incarnation, connection to divine plan, tools available to manifest potential	Rootless, purposeless, lost
Self-contained, powerful	Exhausted and manipulated
Loving, generous, compassionate, nurturing, flexible, self-confident, accepting	Disconnected from feelings, unable to show love, jealous, possessive, insecure, miserly or resistant to change
Compassionate, empathic, nurturing, forgiving, spiritually connected	Spiritually disconnected, grieving, needy; inability to express feelings

CHAKRA ASSOCIATIONS CONTINUED

CHAKRA	COLOR	POSITION	ISSUE
THROAT	Blue	Throat	Communication
PAST LIFE	Light turquoise-green	Behind ears	Anything carried over from past lives
THIRD EYE	Dark blue	Forehead	Intuition and mental connection
SOMA	Lavender	Center of hairline	Spiritual connection
CROWN	Violet	Top of head	Spiritual connection
HIGHER CROWN	White	Above head	Spiritual enlightenment
SOUL STAR	Lavender/white	1 foot above head	Soul connection and highest self illumination
STELLAR GATEWAY	White	Above soul star chakra	Cosmic doorway to reach other worlds

POSITIVE QUALITIES	NEGATIVE QUALITIES
Able to speak own truth, receptive, idealistic, loyal	Unable to verbalize thoughts or feelings, stuck, dogmatic, disloyal
Wisdom, life skills, instinctive knowing	Emotional baggage, insecurity, unfinished business
Intuitive, perceptive, visionary, in the moment	Spaced-out, fearful, attached to past, superstitious, bombarded with other people's thoughts
Spiritually aware and fully conscious	Cut off from spiritual nourishment and sense of inner connectedness
Mystical, creative, humanitarian, giving service	Overly-imaginative, illusory, arrogant, uses power to control others
Spiritual, attuned to higher things, enlightened; true humility	Spaced-out and open to invasion, illusions and delusions
Ultimate soul connection, soul intertwining with physical body together with high-frequency light, communication with soul intention, objective perspective on past lifetimes	Soul fragmentation, open to extra-terrestrial invasion, messiah-complex; rescues not empowers
Connected to highest energies in the cosmos and beyond; communication with enlightened beings	Disintegration; open to cosmic disinformation, unable to function

THE CRYSTAL MEDICINE WHEEL

Traditionally, the medicine wheel teaches the way to balance your life. It is worked in a clockwise direction starting with the south, the place of coming into incarnation. While it is always best to work with an experienced practitioner, the wheel can be used for personal healing and, if you are working alone, the most effective way is to sit facing each direction in turn, holding the appropriate crystal and meditating on a question connected to the energies of that direction and how they have affected your life.

You can also travel the paths between opposite directions to integrate the qualities associated with those directions, such as the path between the south-west (the dream and the way your life is) and the north-east (which helps in understanding the choices you make and how you can facilitate them). The crystals act as storehouses for the information and facilitate your journey to the cardinal and minor points.

Placing your crystals on the appropriate colors helps you to remember the direction associations.

CARDINAL POINTS AND DIRECTIONS

The cardinal points are south, west, north and east, and the minor directions are south-west, north-west, north-east and south-east. Each direction has its specific energy and associations:

Smoky Candle Quartz

SOUTH
The close-to place

GENDER	More feminine than masculine
SEASON	Summer
ELEMENT	Water—rain, river, ocean, lake, blood
WORLD	Plants, trees
TIME	Past
COLOR	Red (blood)
HUMAN ASPECT	Emotions, heart, feelings
HUMAN SHIELD	Inner child—wounded child, child's view
ALLY	Trust and innocence
ENEMY	Fear
PLANETARY CONNECTION	Moon
TOTEMS	Mouse, coyote, snake
CRYSTAL	Smoky Candle Quartz

The south is where you are birthed. Placed here, Candle Quartz makes you feel good about yourself and your body—it is useful for those who find physical incarnation challenging. Candle Quartz restores trust and innocence, bringing healing to the hurt child within and helping in

369

incarnating more fully, surrounded by an aura of unconditional love. It heals the ancestral line* and your karmic* inheritance. Highlighting soul purpose and focusing the life path, Candle Quartz facilitates putting ancient knowledge into practice and brings the totems closer. It assists in understanding how the physical body can be damaged by emotional or mental distress.

SOUTH-WEST
The place of dreams

CRYSTAL	Selenite

In the south-west, Selenite takes you into the place of dreams and dreaming. It reaches other lives and is useful for checking on progress made and for accessing the life plan* for the present life from the between-life state*. Pinpointing lessons and issues that are still being worked upon, it shows how they can best be resolved.

WEST
The looks-within place

GENDER	Feminine
SEASON	Autumn
ELEMENT	Earth—crystal, stone, etc.
WORLD	Mineral
TIME	Present
COLOR	Black

*Selenite
Phantom*

HUMAN ASPECT	Body
HUMAN SHIELD	Adult spirit (manifestation)
ALLY	Intuition, change, death and rebirth
ENEMY	Inertia, death, getting old
PLANETARY CONNECTION	Earth
TOTEMS	Panther/jaguar, owl, crow
CRYSTAL	Smoky Quartz

The west is the place of death and going within. Smoky Quartz teaches how to leave behind anything that no longer serves and it accompanies you through the gates of death into the otherworld and rebirth. One of the most efficient grounding* and cleansing stones available, this protective stone has a strong link with the earth, promoting concern for the environment and suggesting ecological solutions. Alleviating ambivalence about being in incarnation, Smoky Quartz helps in tolerating difficult times with equanimity, fortifying resolve. It assists acceptance of the physical body and the sexual nature, enhancing virility and cleansing the base chakra so that passion flows naturally.

Smoky Quartz

NORTH-WEST
The place of habits, patterns and routines

CRYSTAL	Chlorite Phantom Quartz (Shaman Quartz)

This is the place where the habits of the past must be challenged. Shaman Quartz assists in clearing cellular memory* and healing the present-life ancestral line, opening the way for changes to occur. Absorbing negativity and environmental pollutants, this stone clears

Shaman Quartz

a build-up of stagnant energy anywhere in the body or environment. This stone assists with the removal of energy implants*, accessing their source in this or any other lifetime. Chlorite has strong associations with nature and with Mother Earth.

NORTH
The knowing place

GENDER	More masculine than feminine
SEASON	Winter
ELEMENT	Air—the four winds
WORLD	Animal
TIME	Future
COLOR	White
HUMAN ASPECT	Mind: heart-mind, thinking-mind, functioning-mind, small-mind
HUMAN SHIELD	Adult—world view
ALLY	Balance, knowledge, wisdom
ENEMY	Knowledge without wisdom
PLANETARY CONNECTION	The stars
TOTEMS	Wolf, horse, buffalo
CRYSTAL	Quartz

Clear Quartz point with barnacle and bridge

In the north, Quartz helps to focus and integrate different levels of the mind, facilitating inner wisdom and taking a wider perspective on life. It enhances metaphysical abilities* and attunes to spiritual purpose, bringing about a balance between heart, mind, body and soul. A master healer for any condition, multi-dimensional cellular memory repairer and efficient receptor for programming (see page 358), Clear Quartz works on all levels of being and has the ability to dissolve karmic seeds (the patterns and imprints from former lives that may become activated and result in dis-ease*, relationships or events in the present life).

NORTH-EAST
The place of choices

CRYSTAL	Amethyst

In the north-east, Amethyst facilitates the decision-making process, bringing in common sense and spiritual insights, and also improves motivation, making you more able to set realistic goals and put decisions and insights into practice. It assists in the assimilation of new ideas and connects cause with effect. Amethyst balances out highs and lows, aiding emotional and spiritual centering.

Amethyst

EAST
The sees-far place

GENDER	Masculine
SEASON	Spring
ELEMENT	Fire
WORLD	Human
TIME	Beyond time
COLOR	Yellow/gold—the morning star

373

HUMAN ASPECT	Spirit
HUMAN SHIELD	Magical child—inspiration
ALLY	Illumination, enlightenment, beauty, pure pleasure
ENEMY	Misuse of power
PLANETARY CONNECTION	Sun
TOTEMS	Eagle, hawk, condor
CRYSTAL	Citrine

The east is the place of conception. Citrine carries the power of the rising sun to illuminate your life and touch the spark of pure spirit within your self. Lighter shades of Citrine govern the physical body and its functions, and darker shades the spiritual aspects of life. Citrine helps in moving into the flow of feelings and becoming emotionally balanced. It absorbs, transmutes and grounds negative energy and protects the environment. In the east of the crystal medicine wheel, it is particularly beneficial for attracting abundance and enhancing creativity.

Natural citrine

SOUTH-EAST
The place of the ancestors

CRYSTAL	Spirit Quartz

In the south-east, Spirit Quartz is particularly useful for providing insights into problems experienced within a family, tightly focusing healing that reaches multi-dimensions and reprograms cellular memory, promoting self-forgiveness. Spirit Quartz takes you to meet the spirits of your ancestors and those of the planet, and can be programmed for ancestral healing (see page 358), especially for reframing* the past. In past-life healing, this stone rejigs the etheric blueprint* for the present life, pinpointing significant karmic connections and the gift or karmic justice in traumatic situations.

White Spirit Quartz

CENTER
The place of Above and Below and All That Is

CRYSTAL   Smoky Quartz Elestial

Smoky Quartz Elestial

The center of the medicine wheel represents the Below (Mother Earth) and the Above (Father Earth) and All That Is*. A Smoky Quartz Elestial placed at the center of the wheel bridges Above and Below, bringing the light and wisdom of All That Is to the circle infused with the creative power of Father Sun and the nurturing energy of Mother Earth to create a sacred holding space of infinite possibilities and profound healing.

GLOSSARY

AKASHIC RECORD A record that exists beyond time and space containing information on all that has occurred and all that will occur.

ALL THAT IS Spirit, the Source, the divine: the sum total of everything that is.

AMORPHOUS CRYSTAL No rigid internal organization or structure, energy flows rapidly through; strong acting and instant in effect. *See* Gaia Stone, page 138.

ANCESTRAL-LINE PATTERNS Family patterns and beliefs that have been passed from previous generations to the present.

ASCENDED MASTERS Highly evolved beings who guide the spiritual evolution of the earth and the ascension process.

ASCENSION PROCESS Means by which people seek to raise their spiritual and physical vibrations.

ASTRAL TRAVEL *See* JOURNEYING.

ATTACHED ENTITIES Spirit or alien forms attached to the BIOMAGNETIC SHEATH of a living person.

AURIC SHIELD The edges of the BIOMAGNETIC SHEATH strengthened to provide protection.

BALL FORMATION Emits energy in all directions equally. A window to past or future, balls move energy through time and provide a glimpse of what is to come or what has been. *See* Gaspeite, page 140.

BARNACLE FORMATION Small crystals partially covering a larger crystal. Assists family or community problems, supports group energy and comforts after loss of a loved one. *See* Spirit Quartz pages 300–303; Morion Quartz, page 268.

BETWEEN-LIVES STATE Vibratory state in which the soul resides between incarnations. *See also* PRE-BIRTH STATE.

BIOMAGNETIC SHEATH Subtle energy body (bodies) around the physical body, comprising physical, emotional, mental, KARMIC and spiritual layers.

BLADE FORMATION Flat crystal, useful for clearing past patterns and psychic blockages; the point heals and seals with light. *See* Smoky Lemurian, page 264.

BLUEPRINT Subtle energetic program from which the physical body is constructed. It carries imprints of past life DIS-EASE or injury, emotional traumas and mental constructs from which present-life illness or disability can result.

BOTRYOIDAL CRUST A drusy coating of quartz or other minerals. *See* Hemimorphite, page 154.

BRIDGE FORMATION One crystal linking two others, or across another crystal, bringing together two points of view. *See* Clear Quartz, page 372.

CELLULAR MEMORY Memory of past-life or ancestral attitudes, trauma and patterns deeply ingrained as on-going negative programs, such as POVERTY CONSCIOUSNESS, which create DIS-EASE or are replayed in slightly different forms.

CHAKRA Energy linkage point between the physical and SUBTLE BODIES. Chakra malfunction leads to physical, emotional, mental or spiritual DIS-EASE or disturbance. *See* pages 363–367.

CHANNELING Process through which information is passed from a soul not in incarnation to or through an incarnate being.

CHRIST CONSCIOUSNESS State in which all the life forms of the universe are linked together in universal love and awareness; highest manifestation of divine energy.

CLAIRAUDIENCE Hearing with the psychic ear rather than the physical one; hearing what is inaudible to physical hearing.

CLAIRVOYANCE Ability to discern and communicate with spirits.

COMPANION FORMATION Two crystals entwined and partly growing in each other, or a smaller crystal that grows out of the main crystal. Occasionally, one crystal totally surrounds another. Nurtures, assisting in understanding a relationship better and recognizing how one partner can best support the other without enabling or disempowering. *See* Vera Cruz Amethyst, page 315.

COSMIC ANCHOR Subtle energy conduit down the central line of the body, passing through the earth CHAKRA deep into the earth attaching to the core, and passing via the soul star chakra above the head, upward to the GALACTIC CENTER. Stabilizes core energy and provides a grounding cable for the LIGHTBODY, enabling riding out earth-energy changes and assimilating downloads of high-vibration energy and, where appropriate, grounding it into the earth.

COSMIC CONSCIOUSNESS High state of awareness in which you are part of universal energy.

DANTIEN Small, spirally rotating, power-generating sphere on top of the sacral chakra. If empty or depleted, creative energy cannot function fully, resulting in unbalance. Draining occurs through sexual acts that are not fully loving, overwork and people pulling on your energy.

DENDRITIC Fern-like markings visible within a crystal. *See* Dendritic Chalcedony, page 118.

DEVAS/DEVIC KINGDOM Nature spirits, traditionally believed to rule trees, rivers and mountains.

DIS-EASE State resulting from physical imbalances, blocked feelings, suppressed emotions, karma and negative thinking which, if not reversed, leads to illness.

DNA HEALING It is believed that human DNA originally had 12 strands, which are being reactivated as humanity evolves.

DOUBLE TERMINATIONS Pointed at both ends; breaks old patterns. *See* Sichuan Quartz, page 293.

EARTH HEALING Rectifying distortion of the earth's energy field that has been caused by pollution and destruction of its resources.

ELECTROMAGNETIC SMOG Subtle but detectable electromagnetic field given off by power lines and electrical equipment that has an adverse effect on sensitive people.

EMPATHY NICKS Small chips on crystals that do not detract from their healing power and which may mean the crystal has greater empathy with pain.

ENERGY IMPLANT Vibration, thought or negative emotions implanted in the subtle body by outside sources.

ENTITY Discarnate spirit who hangs around close to earth and may attach to an incarnate being.

ENTITY REMOVAL Detaching discarnate spirit or other being and dispatching it to the appropriate post-death dimension.

ETHERIC BODY Subtle BIOMAGNETIC SHEATH surrounding the physical body.

FLAME Energy field that is part of your greater overall being and which can transform or transmute your vibrations.

GALACTIC CENTER The astrological zodiacal center around which the galaxy revolves, currently at the end of Sagittarius.

GENERATOR Cluster with several points or six facets. Bringing together a group in peaceful harmony, it generates powerful healing energy. Six facets meeting in a sharp point is the optimum shape for generating energy, focusing healing energy and clarity of intention. *See* Aqua Aura Spirit Quartz, page 302.

GEODE Cave-like crystal that amplifies, conserves and slowly releases energy. Beneficial for addictive or over-indulgent personalities. *See* Avalonite, page 61.

GEOPATHIC STRESS Earth stress created by energy disturbance from underground water, power lines and ley lines.

GRIDS/GRIDDING Placing crystals around a building, person or place for energy enhancement or protection—the positioning is best dowsed for.

GROUNDING (1) Creating a strong connection between one's soul, physical body and the earth. (2) Anchoring energies in the earth.

HEALING CRISIS Positive sign that symptoms will soon disappear, marked by a brief intensifying of symptoms.

HIGHER DIMENSIONS/VIBRATIONS Vibrational space or state with a faster and finer vibration not necessarily being located elsewhere. Higher-vibrational states can exist on earth or in crystals.

HIGHER RESONANCE Acts rather like a Higher Self for the base stone, raising the vibrations to the next level.

HIGHER SELF The part of the soul not in incarnation that knows the soul plan for the current and ultimate lifetimes and contains wisdom and gifts garnered in previous incarnations.

HOUSE CLEARING Removing entities and negative energies from a house.

HYPNOTIC COMMANDS Unconscious programs instilled by an external source that 'run' a person, causing them to act in automatic mode.

ILL-WISHING *See* PSYCHIC ATTACK.

IMPLANT *See* ENERGY IMPLANT.

INCLUSION/INCLUDED IN *See* OCCLUSION.

INDIGO CHILDREN Children born with a higher vibration to those already on earth. These children often have difficulty adjusting to the present earth vibration.

INNER CHILD Part of the personality that remains childlike (but not childish) and innocent, or may be the repository of abuse and trauma that requires healing.

INNER LEVELS/DIMENSIONS Levels of being that encompass intuition, psychic awareness, emotions, feelings, subconscious mind and subtle energies.

ISIS FACE Puts you in touch with the goddess within. Healing anything broken—body, mind, emotions or spirit—it integrates spiritual energies into the emotional body and ameliorates over-identification with suffering of others. Helpful for men who want to get in touch with their feeling nature; assists sensitive children to stabilize. Beneficial for anyone facing transition. *See* Amphibole Quartz, page 227.

JOURNEYING Soul leaves the physical body and travels to distant locations. Also known as out-of-body experience and astral travel.

KARMA Dynamic, continuous process of learning and meeting the credits and deficits of previous actions and what is being set in motion now.

KARMA OF GRACE When sufficient has been done, karma can be released and no longer operates.

KARMIC Experiences or lessons arising from or appertaining to a past incarnation. Debts, beliefs and emotions such as guilt are carried over into the present life and create DIS-EASE, but past-life credits and wisdom are available to heal these. Karmic seeds are patterns and imprints from former lives that may become activated and result in dis-ease, relationships or events in the present life.

KARMIC ENMESHMENT Entanglement with another soul that has its roots in past lives in which karma or actions are repeated over and over again.

KUNDALINI Inner, subtle spiritual and sexual energy that resides at the base of the spine and, awakened, rises to the crown chakras.

LIFE PLAN *See* SOUL PLAN.

LIGHTBODY Subtle energy body vibrating at a high frequency. A vehicle for Spirit.

LIGHTWORKER Soul who has undertaken to assist the vibrational shift of the earth by doing their own work and, in so doing, stimulates others to evolve.

LONG-POINT CRYSTAL Focuses energy in a straight line. Pointed toward the body it rapidly transmits energy, or draws it off if turned away. *See* Lemurian Seed, pages 263–265.

LOWER WORLD The shamanic lower world is that of the earth and the subconscious mind. *See also* UPPER WORLD.

MATRIX The bedrock on which crystals are formed.

MENTAL INFLUENCES Effect of other people's thoughts and strong opinions on your mind.

MENTOR FORMATION Acts as a teacher stone and conveys ancient wisdom downloading information from the AKASHIC RECORD and sharing knowledge, bringing the highest dimension to the work.

MERIDIAN Subtle energy channel that runs close to the surface of the skin, or the planet, and contains acupuncture points.

MERKABA Complex geometric shape said to assist consciousness evolution and the activation of the LIGHTBODY.

METAPHYSICAL ABILITIES/GIFTS Abilities such as CLAIRVOYANCE, telepathy, healing.

MIASM Subtle imprint of an infectious disease or traumatic event from the past that has been passed down through a family or place.

NEGATIVE EMOTIONAL PROGRAMMING 'Oughts' and 'shoulds' and emotions such as guilt instilled in childhood or other lives that remain in the subconscious and influence present behaviour, sabotaging effects to evolve until released.

OCCLUSION Inclusion formed from a deposit of another mineral within a Quartz crystal, but may be attached to an external face and show through; radiates energy of the mineral focused and amplified by the surrounding Quartz.

OUT-OF-BODY EXPERIENCE *See* JOURNEYING.

PLANETARY GRID Subtle and invisible earth energy lines that cover the planet rather like a spider's web.

POVERTY CONSCIOUSNESS Ingrained belief that it is somehow right and meritorious to suffer poverty and lack.

PRE-BIRTH STATE Dimension inhabited by the soul before birth.

PROJECTION Seeing and disliking in others characteristics that we cannot accept are actually part of ourselves.

PSYCHIC ATTACK Malevolent thoughts or feelings toward another person, whether consciously or unconsciously directed, creating DIS-EASE and disruption in that person's life.

PSYCHIC VAMPIRISM Ability to draw off or 'feed on' the energy of others.

PSYCHOPOMP The conveyor of souls to the next world.

PYRAMID Amplifying and tightly focusing energy through the apex, this shape draws off negative energies and blockages from the chakras, replenishing with vibrant energy. *See* Heulandite, page 158.

QI Life-force that energizes the physical and SUBTLE BODIES.

RADIONIC Method of diagnosis and treatment at a distance.

RAISING VIBRATIONS Bringing the HIGHER SELF into line with the soul's purpose, and aligning the physical body and the LIGHTBODY.

REFRAMING Seeing a past event in a different, more positive light so that the DIS-EASE it is creating is healed.

REIKI Natural hands-on method of healing. Healing passes through the practitioner to the recipient or is sent at a distance.

SCEPTER Formed from a central rod around which another crystal grows. Reversed scepter is a small crystal point emerging from a larger base. Directs healing to core of a problem or to subtle bodies. DIS-EASE is dissolved and energies restructured at all levels of being as appropriate. Scepters are excellent for reclaiming power. *See* Orange River Quartz, page 272; Smoky Amethyst Brandenberg, page 234.

SCRYING Using a crystal to look into the future or past.

SELF-HEALED CRYSTAL Many small terminations where the crystal has broken from its base and healed the break by laying down fresh crystal. This formation has an impressive knowledge of self-healing, teaching how to become whole again no matter how damaged and wounded you are. *See* Lemurian Seed, page 263.

SHADOW QUALITIES/ENERGIES Qualities that are repressed or denied and exist out of conscious awareness within the subconscious mind.

SHAMANIC ANCHOR Conduit that helps to bring earth or galactic energies into the physical body during upper- or lower-world journeying; a cord to guide return.

SILVER CORD Link between the physical and ETHERIC BODY that goes from the soma CHAKRA to the etheric body.

SOUL FRAGMENTS *See* SOUL PARTS.

SOUL GROUP Cluster of souls who have traveled together throughout time, all or some of whom are in incarnation.

SOUL IMPERATIVE Past-life agendas and unfinished business that operate unconsciously to motivate the present life. Includes past-life promises and purposes that drive the soul forward from life to life and which draw past partners back into your orbit in the guise of lovers—or enemies.

SOUL LINKS Connections between members of a SOUL GROUP.

SOUL PARTS The soul is the vehicle for carrying the eternal spirit. Soul parts are part of the soul not presently in incarnation, which include, but are not limited to, soul fragments that split off. *See also* SOUL RETRIEVAL.

SOUL PLAN Soul's intention and learning-plan for the present life, which may have been carefully reviewed in the between-life state or may be a knee-jerk reaction to karmic causes.

SOUL RETRIEVAL Trauma, shock or abuse, and even extreme joy, cause a part of the soul energy to leave and remain stuck at a certain point in life or at a past-life death. A soul-retrieval practitioner or shaman retrieves the split-off part, bringing it back to the present-life body.

SOULMATE CONFIGURATION *See* TWINFLAME CONFIGURATION.

SPIRIT RELEASE *See* ENTITY REMOVAL.

STAR CHILDREN Beings from other planetary systems who have incarnated on the earth to help its spiritual evolution.

SUBTLE BODIES Layers of the BIOMAGNETIC SHEATH.

SUBTLE ENERGY FIELDS Invisible but detectable energy field that surrounds all living beings.

TABULAR FORMATION Two wide sides result in a flat crystal; energy flows freely. It removes confusion, misinterpretation and misunderstanding and aids communication at all levels. Links two points, bringing about perfect balance. *See* 'Citrine' Lemurian, page 264.

TANTRIC TWIN Two identical crystals aligned side by side but not sharing a base. Ideal for two people working together as equals, spiritually or materially. Tantric twins harmonize and integrate different levels of being. A double-terminated tantric twin is perfect for the ASCENSION PROCESS.

TELLURIC CURRENTS Powerful earth energy currents that run around and through the earth's mantle.

THOUGHT FORMS Forms created by strong positive or negative thoughts that exist on the etheric or spiritual level and affect a person's mental functioning.

TRIPLE-BURNER MERIDIAN Meridian concerned with temperature control.

TWINFLAME/SOULMATE CONFIGURATION Two equal-sized crystals on the same base (the difference is in the programming). Twinflame bonds two people into a close and intimate relationship, teaching how to be unique and separate while united in equal partnership, creating interdependence and deep intimacy. The closer the points are in size, the more harmonious the partnership. Soulmates share KARMIC lessons, twinflames mutual support and unconditional love. Without a common base, union tends to be mental and spiritual rather than emotional and physical. An unequal twinflame brings unconditional love to a relationship such as parent–child, employer–employee, creating alignment and greater harmony. Place twin crystal farthest right from the door. *See* Orange River Quartz, page 272.

UPPER WORLD The shamanic upper world is that of the stars and the conscious and higher mind. *See also* LOWER WORLD.

VIBRATIONAL ENERGY DOWNLOADS Influxes of energy that will raise the consciousness of humanity and are 'downloaded' into the physical level of being, but may take time to process and come into awareness.

INDEX

USEFUL INFORMATION

FURTHER READING

Hall, Judy, *The Crystal Bible*, Godsfield, London, 2003

Hall, Judy, *Crystal Prescriptions*, O Books, Ropley, 2005

Hall, Judy, *The Crystal Zodiac*, Godsfield, London, 2005

Hall, Judy, *Good Vibrations: Energy enhancement, psychic protection and space clearing*, Flying Horse Books, Bournemouth, 2008

WORKSHOPS AND TRAINING ORGANIZATIONS

United Kingdom
Judy Hall workshops
www.judyhall.co.uk

Affiliation of Crystal Healing Organisations (ACHO)
www.crystal-healing.org/schools.htm

Institute of Crystal and Gem Therapists
www.mcscourses.co.uk/xtherapy.html

International Association of Crystal Healing Therapists (IACHT)
www.iacht.co.uk

United States
The Association of Melody Crystal Healing Instructors (TAOMCHI)
www.taomchi.com

AUTHOR ACKNOWLEDGMENTS

My deepest thanks to Ray Berry for the Lemurian medicine wheel experience and the directions data in Quick Reference. To crystal suppliers and eBay sellers from whom I sourced stones, thanks for sterling service and apologies I cannot name you. As always, thanks to Jacqui Malone for her knowledge and amazing stones, and to Sue and Simon Lily for the Bluestone gift and enduring friendship. To participants on my workshops, Dawn Robins, Jacki Dixon and everyone who helped me to explore the properties of these beautiful stones heartfelt blessings, and to my agent Chelsey Fox for patience and for making it work, thank you.

PICTURE ACKNOWLEDGMENTS

All photography © Octopus Publishing Group Limited, with the exception of the following:

Alamy/North Wind Picture Archives 17. Catherine Best Ltd. 24. Corbis/1996–98 AccuSoft Inc., All right/Robert Harding World Imagery 15 bottom. Nasa/GSFC, Jacques Descloitres, MODIS Land Rapid Response Team 33 bottom.

Executive Editor: Sandra Rigby
Senior Editor: Fiona Robertson
Executive Art Editor: Sally Bond
Designer: Julie Francis
Photographer: Andy Komorowski
Production Controller: Linda Parry
Picture Researcher: Jennifer Veall